Making Room for the Future: Rebuilding California's Infrastructure

• • •

David E. Dowall
Jan Whittington

2003

PUBLIC POLICY INSTITUTE OF CALIFORNIA

Library of Congress Cataloging-in-Publication Data
Dowall, David E.
Making room for the future : rebuilding California's infrastructure / David E. Dowall, Jan Whittington.
p. cm.
ISBN: 1-58213-045-0
1. Infrastructure (Economics)—California. 2. California—Economic policy. I. Whittington, Jan, 1965-. II. Title.

HC107.C23C337 2003
363'.09794—dc21 2002156314

PPIC does not take or support positions on any ballot measure or state and federal legislation nor does it endorse or support any political parties or candidates for public office.

Research publications reflect the views of the authors and do not necessarily reflect the views of the staff, officers, or Board of Directors of the Public Policy Institute of California.

Foreword

California has an infrastructure problem, and its causes are many. Population growth has outstripped the expansion of public facilities, and deferred maintenance has left a good deal of existing infrastructure in poor repair. Environmental concerns have constrained the feasible options for building new schools, roads, and water projects, and some localities have been unable to gain voter approval for new bond-financed construction. User fees are unpopular with users and therefore with politicians. As a consequence, demand for the state's aging infrastructure is increasing, yet we see continuing resistance to the taxes and outlays needed to maintain, renew, and expand public facilities.

Sacramento has done much in the last few years to break this logjam. In 1999, Governor Davis created a Commission on Building for the 21st Century, which conducted a thorough review of the state's infrastructure problems and solutions. Governor Davis also signed Assembly Bill 1473 into law to foster more strategic infrastructure planning, and voters approved the bond issues the legislature placed on the 2002 ballot. Assembly Constitutional Amendment 11, which the legislature approved for the 2003 ballot, will ask voters to approve a budgetary set-aside for infrastructure whenever expenditures increase from year to year.

To assist Sacramento in its work, PPIC asked David Dowall and Jan Whittington to explore the infrastructure needs and challenges of three key sectors: education, transportation, and water. In *Making Room for the Future: Rebuilding California's Infrastructure*, the authors examine, among other things, the challenges that cut across all three sectors, including a lack of state oversight, burdensome regulations, inaccurate cost estimating, and local resistance to regional solutions. They note the advantages of a more predictable finance system that also links fees to benefits. They emphasize the importance of balancing efficiency and equity and identify precedents in the public utility sector for doing so. They also maintain that enhanced project delivery and demand management—regulating the demand for infrastructure services through pricing and conservation programs—are essential if California is to address its infrastructure problems effectively. Most important, perhaps, the authors note that California's infrastructure problems have solutions but that these solutions require creativity, flexibility, and long-term thinking—characteristics that have not dominated capital planning in the last three decades.

Making Room for the Future concentrates on problems that are deeply embedded in the way we plan, build, and finance infrastructure in California. As a result, it makes an important contribution to the analysis of the state's public policy options. In doing so, we hope, it also contributes directly and helpfully to California's efforts to rebuild itself in the 21st century.

David W. Lyon
President and CEO
Public Policy Institute of California

Summary

Introduction

Projections suggest that by the year 2020, California's population will surpass 45 million. How well the state responds to this growth will largely define California's prosperity and quality of life for decades to come. The state must meet two challenges—shore up its aging stocks of infrastructure and build new facilities and networks to accommodate 16 million more people. Unfortunately, there isn't much time. The state is out of highway capacity, mobility is plummeting, and access to educational facilities is becoming even more difficult despite realization of the overarching importance of having a well-educated labor force. The crunch in the water sector is coming at the precise time of an awareness that water resources must be managed differently—balanced among environmental, urban, and agricultural sectors. As the state squeezes up against capacity constraints, its infrastructure systems are also being throttled by increasing demand from population and economic growth and from pressures to increase infrastructure standards.

The overarching purpose of this study is to help policymakers in Sacramento and across the state more effectively address infrastructure needs. It analyzes the issues and opportunities confronting three of the state's major infrastructure responsibilities—education, water, and transportation. We have explored the challenges faced by each sector and identified a range of policy tools that can be used to improve the efficacy and efficiency of infrastructure service delivery. Our assessments of education, transportation, and water supply have uncovered an array of daunting infrastructure challenges.

Failure to Link Strategic and Capital Planning

Most sectors engage in some form of planning, but few agencies rigorously link strategic planning with capital planning. Even fewer provide long-term financial plans for the delivery of infrastructure services. Most agencies do not explore alternative forms of service delivery or identify noncapital alternatives for meeting future needs. This traditional supply-side planning made sense in the 1950s when the sectors were in their infancy, California was growing rapidly, and there was a broad consensus in support of growth. But now, the environment has changed. Not all citizens view the state's economic and demographic growth as desirable. Our capital planning process has become politicized, based mostly on pork-barrel deal-making. In short, the context in which the state plans and funds capital infrastructure investments is vastly different now than during the Earl Warren and Pat Brown eras.

No Multisectoral Vision for Infrastructure Investment Planning

California has not attempted multisectoral planning since the Jerry Brown administration, when *An Urban Strategy for California* was drafted. This plan called for more compact urban development. Policies were proposed to encourage the redevelopment of inner cities and older suburbs. New greenfield development was to be discouraged. A major element of the strategy's policy framework was to channel state infrastructure investments into urban areas. With the adoption of Assembly Bill (AB) 1473 each agency is now required to develop strategic plans. However, there are no guidelines for formulating multisectoral infrastructure programs for California.

Lack of Interest in Demand Management

Most sectors have not considered how to use demand management as a tool for meeting strategic objectives. The water supply sector seems to be the one exception—urban water districts across the state, working in concert with the Department of Water Resources have implemented a range of demand management policies to promote water conservation. Although there are some signs that demand management is slowly being introduced to the agricultural sector, there has been little interest elsewhere. Until very recently, K–12 and higher education have not embraced demand management as a policy option. Fortunately, the legislature has pressed higher education to consider year-round operation as a demand management tool to squeeze more capacity out of existing capital infrastructure.

There has been considerable research on the use of demand management in transportation to cope with highway congestion. Despite the use of congestion pricing on SR 91 and I-15 in Southern California, and bridges and tunnels into New York City, state transportation planners seem frightened by the concept. We acknowledge that there are serious equity effects associated with the application of congestion pricing; however, as we point out, there are numerous ways that the effects can be circumvented—through tax rebates, transit vouchers, and so forth.

Declining Real User Fee Base for Many Services

In some cases, California infrastructure services are financed through user fees or charges. Real, inflation-adjusted fees have not kept pace with the cost of services. Educational fees for higher education—California Community Colleges, California State University and University of California have all fallen since 1994. Efforts by both UC and CSU to raise fees have been rebuffed for over seven years by both Republican and Democratic governors. In the transportation sector, California's gasoline taxes fell by 50 percent in real terms between 1950 and 1998.

Fee increases need not adversely affect the poor. There is a long tradition of offering low-income households "lifeline rates" for privately provided public utilities (telephone, electricity, and gas). It seems to us that fees and charges can be raised while protecting low- and moderate-income households through lifeline rates, financial aid (for higher education), and tax rebates.

Unpredictable Funding

Evidence provided on the capital funding of education and transportation clearly reveals that state support has been erratic. Funding of infrastructure varies from year to year. With such volatility it is extremely difficult to adequately plan and program infrastructure investments.

Imbalanced State-Local Funding Shares

We explore the question of how to balance the division of funding between state and local governments. We conclude that more attention needs to be given to the benefit principle of taxation; that is, to the extent possible, levy taxes on those who benefit from the provided service. This suggests that there should be some allocation of costs across users, local taxpayers, and state taxpayers. Unfortunately, pragmatic politics has trumped economic principles, and the state has stepped in to provide assistance to local governments. This is most prevalent in K–12 funding of school facilities and of community colleges.

Poor Project Execution and Service Delivery

Our review of the delivery of infrastructure capital projects turned up a number of problem areas and issues. In the case of transportation projects, Caltrans process is cumbersome and time-consuming. Audits of capital project delivery for CSU revealed excessive handoffs and repetitive reviews. In the case of Caltrans, there has been a reluctance to partner with the private sector. Unlike many other state departments of transportation, Caltrans has refused to contract out planning, design, and management work. As a result, projects take from 7 to 23 years to complete.

Failure to Maintain Infrastructure Investments

California has a deferred maintenance crisis on its hands. Our assessment uncovered extensive deferred maintenance backlogs in educational facilities and transportation facilities. The UC system and particularly UC Berkeley do not adequately fund the maintenance of their facilities. UC spends approximately 1.7 percent of the total replacement cost of their facilities on annual maintenance. The U.S. General Accounting Office recommends a minimum of 3 percent per year, and private universities in California spend 4 percent. As a consequence, deferred maintenance in higher education exceeds $2 billion dollars.

Deferred maintenance in the transportation sector is also a major problem. *Transportation California* recently reported that the state ranked 48th in the nation in terms of road condition. Despite the planning and maintenance efforts of Caltrans and local governments across the state, maintenance expenditures have not kept pace with highway usage—vehicle miles traveled.

The water supply sector also suffers from deferred maintenance and it also needs to upgrade its systems to meet new, more stringent environmental standards. Overall, California's water supply and wastewater treatment systems maintenance backlog is estimated to stand at $40 billion.

What Should the State Do?

As a starting point, the state needs to introduce strategic planning and link it with agencies' capital planning. This process is under way with the implementation of AB 1473. However, the state needs to think about how to foster multisectoral investment planning. The state needs to develop a vision for the future growth of California and use it to plan and prioritize infrastructure investments in water supply, transportation, education, and other services. This could be carried out in a number of ways. One way is to develop a series of regional or metropolitan plans that consider how to link transportation and land-use planning with other infrastructure services. The plans could be then integrated to form the basis of a statewide strategic plan for California. A more centralized approach would be to develop a statewide development plan. We actually have some examples of this—*The California Tomorrow Plan* (Heller, 1972), and the Brown administration's *An Urban Strategy for California* (Office of Planning and Research, 1978).

Define California's Vision for the Future and Use It to Plan Infrastructure Investments

The state government needs to define and implement its vision of performance-based efficient government service delivery. It needs to link agency-related goals and missions with the capital decisionmaking process for infrastructure investment. This means being absolutely sure that the new investment is needed and that the performance gap cannot be met in some other way. It means carefully assessing if there are ways to shift the provision of the service to other entities. It means carefully assessing if there are ways of creatively financing required infrastructure or developing collaborative partnerships to provide services. Finally, it means determining how to most efficiently provide services, by enhancing project delivery.

Introduce Demand Management to Infrastructure Planning

California cannot possibly accommodate future growth without considering demand management. The state needs to embrace demand management policy tools and use them to better utilize existing facilities. This means fostering conservation in both urban and agricultural water-use sectors. It means implementing road pricing to mitigate traffic congestion and to begin to "level the playing field" between single occupancy auto use and transit. Land-use planning should be geared more to transit and the state should offer incentives to encourage alternatives to auto travel.

In the case of higher education, operating year round makes good sense by providing incentives for students to move through colleges and universities at a faster rate. In the case of water supply, the state should continue to promote conservation and conjunctive use of surface and groundwater resources and devote more effort to promoting water recycling and reuse.

Review and Adjust User Fees and Charges and Develop Ability-to-Pay Offsets

Where the state uses fees and charges to finance infrastructure, it needs to raise rates to recover from years of stagnation The DWR and the myriad of urban and agricultural districts need to revise their pricing policies to promote water conservation. This means using increasing block rate tariffs in urban areas and linking them with the California Irrigation Management Information System to adjust blocks to weather conditions. Agricultural pricing needs to promote more flexibility in cropping patterns and to develop best-practice irrigation.

The state's reliance on user fees and taxes to fund highways has broken down. The challenge facing the transportation sector is to increase gasoline taxes and vehicle registration fees and to implement a range of programs to promote transit and carpooling. Higher parking fees, telecommuting, and nonauto alternative forms of transportation would make great sense. The biggest challenge is to implement a congestion pricing system on the state's congested bridges and highways. A demonstration project to address equity effects should be launched.

Higher education is even more problematic since it is the quintessential merit good. However, there are ways to adjust prices to foster more revenues while maintaining and enhancing quality. Tuition should be based on means testing, with scholarships and financial aid given to those needing it. Fees should encourage students to move through the system—pricing should be used to foster faster time to degree in the UC and CSU systems. Fees for courses in community colleges should differentiate between vocational and university preparatory courses and those aimed at senior and leisure markets.

The fees of professional schools and colleges should be increased to more closely approximate actual costs, particularly in areas where students receive high starting salaries. Exceptions and fee waivers could be given to students willing to enter public or community service careers upon graduation. If fee structures can be increased and more of the burden placed on users and beneficiaries, more resources will be available to support systemwide growth and modernization.

Exceptional care must be taken to ensure that fee adjustments do not limit the access of low- and moderate-income households to services. This requires that the state offer a range of offsets—lifeline rates, financial aid, and tax rebates.

Make Capital Funding More Predictable

Sacramento needs to move beyond its current pork-barrel method of allocating funds for capital investment. Capital outlays need to be geared to strategic capital planning.

Introduce Accountability Measures to Foster Enhanced Project Delivery

A common theme that we uncovered in our assessments is the lack of accountability in infrastructure provision. Many state agencies face no competition and are not client-oriented. The state needs to consider how to increase the accountability of state infrastructure providers. The most appropriate place to start is to develop agency strategic plans that establish goals and standards of performance for meeting client needs. These goals and standards should be regularly used to assess agency performance. Evaluation of agencies' service needs to be frequent and ongoing.

Accountability alone will not deliver improved service. The state needs to provide clear and strong incentives to reward high-level performance. Personnel reviews, salary merit increases, and bonuses could play a useful role. Competition should also be introduced, so that public service providers are forced to compete with private firms for the right to provide client services.

Introduce Lifecycle Costing and Management

State decisionmakers and policy analysts are far too preoccupied with first costs. Instead, the state needs to develop a new approach to assessing its capital outlay decisions. The approach should focus on lifecycle costs, that is, the total costs of building, operating, and maintaining a capital asset. The lifecycle approach looks beyond procurement costs and considers ongoing maintenance costs. These costs should be included as part of the budget for the facility. Funding for maintenance needs to be encumbered when an asset is put in place.

The state needs to hold agencies accountable for the maintenance of their capital facilities. At a minimum, this requires much better reporting of facilities' condition. Agencies should be required to report deferred maintenance backlogs and to develop five-year plans for eliminating deferred maintenance. The state needs to fund these plans.

Where Should the State Start?

Our sense is that the state should develop a strategy and framework for overhauling its infrastructure problems. The strategy should consist of short-, medium-, and long-term actions to address the problems and issues that we have outlined above.

Under AB 1473, the governor is required to submit a Five-Year Capital Plan to the legislature. This plan should serve as the basis for charting out the course of actions that need to be taken. The plan should be divided into three phases: immediate steps to relieve costly congestion and infrastructure effects, near-term efforts to begin to address infrastructure service shortfalls over a two- to five-year period, and a long-term overhaul to remove structural and institutional impediments to infrastructure provision. What might these look like?

Immediate Actions—Demand Management and Pricing

Demand management interventions will have the quickest effect. They can create capacity in weeks or months and they do not rely on capital outlays. In areas of the state that face extreme and costly traffic congestion, we propose implementing congestion pricing pilot projects. In the Bay Area, for example, peak hour tolls should be imposed for a one-year trial. In conjunction with the tolling, the state should offer commuters discounted (or perhaps even free) vouchers for public transit use.

The state's gasoline taxes should be scheduled for a 20 percent increase per year over the next five years. The state should also consider requiring that local governments levy parking excise taxes on all municipal and private parking lots and structures.

The state should aggressively encourage the rollout of urban water conservation programs to all municipal districts. This might be effected by requiring that urban water districts adopt the Department of Water Resources memorandum of understanding on urban water conservation. Similar action is needed for agricultural water districts as well. The state should accelerate the conversion of water tariffs to a full cost recovery basis.

For higher education, the state should mandate a through review of capital planning at the CCC and UC systems. Such a review should be modeled on the recent assessment carried out for CSU. Student fees should be increased for all systems and additional financial aid should be offered on a means-tested basis. At CSU and UC, students should be encouraged to graduate in four years.

Medium-Term Actions—Institutional and Financial Restructuring

Over the next five years, the state should work to restructure its infrastructure institutions. The AB 1473 process should be used to foster more strategic planning and a closer linking of strategic and capital planning. The state needs to develop accountability systems to measure agency performance. Incentives (both positive and negative) need to be developed to spur more efficacious performance.

Over the next two to five years, as user fees and beneficiary charges are raised to reflect cost of service provision, the state should restructure its systems of infrastructure finance. This should include dedicated full funding of maintenance, programming of capital outlay grants to sectors based on demand, and a balancing of pay-as-you-go and debt financing to introduce more predictability to infrastructure capital investment.

Long-Term Actions—Create a Vision and Make Infrastructure Policy More Integrated and Multisectoral

In the long term, over the next 10–20 years, the state should work to develop a vision for the future economic and physical development of California. The vision should link land-use and environmental planning with economic development and infrastructure investment. The vision and the plan should serve as a basis for planning and programming multisectoral infrastructure investments. What is important is to start the process of integrated planning. As President Dwight Eisenhower said, "plans are nothing, planning is everything." We need the process if we are to ensure prosperity for tomorrow's Californians.

Contents

Foreword iii
Summary v
Figures xix
Boxes xxi
Tables xxiii
Acknowledgments xxv
Acronyms xxvii

1. INTRODUCTION 1

2. CALIFORNIA'S INFRASTRUCTURE LEGACY 5
   Population Growth and Infrastructure Services 6
   The Era of State Building—1950–1970 10
   Living Off the Legacy 14
   Facing the Future 18
   Conclusions 21

3. THE CROWN JEWELS 23
   Education 23
      K–12 Education 23
      Higher Education 27
   Transportation 35
      The State's Transit System 37
      Management of the System 39
      Maintenance 44
   Water Supply 45
      The U.S. Bureau of Reclamation 49
      The California Department of Water Resources 55
      Groundwater Supply 57
      CALFED 58

4. IS CALIFORNIA PREPARED FOR THE FUTURE? 61
Introduction 61
K–12 Education 61
Unstable and Insufficient Financing 61
Lack of Planning and Record-Keeping 62
Shifting Regulations 64
Lack of State Oversight 65
The State Architect Bottleneck 66
Higher Education 68
Projections and Planning 68
Inadequate Data and Estimates of Need 69
State Funding Shortfalls 70
Inadequate Data Collection for CCC 71
Transportation 73
Slow and Expensive Project Delivery 73
Lack of Approved Plans 74
Cost-Estimating 76
One-Hat Project Management and STIP Incentives 78
Maintenance 82
Structural and Cultural Barriers 83
Water 84
"Groundwater Is Akin to the Right of Free Speech" 85
Local Agencies and State Oversight 89
Dam Safety 92
Water Policy and Politics 92
Conclusion 94

5. PLANNING FOR THE FUTURE 95
California's Capital Budgeting Process 96
The Need for Strategic Planning 99
Linking Capital Budgeting and Strategic Planning 102
U.S. Bureau of Reclamation: A Best-Practice Model of Capital Decisionmaking 105
State-Level Strategic Plans 108
Minnesota 108
New Jersey 110
Washington 112

6. MANAGING THE DEMAND FOR INFRASTRUCTURE SERVICES . . . 115
Managing Water Demand . . . 117
Demand Management in Education . . . 123
Transportation Demand Management . . . 129
Conclusion . . . 135

7. RECOVERING INFRASTRUCTURE COSTS: BALANCING EFFICIENCY WITH EQUITY . . . 137
Trends in Cost Recovery . . . 140
Transportation . . . 140
Water Prices . . . 141
Higher Education . . . 142
Tackling Adverse Equity Effects . . . 146
How Should the State Set Tariffs? . . . 149

8. FINANCING CALIFORNIA'S INFRASTRUCTURE . . . 153
Improving Infrastructure Finance . . . 154
Recommended Actions . . . 156

9. ENHANCING PROJECT AND SERVICE DELIVERY . . . 163
Better Project Execution . . . 163
Santa Clara County Traffic Authority . . . 163
California State University System . . . 166
Joint-Use Facilities . . . 172
Public-Private Partnerships . . . 175
Outsourcing, Competition, and Accountability . . . 177

10. DEFERRED MAINTENANCE . . . 183
California's Deferred Maintenance Backlog . . . 184
Higher Education . . . 186
Transportation . . . 189
Water Supply . . . 195
What Should the State Do About Deferred Maintenance? . . . 196
Lifecycle Maintenance . . . 196

11. POLICY RECOMMENDATIONS . . . 199
Where Should the State Start? . . . 202
Immediate Actions—Demand Management and Pricing . . . 202

Medium-Term Actions—Institutional and Financial Restructuring 203
Long-Term Actions—Articulate a Vision and Make Infrastructure Policy More Integrated and Multisectoral 204
Bibliography 205
About the Authors 223
Related PPIC Publications 225

Figures

2.1. California State Population, 1930–2000 7
2.2. Real Per Capita State Operations Expenditures, 1930–2000 8
2.3. Real Per Capita State-Provided Local Assistance, 1930–2000 8
2.4. Real Per Capita State Capital Outlay, 1930–2000 9
2.5. Real Per Capita General Obligation Bond Debt, 1930–2000 10
2.6. K–12 Enrollment and Real Capital Outlay, 1951–1970 12
2.7. Higher Education Enrollment and Real Capital Outlay, 1955–1970 13
2.8. VMT and State Lane Mile Trends, 1957–1970 13
2.9. Water Storage Capacity and Population Trends, 1950–1970 14
2.10. K–12 Enrollment and Real Capital Outlay, 1985–1996 15
2.11. Higher Education Enrollment and Real Capital Outlay, 1970–2000 16
2.12. VMT and State Lane Mile Trends, 1970–2000 17
2.13. Water Storage Capacity and Population Trends, 1970–2000 17
2.14. California Population Projections, 2000–2040 19
2.15. K–12 Enrollment Projections, 2000–2001 to 2008–2009 20
2.16. Higher Education Enrollment Projections, 1999–2008 . . 20
3.1. State K–12 School Building Funding Process Under SB 50 School Facilities Program 26
3.2. California Community College Capital Outlay Process . . 29
3.3. California State University Capital Outlay Process 32
3.4. University of California Capital Outlay Process 34

3.5. Caltrans and California Transportation Commission STIP Process 40
3.6. Regional Offices of the U.S. Bureau of Reclamation 50
3.7. California Service Areas for Colorado River Water 52
5.1. The Capital Decisionmaking Framework 103
5.2. New Jersey State Strategic Infrastructure Planning Process 112
7.1. California State Gasoline Tax in Real 1997 Dollars 140
7.2. Real Wholesale Water Prices from the State Water Project 141
7.3. Real Resident Undergraduate Student Fees 144
8.1. State Funding of Higher Education Capital Outlay, 1980–2001 157
9.1. Santa Clara County Traffic Authority Management Model 164
10.1. Effect of Adequate and Timely Maintenance and Repairs on the Service Life of an Asset 185
10.2. Facilities Maintenance Expenditures Versus Replacement Cost, 1999 187
10.3. Real Road Maintenance Expenditures per 100 VMT . . . 191
10.4. Metropolitan Transportation Commission Pavement Condition Index Versus Maintenance Expenditures per Mile, 1996–1997 194

Boxes

6.1. Urban Best Management Practices 118
6.2. Efficient Water Management Practices for California's Agricultural Suppliers 122
7.1. PG&E's CARE Program 148
7.2. EBMUD's CAP 149

Tables

3.1. California Public Education Facilities and Enrollment, 2000 24
3.2. State Road Transportation Network, 2000 36
3.3. The State Transit System, 1998 38
3.4. California's Surface Water Storage Capacity, by Agency with Greater Than 250,000 Acre-Feet of Storage Capacity 46
3.5. Major Conveyance, by Agency 47
3.6. Local Water Supply Agencies in California 48
3.7. State and Federal Agencies of CALFED 59
5.1. Typical Strategic Planning Process in the Public Sector . . 100
5.2. Sample of USBR's Annual Performance Measures 106
5.3. Sample of Additional Features Required by GPRA for the USBR 107
6.1. Block Prices for the Irvine Ranch Water District 119
6.2. Sample Rates for Irvine Ranch Water District Residential Customers 119
6.3. Estimated Surplus FTE Student Capacity, 1998–1999 . . 124
6.4. Estimated Surplus FTE Student Capacity and Projected Need 124
6.5. Estimated Capital Costs of Meeting Higher Education Enrollment Growth 125
6.6. Estimated Capital Cost Savings from Year-Round Operation 126
6.7. University of California General Assignment Classrooms and Teaching Labs 126
6.8. The University of California's Classroom and Teaching Lab Utilization, 1997 127
6.9. Percentage Graduation Rates for Freshmen Entering in Fall 1990 128
6.10. Percentage Graduation Rates of Community College Transfers in Fall 1992 128

6.11 Cost-Effectiveness of TDM Projects in the South Coast Air Quality Management District 136
7.1. DWR Survey of Agricultural Surface Water Retail Prices, 1996 143
7.2. Income Distribution Trends of California Single and Joint Return Taxpayers, 1975–1998 146
8.1. Ten-Year Capital Requirements, 1999–2009 153
8.2. Estimates of Capital Allocation Spending for Higher Education Institutions 159
8.3. Possible Effects of Student Facilities Fees, 1999–2000 . . . 161
9.1. CSU's Restructured Capital Outlay Process 168
9.2. Overview of Outsourcing by State Highway Departments, 1997 178
9.3. Trends in State and Local Government Service Outsourcing 179
10.1. Trends in Highway Maintenance 190
10.2. Pavement Expenditure and Pavement Condition Index . . 193

Acknowledgments

The authors wish to acknowledge the assistance of over 100 governmental employees who provided us with invaluable insights. This research would not have been possible without the generous access and thoughtful interviews provided by

- Staff to Gray Davis, Governor of California,
- The California Department of Finance,
- Staff to the Commission on Building for the 21st Century,
- The Office of Public School Construction, California Department of General Services,
- State Architect, California Department of General Services,
- The School Facilities Planning Division, California Department of Education,
- Real Estate Services Division, California Department of General Services,
- The offices of numerous local unified school districts,
- The California Community College Chancellor's Office,
- California Community College District Offices,
- The California State University, Office of the Chancellor,
- The University of California, Office of the President,
- Staff to the California Transportation Commission,
- The District and State Offices of the California Department of Transportation,
- The Metropolitan Transportation Commission, San Francisco Bay Area,
- San Diego Metropolitan Transit Development Board,
- Transportation Corridor Agencies, Orange County,
- University of California, Pavement Research Center, Institute for Transportation Studies,
- The California Department of Water Resources,

- Staff to the California Water Commission,
- Staff to the California State Water Resources Control Board,
- CALFED,
- The Mid-Pacific Region, Bureau of Reclamation, U.S. Department of the Interior,
- The Lower Colorado Region, Bureau of Reclamation, U.S. Department of the Interior,
- Metropolitan Water District of Southern California,
- San Diego County Water Authority,
- San Diego Association of Governments,
- Westlands Water District,
- Participants in the Public Policy Institute of California's Forum on Infrastructure, February 2001,
- Participants in the California Foundation on the Environment and Economy Seminar Series of Infrastructure, May 2001, October 2001, and May 2002.

The authors would also like to thank our research assistants, all graduate students at UC Berkeley, for their invaluable work during the first 18 months of the project: Katherine Florey, Yasuyuki Motoyama, Larissa Muller, and George Woodward. We received valuable comments on a draft manuscript from Michael Dardia, Joyce Peterson, Peter Richardson, Michael Teitz, and Chris Weare of PPIC. Robert Poole of the Reason Foundation provided extensive comments on Chapters 7–10. Gerald Beavers, formerly of the Legislative Analyst's Office, provided extensive comments on the entire draft. William Hauck of the California Business Roundtable, Fred Silva of PPIC, and Patrick Mason of the California Foundation on the Environment and Economy counseled us on California infrastructure politics. Although all of these people improved the final product, the responsibility for any error of fact or interpretation rests with the authors.

Acronyms

AB	Assembly Bill
ASF	Assignable square feet
BMP	Best management practice
CARE	California Alternative Rates for Energy
CASA	California Annual School Allotment
CCC	California Community Colleges
CCCCO	California Community College Chancellor's Office
CDE	California Department of Education
CIMIS	California Irrigation Management Information System
COBCP	Capital Outlay Budget Change Proposal
CPDC	Capital Planning, Design, and Construction
CPEC	California Postsecondary Education Commission
CSR	Class Size Reduction
CSU	California State University
CTC	California Transportation Commission
CTR	Commute trip reduction
CVP	Central Valley Project
CVPIA	Central Valley Project Improvement Act
DOF	Department of Finance
DSA	Division of the State Architect
DWR	Department of Water Resources
EPA	Environmental Protection Agency
ER	Emission reduction

EBMUD	East Bay Municipal Utility District
ESA	Endangered Species Act
EWMP	Efficient Water Management Practices
FPP	Final Project Proposal
FTE	Full-time-equivalent
GAO	General Accounting Office
GASB	Government Accounting Standards Board
GPRA	Government Performance and Results Act
HOV	High occupancy vehicle
ITIP	Interregional Transportation Improvement Program
IPP	Initial Project Proposal
IRWD	Irvine Ranch Water District
LAO	Legislative Analyst's Office
LHC	Little Hoover Commission
MAF	Million acre-feet
MMWD	Marin Municipal Water District
MOA	Memorandum of Agreement
MOU	Memorandum of Understanding
MTC	Metropolitan Transportation Commission
MTDB	Metropolitan Transit Development Board
MWD	Metropolitan Water District
O&M	Operations and maintenance
OMB	Office of Management and Budget
OPSC	Office of Public School Construction
PPD	Physical Planning and Development
PSR	Project Study Report
PUC	Public Utilities Commission
RoW	Right of Way

RTIP	Regional Transportation Improvement Program
RTPA	Regional Transportation Planning Agency
SAB	State Allocation Board
SB	Senate Bill
SCAQMD	South Coast Air Quality Management District
SCCTA	Santa Clara County Traffic Authority
SDCWA	San Diego County Water Authority
SHOPP	State Highway Operations and Protection Program
STIP	State Transportation Improvement Project
SWP	State Water Project
SWRCB	State Water Resources Control Board
TAF	Thousand acre-feet
TDM	Transportation Demand Management
UC	University of California
UCI	University of California, Irvine
UCOP	U.C. Office of the President
ULFT	Ultra-low-flow toilet
USBR	U.S. Bureau of Reclamation
VMT	Vehicle miles traveled
VMTR	Vehicle miles traveled reduction
VTR	Vehicle trip reduction

1. Introduction

Throughout the 1980s, policymakers, engineers, and economists across the nation expressed their deep concern about the nation's inadequate infrastructure investments.[1] Commentators frequently lamented the lack of maintenance of the nation's highways, water supply systems, and schools. Their research also indicated that capital spending on critical infrastructure was not keeping pace with depreciation and obsolescence and that network infrastructure was not expanding to meet growing demand.

In California, state officials expressed similar concerns about the state's poor infrastructure conditions. In *Rusty Hinges on the Golden Gate* (California Legislature, 1983), Governor Deukmejian's staff examined whether the national assessments of infrastructure adequacy also applied to California. Although the study concluded that problems of widespread deferred maintenance were not as severe in California as in other parts of the country, it noted that California's investment in infrastructure had lagged during the 1970s and 1980s. The study went on to identify the reasons for inadequate infrastructure investment: the issue's low visibility, unstable and uncertain funding procedures, institutional and organizational inefficiencies, and limited local fiscal capacity following the passage of Proposition 13.

Sacramento policy analysts went on to offer a range of proposals to remedy the infrastructure problem. These proposals included setting up a new state funding authority for infrastructure investment and launching a series of new bond initiatives. Analysts also proposed looking at administrative reforms to improve infrastructure delivery. These reforms included redividing state and local infrastructure responsibilities, reviewing infrastructure standards and their effects on

[1]For example, see Choate and Walters (1981) and Peterson (1979).

investment costs, and launching public works projects during downturns in the economy, when construction costs are lower.

The report and its recommendations were largely ignored, and as the state's economy deteriorated during the late 1980s and early 1990s, concerns about infrastructure were displaced by more pressing issues. Moreover, California lost population and the state's economy shed over one million jobs during the recession of the early 1990s. Concerns about inadequate infrastructure receded as the demand for infrastructure services declined in the industrial, commercial, and residential sectors.

When the California economy began roaring back to life in the mid-1990s, the demand for infrastructure services increased sharply. Between 1993 and 2000, California added 2,953,000 jobs, and 3,168,000 people. Almost immediately, the state's creaky infrastructure became overwhelmed. Traffic congestion increased, enrollment pressures began to affect K–12 and higher education facilities, and water supply conflicts between urban and agricultural interests surfaced. The California Business Roundtable was one of the first groups to raise concerns about the state's infrastructure, noting that spending on infrastructure did not match demand pressures (California Business Roundtable, 1998). The Legislative Analyst's Office began a series of publications directed at reforming infrastructure policy.[2] Pressure from business groups and the general public created a new climate and stimulated a renewed interest in infrastructure planning issues in the state. With the new administration in 1999, Governor Gray Davis formed the Commission on Building for the 21st Century, a blue-ribbon committee formed to assess infrastructure issues and formulate policy options for improving infrastructure quality.

In 1999, PPIC commissioned two studies of infrastructure policy. The first examined the current form and process of infrastructure planning and investment decisionmaking in California (Neuman and Whittington, 2000). The second compared California's basic approach to infrastructure planning and policymaking against best practices in

[2]See, for example, Legislative Analyst's Office (1995, 1998b, 1999).

other states and countries and offered a range of policy options for improving infrastructure planning and policymaking (Dowall, 2000).

The present report builds on these two studies and deepens their analyses. Its main purpose is to help policymakers in Sacramento and across the state address infrastructure needs more effectively by addressing the following six questions:

- How can strategic planning be used to structure long-term capital planning and budgeting?
- What role can demand-side analysis and management play in setting levels of infrastructure service provision?
- How can pricing be used to ensure access while promoting efficient asset utilization?
- What are the best ways to finance infrastructure investment?
- How might the state enhance the efficiency of project delivery, either in-house or with private partners and competitors?
- What are the most effective methods for tackling deferred maintenance?

In effect, it takes the policy options from Dowall's study and matches them to the institutional analyses of the Neuman and Whittington study. It also develops case studies of infrastructure planning in three critical sectors—education, transportation, and water supply—and explores how current practices can be improved through a range of policy and institutional reforms. In this sense, the report is both evaluative and prescriptive.

The report's structure is as follows. Chapter 2 examines long-term trends in real per capita infrastructure spending, government expenditures, and bond financing. Chapter 3 describes the state's three key infrastructure systems—education, transportation, and water supply—and the next chapter evaluates them. Chapter 5 considers the role of strategic planning and offers best-practice examples of capital investment decisionmaking. Chapter 6 explores the role of demand management in infrastructure provision, offering examples from each of the three sectors. Chapter 7 discusses the role of pricing in infrastructure delivery, exploring both efficiency and equity issues. Chapter 8 considers the state's current approach to financing infrastructure, identifies some of its weaknesses, and offers five recommendations for addressing those weaknesses. Chapter 9 presents a wide range of techniques for enhancing the efficacy and efficiency of program delivery. Chapter 10 discusses deferred maintenance issues, and Chapter 11 summarizes the main findings and recommendations.

2. California's Infrastructure Legacy

In 1949, Carey McWilliams published *California: The Great Exception*, a classic characterization of the state's extraordinary development from statehood to its centenary. As the title suggests, McWilliams portrayed the state's dynamic growth, which seemed to be boundless, as an exception to rules and convention.

> California, the giant adolescent, has been outgrowing its governmental clothes, now, for a hundred years. The first state constitution was itself an improvisation; and, from that time to the present, governmental services have lagged far behind population growth. . . . The state is always off balance, stretching itself precariously, improvising, and seeking to run the rapids of periodic tidal waves of migration. Right now it is trying to negotiate the latest and the most dangerous of these recurrent "rapids" (p. 17).

The rapids to which McWilliams refers were the massive demands of the period immediately following the World War II. Because the war forced California to defer expensive infrastructure investments, victory brought with it the need for public investment, especially in the face of increasing demand for infrastructure services by returning veterans and their fast-growing families.

McWilliams's characterization was essentially correct. Under the leadership of Earl Warren and Pat Brown, California invested massively in public infrastructure, especially highways, higher education facilities, and water projects. These and other public investments provided the foundation for California's growth and prosperity from 1950 to 1970. What McWilliams did not foresee was the downturn in state leadership in infrastructure deployment and provision following that period. For a variety of reasons, Sacramento slashed spending on infrastructure investment from 1970 onward. By the late 1990s, that neglect threatened the state's economic prosperity.

This chapter traces the history of the state's infrastructure investments and their consequences, paying special attention to the last two decades, when the state turned away from its infrastructure commitments and struggled with droughts, rotating blackouts, traffic congestion, and inadequate school facilities. Will California sidestep these problems? Will it successfully run this new set of "rapids" and rebuild its monumental infrastructure systems? The answer depends on many factors, such as how fast the state's population and economic base grow, and how fast it is able to modernize and expand its infrastructure.

Population Growth and Infrastructure Services

Demand for infrastructure has always been driven by population growth, which has been the rule in California since the Gold Rush. That growth was reinforced by the completion of the Transcontinental Railroad in 1869, mass migration from the Dust Bowl during the 1930s, the expansion of defense-related industries during World War II, the postwar baby boom, the emergence of Silicon Valley, and increased immigration since the mid-1980s. World War II was an especially notable growth period. Over 1.9 million new residents arrived between 1940 and 1945, when the state's manufacturing output tripled. In the subsequent 25 years, the state's population grew by about 500,000 per year, overtaking New York as the nation's largest state in 1963 (California Department of Finance, 2000). Between 1950 and 1970, the state's population doubled from 10 million to 20 million (Figure 2.1).

Although it seems self-evident that infrastructure investment should keep pace with population growth, this equation has not always been acknowledged in Sacramento. One way to see whether investments have kept pace with demand is to compare real per capita state spending over time across the three categories of state expenditures: operations, local assistance, and capital outlay.

State expenditures for operations consist largely of staffing costs but also include routine maintenance, repair, equipment, deferred maintenance, and the leasing of facilities without the option to purchase. The gradual increase in real, per capita operations is a direct indication of

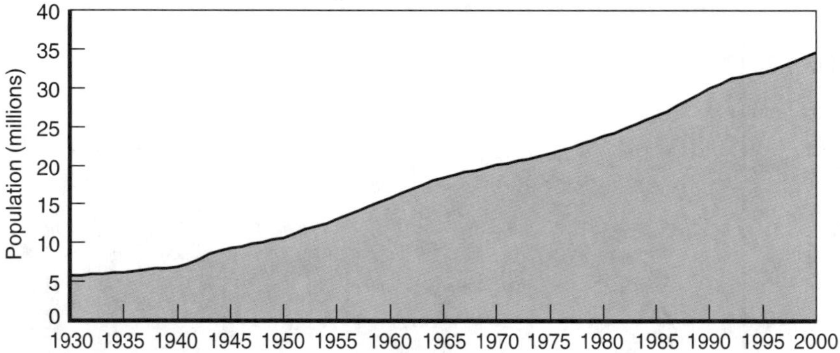

SOURCE: California Department of Finance (2000).

Figure 2.1—California State Population, 1930–2000

the expansion of government agencies and their costs over time (Figure 2.2).[1] In 1960, state government consisted of 22 departments and spent about $250 per capita on operations. Today the state has 64 departments and eight agencies, and expenditures for operations are well above $700 per capita.

The state also allocates considerable funds to local governments throughout California (Figure 2.3). Local assistance consists of grants to local agencies for the operation, maintenance, acquisition, or development of facilities or land. These grants may be used for school construction, local police assistance, and financial support to comply with state regulations.

Like operations, state expenditures for local assistance have outpaced population growth. Considerable growth took place in the 1960s, topped by a spike in local assistance in 1978, the year California voters passed Proposition 13. Local assistance surged again in the late 1990s. In the 1950s, only about $400 per capita was funneled annually from the state to local governments as local assistance. By the end of the century that figure was over $1,900.

---

[1]California state expenditures were compiled from annual issues of the *California Statistical Abstract* and *Governor's Budget Summary*, both published by the California Department of Finance.

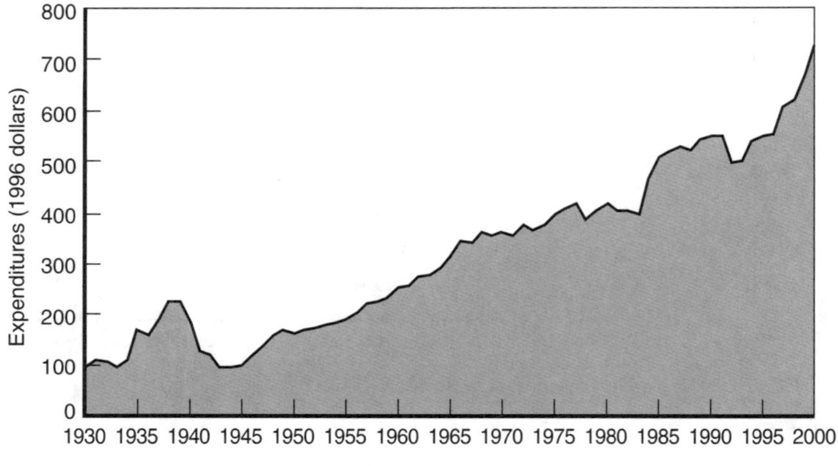

Figure 2.2—Real Per Capita State Operations Expenditures, 1930–2000

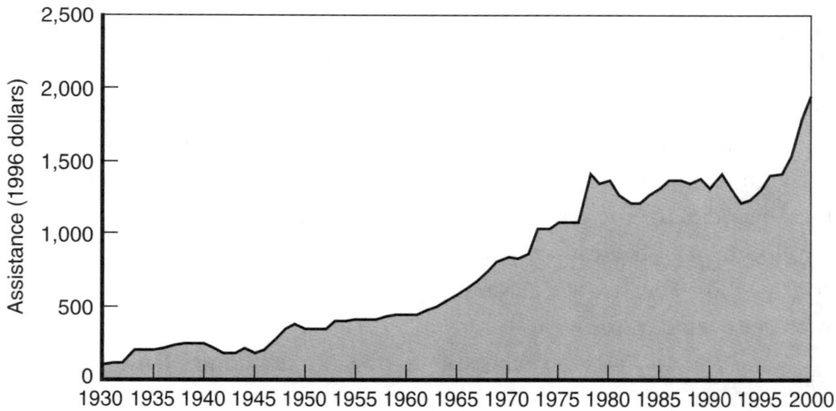

Figure 2.3—Real Per Capita State-Provided Local Assistance, 1930–2000

Capital outlay funds land acquisition, the cost of planning and constructing new buildings, additions to and modifications of existing buildings, leases for buildings with the option to purchase, and related equipment (Figure 2.4). Capital outlay spending reflects the state's investment in physical plant and equipment—facilities and infrastructure. It is the best available measure of trends in the state-

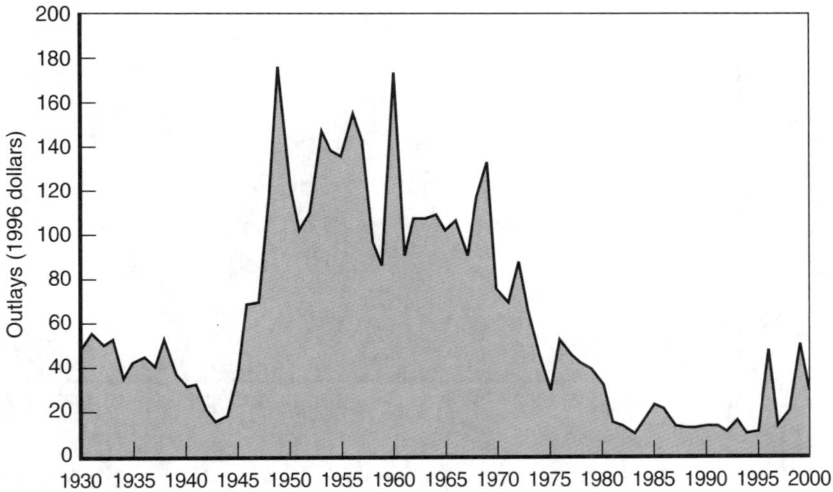

Figure 2.4—Real Per Capita State Capital Outlay, 1930–2000

funded investment of infrastructure. Comparison of Figures 2.2 and 2.3 with Figure 2.4 suggests that real per capita spending on capital outlays has fallen off since the 1970s, whereas spending for operations and local assistance has risen. Although the state's real per capita investment in capital outlay was between $100 and $160 per capita from 1945 to 1970, that figure averaged about $30 in the late 1990s.

In some ways, the decline in capital outlay spending in the 1970s is no surprise. The basic infrastructure systems for education, water, and transportation were already in place, and most were designed to accommodate future growth. The low per capita spending throughout the 1980s and 1990s, however, is cause for deep concern. Buildings, roadways, and hydroelectric dams have limits to their life expectancy; materials begin to fail, operations are curtailed, and safety becomes an issue. Many of the state's facilities were designed and constructed in the 1950s and 1960s and have already reached the end of their designed lives.

These declines in "pay-as-you-go" infrastructure financing were not entirely offset with increases in long-term financing (Figure 2.5). In the postwar period, real per capita general obligation bond indebtedness

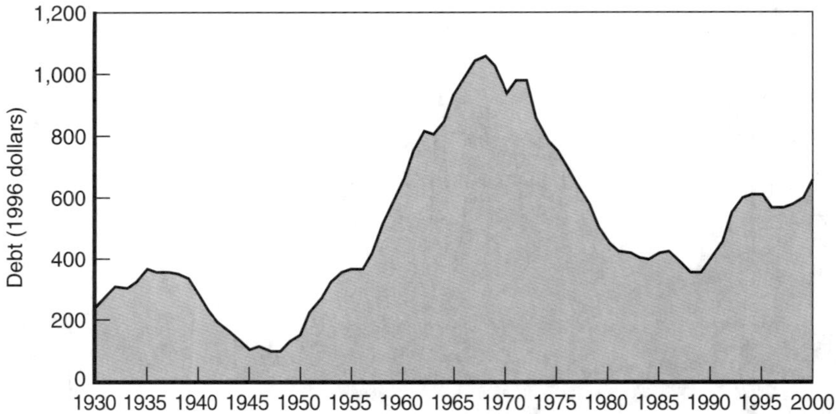

Figure 2.5—Real Per Capita General Obligation Bond Debt, 1930–2000

lagged about ten years behind capital outlay expenditures. In the 1960s, that bond debt climbed to $1,000 per capita and slowed to about $400 from the 1980s to the mid-1990s. During the 1990s, bond indebtedness began rising again, in large part as a result of bond financing for higher education and local K–12 facilities.

The overall expenditure pattern is clear. Under mounting pressure from state operations and local assistance, real per capita infrastructure expenditures have declined, and only part of this decline has been offset with long-term financing. But these patterns do not explain the motives behind decisionmaking at the state level. Why have operations and local assistance grown out of proportion with the state's population? How did the state obtain the political momentum necessary to invest heavily in infrastructure following World War II?

The Era of State Building—1950–1970

Although the Pat Brown era (1958–1966) is often regarded as the Golden Age of California's infrastructure investment, California's prosperity during this period drew from a variety of sources, including increased federal spending, a boom in established industries, and overwhelming bipartisan support for investment in infrastructure.

In many ways, Pat Brown brought the New Deal to California. The warning of a "tidal wave" of population growth sounded by Carey

McWilliams fit neatly into the public investment policies of Keynesian economics and the fears of postwar depression that gripped the state in the late 1940s. Pat Brown had moved from the Republican to the Democratic party in 1934, and his ideas for addressing growth through public investment rang with New Deal confidence (Rapoport, 1982, p. iii).

Successive investments in rail, power, water, roads, and military facilities through the first half of the 20th century had set California up for an unprecedented economic boom. Shipbuilding came and went with World War II, but the aircraft industry continued to grow, as did the automobile industry, the motion picture industry, and the steel industry. Branch plants sprang up from established manufacturing firms on the East Coast, as did regional offices in downtown Los Angeles and San Francisco. Supermarkets dotted the Southern California landscape, as did canning and frozen food facilities. Peacetime allowed for the resumption of industrial and durable goods production, which was hindered only by the advent of the Korean War (1950–1953).

Brown rose through the state's political ranks in a way that could not be repeated today. Since 1911, California had allowed candidates to seek the nominations of both parties. Earl Warren, the state's only three-term governor, won the gubernatorial nominations of both parties in 1946. With Governor Warren's backing, Brown became attorney general and the only Democrat for statewide office to survive a 1950 Republican landslide. After serving two terms, he ran for governor in 1958, winning 54 of the state's 58 counties. In the same year, the Democrats came to control both houses of the state legislature for the first time in 80 years. In 1962, Brown won re-election over the bruised but formidable former vice president, Richard Nixon.

Brown was determined to establish tuition-free education through the university level, widespread systems of mass transit and highways, and abundant water supplies for both agricultural users and urban residents. During these unprecedented times of political cohesion and economic prosperity, the state invested heavily in its three signature infrastructure systems: highways, education, and water projects.

Enrollment in K–12 increased by 150 percent between 1951 and 1970 as returning veterans started families. K–12 facilities had the slack to absorb much of the new enrollment up to the 1960s. However, by 1963 real state and local capital investment in K–12 facilities increased, rising by over 40 percent and continuing for six years. During the 1960s, state and local school districts invested $800 million in new school construction (Figure 2.6).

Enrollment in higher education also increased during the 1950s and 1960s, as veterans flooded into colleges and universities across the state. Between 1956 and 1970, enrollment increased over 300 percent. Capital outlays for higher education also trended upward during the 1950s and 1960s, as had outlays for K–12 (Figure 2.7). Enrollments and capital spending increased in all three segments of higher education: the University of California (UC), California State University (CSU), and California Community Colleges (CCC). Funding of capital projects in all three segments rose and fell dramatically, peaking in the mid-1960s with the addition of several new campuses.

Californians took to the highways as well. Vehicle ownership increased dramatically after the war, and total state highway lane miles increased by nearly 30 percent between 1957 and 1970. Even this massive construction effort did not keep pace with the increase in vehicle miles traveled (VMT); during the same period, VMT increased 117 percent (Figure 2.8). Although congestion levels were relatively low in

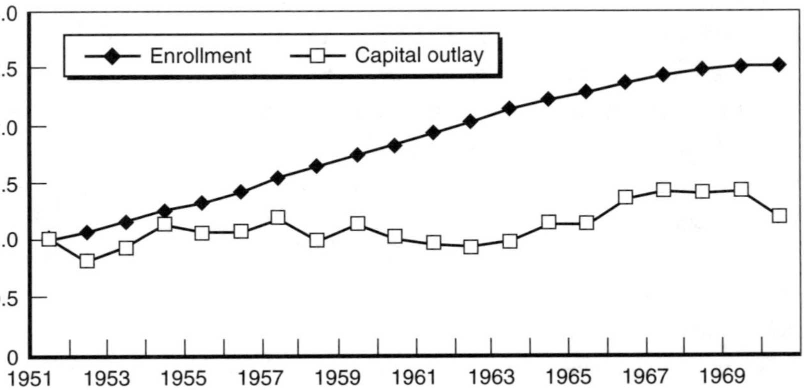

Figure 2.6—K–12 Enrollment and Real Capital Outlay, 1951–1970 (indexed 1951 = 100)

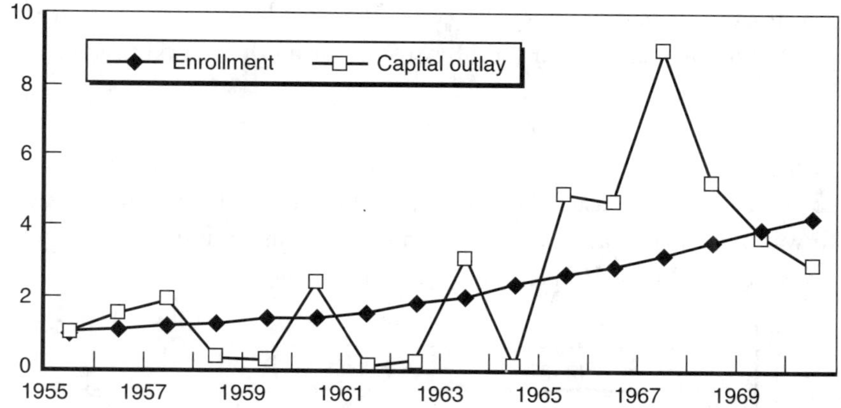

Figure 2.7—Higher Education Enrollment and Real Capital Outlay, 1955–1970 (indexed 1955 = 100)

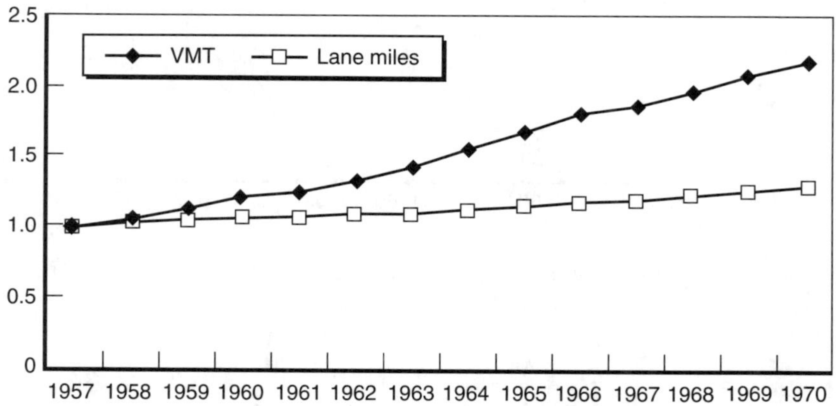

Figure 2.8—VMT and State Lane Mile Trends, 1957–1970 (indexed 1957 = 100)

the 1960s, the rapid growth of VMT foreshadowed massive congestion problems for the 1990s.

During the 1950s and 1960s, the state more than doubled its water storage capacity. Surface water storage capacity increased by 115 percent between 1950 and 1970, as a result of massive construction efforts for the State Water Project and lingering construction for the U.S. Bureau of

Reclamation's Central Valley Project. This growth outpaced the state's population increase, which was 88 percent during this period (Figure 2.9).

By and large, state government provided the leadership in infrastructure provision. The State Water Project, the state highway program, and the Master Plan for Higher Education all charted the way forward. Growth was good, and few argued against infrastructure investments. In the 1970s, things began to change.

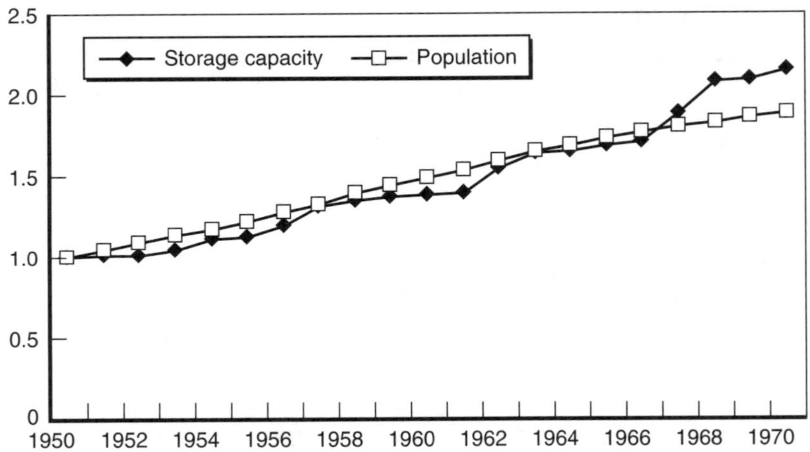

Figure 2.9—Water Storage Capacity and Population Trends, 1950–1970 (indexed 1950 = 100)

Living Off the Legacy

Three forces put the brakes on California's infrastructure program. The first was Ronald Reagan's ascendance in 1966. Reagan's skepticism about public spending led to decreases in capital investment. The second factor was the growth of the environmental movement and the proposition that small is beautiful. After Reagan, Californians elected a governor who believed in and implemented these ideas—Jerry Brown. Many Democrats expected a capital spending program to restart the state's growth machine, but Brown slowed infrastructure investment, claiming that there were limits to California's growth. The third force was the passage of Proposition 13 in 1978, which required a supermajority to approve local bond issues and the imposition of new taxes. Proposition 13 was widely perceived as a revolt against taxation and government expansion. Taken together, these forces led to smaller capital investments at the state level.

In the case of education, the 1970s started out with a baby bust, as K–12 enrollment declined 12 percent between 1970 and 1983. This decline provided some breathing room for schools, but by 1984, enrollments started to increase again. By the end of the century, K–12 enrollment was 31 percent higher than in the 1970s, and over 48 percent above the 1983 enrollment trough (Figure 2.10). After the baby bust, state and local capital expenditures managed to increase by over 50 percent above 1970 levels. However, in the aftermath of Proposition 13, capital outlays for K–12 became much more dependent on state support, and investments in K–12 facilities started to mirror the rise and fall of investment in higher education. During the initial stages of the resurgence (1985–1993), capital investment poured into K–12 schools. This flow of investment was not sustained. Real capital outlays declined as local districts had more and more difficulty raising funds for construction and repair, compounded by the deep recession of the early 1990s.

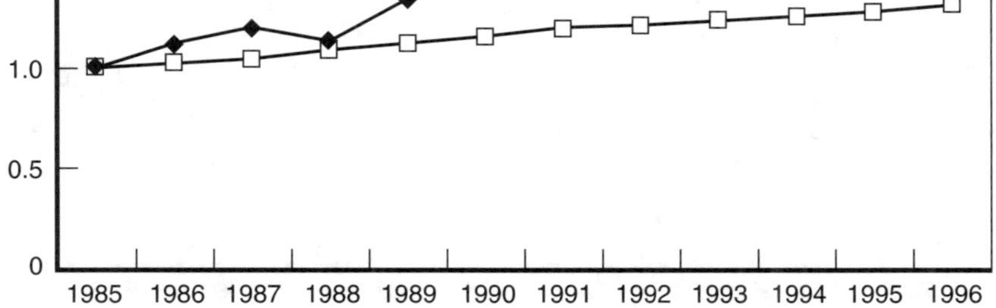

Figure 2.10—K–12 Enrollment and Real Capital Outlay, 1985–1996 (indexed 1985 = 100)

The situation in higher education was somewhat different. Enrollment in the three systems increased by 70 percent between 1970 and 2000. Although higher education did experience an enrollment bust in the late 1970s and early 1980s, it was less severe than that affecting K–12 enrollment. Another key difference between K–12 and higher education is the erratic nature of higher education facilities funding (Figure 2.11). Capital funding in higher education doubled, tripled, or dipped far below 1970 levels with only the slightest resemblance to enrollment.

In the transportation sector, the 1970s, 1980s, and 1990s marked incredible growth in VMT, which increased by 175 percent between 1970 and 2000 (Figure 2.12). At the same time, lane miles increased only about 20 percent. As a result, congestion has worsened across almost all of California's urban centers, some of which now rank as the most congested metropolitan areas in the nation (Texas Transportation Institute, 2001).

By the 1970s, practically all of the planned surface water storage for the State Water Project and Central Valley Project was complete, but other potential sites faced competing demands from a growing environmental movement. Surface water capacity grew by only 20 percent over the 1970–2000 period, whereas population increased by 73 percent (Figure 2.13).

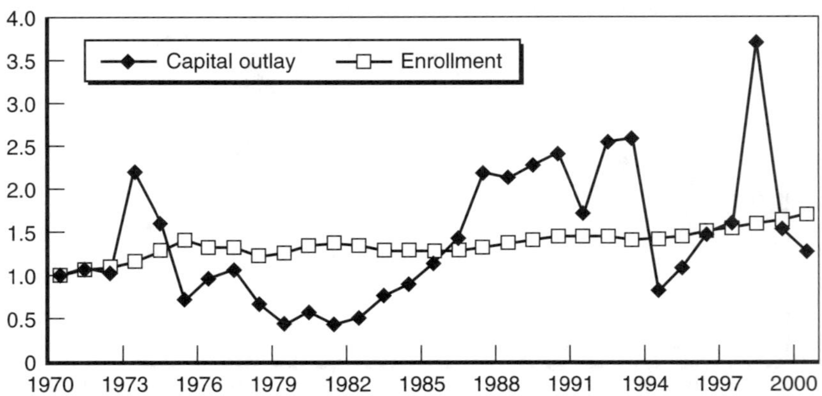

Figure 2.11—Higher Education Enrollment and Real Capital Outlay, 1970–2000 (indexed 1970 = 100)

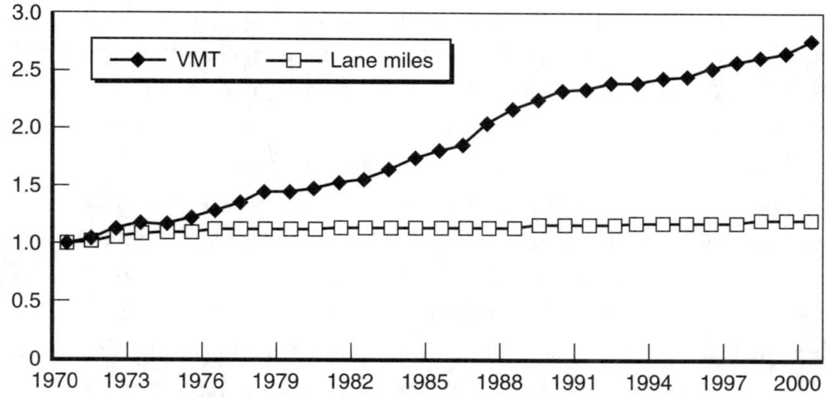

Figure 2.12—VMT and State Lane Mile Trends, 1970–2000 (indexed 1970 = 100)

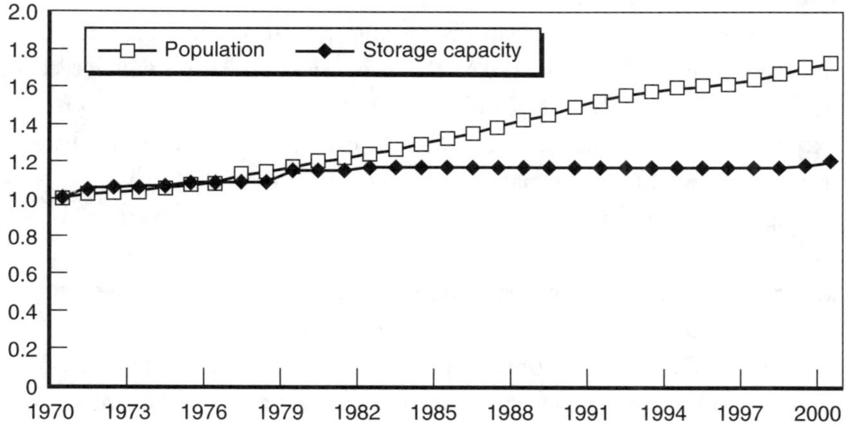

Figure 2.13—Water Storage Capacity and Population Trends, 1970–2000 (indexed 1970 = 100)

Overall, the state's ability to plan, design, and fund capital infrastructure seems to have run into serious problems. In some cases, the problem is financial; for example, Proposition 13 impaired local government's ability to fund K–12 facilities and local roads. In higher education, too, financial constraints and an aversion to fee hikes have created an unstable funding base. In the case of transportation, environmental reviews have made it more difficult to develop highways, but there is also a serious problem with declining real gasoline taxes and user charges. As a result, funds for transportation investment have been constrained. In the case of water supply, environmental concerns have made it difficult to expand surface water storage facilities.

When the economy rebounded in the 1990s, infrastructure planners realized that the state faced severe shortages of capacity. Schools and colleges were crowded, and traffic congestion was commonplace. No electricity plants were built between 1988 and 2000—a quiet broken by deregulation, accusations of market manipulation, and rolling blackouts. Moreover, a water crisis loomed on the horizon (Association of California Water Agencies, 1999).

Facing the Future

A new tidal wave of demand is coming to California. According to the Department of Finance (DOF), California's population will exceed 45 million by 2020 (Figure 2.14). By 2040, that figure is expected to exceed 58 million. Natural increase—the excess of births over deaths—is expected to emulate the pattern of the postwar period. Both immigration and domestic migration are expected to contribute to California's population growth as well. These increases will create additional demands for infrastructure; indeed, the strains will be even greater as the existing stock of infrastructure ages.

How these infrastructure demands manifest themselves depends largely on two factors—age structure and spatial patterns. According to the DOF, the child cohort (newborns to age 18) is expected to be the fastest growth segment of the population. Between 2000 and 2020, California will add 2.7 million children to its population. This increase will generate enormous demands on K–12 education. Increases in the age 18–24 cohort—those most likely to attend community colleges and universities—will also be significant. Between 2000 and 2020, this cohort will increase by one million, leading to substantial pressures on higher education.

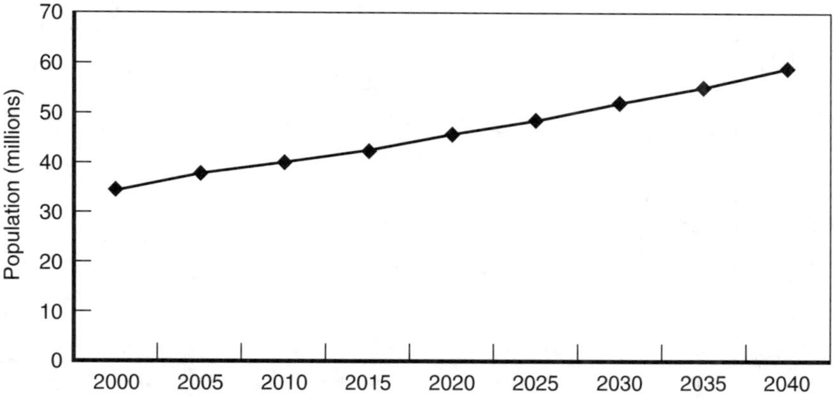

SOURCE: California Department of Finance (2000).

Figure 2.14—California Population Projections, 2000–2040

Enrollment projections for K–12 enrollment are expected to slow over the next ten years, providing welcome relief to many school districts around the state (Figure 2.15). After 2010, however, K–12 enrollment is expected to increase through 2040, as fertility rates increase with the state's changing ethnic composition.

Increases in higher education enrollment are not expected to follow the K–12 pattern of decline. California can expect sharp increases in enrollment over the next ten years in all three state higher education systems (Figure 2.16). The principal reason for the high rates of increase is demographic: The children of the baby boomers are now entering colleges and universities. An additional factor is the growing rate of enrollment in higher educational institutions. Both factors indicate that demand pressures will be acute in the higher education sector.

Where will all these new Californians live? The answer to this question will greatly affect demand for infrastructure investment. If developed areas can accommodate much of this population increase, the state can avoid developing new infrastructure networks in greenfield areas. A recent study estimates that approximately 95 percent of 2000–2020 population growth will be located in the state's urban and

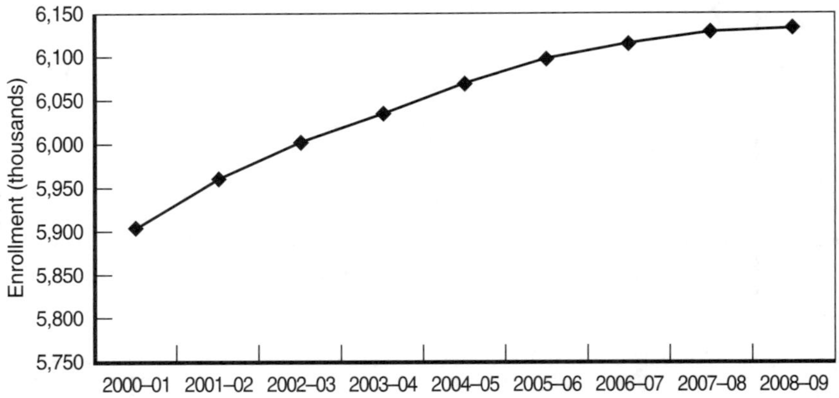

SOURCE: California Department of Finance (2000).

Figure 2.15—K–12 Enrollment Projections, 2000–2001 to 2008–2009

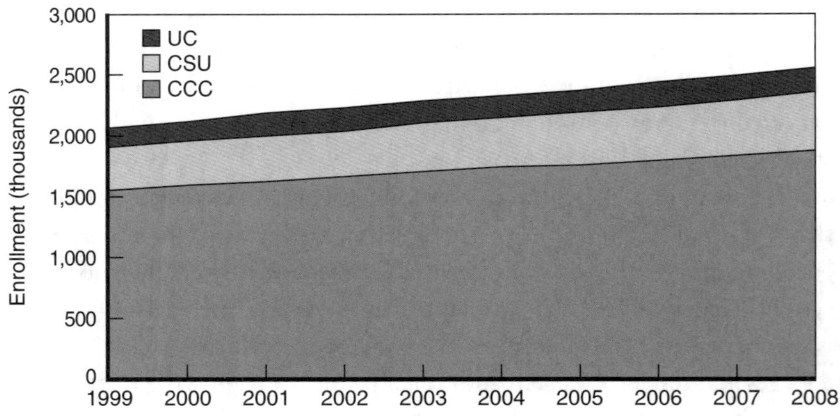

SOURCE: California Department of Finance (2000).

Figure 2.16—Higher Education Enrollment Projections, 1999–2008

metropolitan counties (California Department of Housing and Community Development, 2000). Three areas—greater Los Angeles, the San Francisco Bay Area, and San Diego—are projected to account for 68 percent of the total increase in population. Almost 23 percent of the growth is expected to occur in urbanizing regions within the Central

Valley such as Sacramento, Fresno, Bakersfield and Stockton. The remaining 9 percent will be dispersed across rural areas of the state.

Conclusions

According to Treasurer Phil Angelides, California's growth over the next 20 years will involve five million new jobs, goods and services for 12 million new residents, homes and facilities for over four million new households, and educational facilities for upward of two million new schoolchildren. Is the state ready to accommodate this demand? Much of California's infrastructure is overused, old, and obsolescent. Many facilities, already well past their intended lifespan, are bursting at the seams from constant, daily pressure and lack of maintenance. According to the Legislative Analyst's Office, California needs to overhaul its infrastructure systems (Legislative Analyst's Office, 1998b). The next two chapters provide a detailed assessment of California's crown-jewel infrastructure sectors—education, transportation, and water.

3. The Crown Jewels

Although California's population continues to increase rapidly, policymakers and taxpayers have tightened the spigot of capital outlays, choosing instead to spend on operations and local assistance. As a result, infrastructure supply has not matched demand in three sectors critical to California's economy—education, transportation, and water supply. Each of these complex sectors is managed according to its particular mandates, style, and decisionmaking processes. This chapter looks more precisely at the way the state plans, budgets, finances, constructs, and maintains these infrastructure systems. Along with the next chapter, it also offers a snapshot of the state's current physical and institutional capacity.

Education

California's public education system comprises K–12 public schools and the UC, CSU, and CCC systems. As the previous chapter indicated, the postwar boom remains the most significant period of physical expansion for this sector. Largely as a result of that expansion, California today has the largest system of K–12 and higher education facilities in the nation (Table 3.1). These four institutions are managed by state agencies whose organizational structures and processes bear little resemblance to one another. The following sections examine each sector, beginning with K–12 education.

K–12 Education

Unlike other sectors studied in this report, K–12 schools are governed locally by elected school boards. This fact would suggest a minimal role for the state, but funding trends have made Sacramento a major player in K–12 education. Throughout the early 1960s, school boards raised more than half their revenue through property taxes. Because property tax revenues reflected district wealth, school revenues

Table 3.1

California Public Education Facilities and Enrollment, 2000

System	Schools/ Campuses	Enrollment
K–12	8,761	6,050,900
CCC	109	1,558,500
CSU	23	367,400
UC	9[a]	183,400
Total	8,902	8,160,200

SOURCE: California Department of Finance (2001a); California Postsecondary Education Commission (2002).

[a]The opening of UC Merced gives UC a systemwide total of 10 campuses.

differed dramatically across districts. In the 1970s, the California Supreme Court ruled that this system violated the equal protection clause of the Fourteenth Amendment. A few years later, Proposition 13 transferred property taxes to state control and cut their value by 57 percent.

Despite increased state spending since that time, spending per pupil in California has declined more than 15 percent relative to that in other states. School districts dealt with the budget shortfall by allowing class sizes to climb, lobbying the state for additional funds, and seeking voluntary contributions.[1] Strapped for funds, many school districts deferred maintenance and sought to build schools at the lowest possible cost within the shortest possible timeframe. By the early 1990s, student achievement test scores had plummeted to the bottom of state rankings.[2] Some parents reacted by removing their children from district control; state laws were amended in 1992 to allow the formation of charter schools, which now number more than 274 statewide (WestEd and U.S.

---

[1]Since that time, the Class Size Reduction (CSR) initiative effectively limited class sizes through the third grade statewide; see Jepsen and Rivkin (2002).

[2]In the 1992, 1994, and 1998 reading tests, and the 1992 and 1996 math tests of the National Assessment of Educational Progress, California ranked in the bottom three states; see Sonstelie et al. (2000).

Department of Education, 2001). Other families paid premiums for houses in districts known for high test scores. Among the state's wealthiest families, private school enrollments rose significantly.

As financial authority for K–12 education shifted to the state, school construction has come to rely on the passage of statewide bonds. Since 1974, California voters have authorized nearly $29 billion in state general obligation bonds for the construction and rehabilitation of K–12 facilities (California Department of Finance, 2001a). Almost one-third of this funding came in 1998 with Proposition 1A, a $9.2 billion bond issue intended to provide class size reduction, accommodate growth, repair older schools, and provide wiring and cabling for education technology. Of this total, $6.7 billion was devoted to K–12 spending. These funds were intended to last at least four years (California Department of Finance, 2001b). As of November 5, 2002, only $550 million remained to be allocated (California Secretary of State, 2002). The largest of these bond measures was authorized in the November 5 election of 2002. Proposition 47 will provide $13.05 billion in funds: $11.4 billion for K–12 facilities and $1.65 billion for higher education.

The November 2000 passage of Proposition 39, which lowered the threshold for passing local bonds to 55 percent, suggests that local governments may now be able to pass the bonds necessary to grow with their school-age populations. As of April 2002, 110 local K–12 bond measures, authorizing $11.5 billion have passed (California Department of Finance, 2002). The Legislative Analyst's Office estimates that the state's cost of building necessary for today's K–12 facilities, assuming that local governments raise funds to match the state's commitment, amounts to roughly $20 billion (California Secretary of State, 2002).

As the current regulatory process for distributing state K–12 capital outlays, Proposition 1A and its implementing regulations merit close review. Articulated in Senate Bill 50 in August 1998, these regulations instituted a streamlined process for project approval, fund allocation, and capital outlays (Figure 3.1). Central to SB 50 is the School Facilities Program, which provides funding for new construction, modernization, deferred maintenance, relocatable classrooms, and hardships. Instead of using past methods, such as measuring cost per square foot for projects,

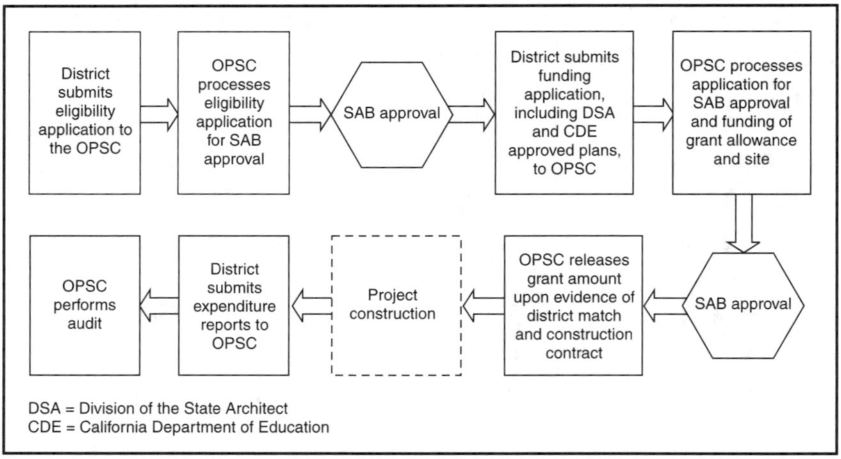

SOURCE: California Department of General Services (2002).

Figure 3.1—State K–12 School Building Funding Process Under SB 50 School Facilities Program

the program grants funds on a per-pupil basis. New construction funding is provided to districts in the form of 50-50 state-local matching funds; modernization funding is provided on an 80-20 basis. Local districts raise matching funds through local bonds, developer fees, federal grants, Mello-Roos districts, and other sources. Districts that meet one of several criteria—including the failure of two local bonds—can qualify for additional hardship funding from the state. Two units of the Department of General Services—the State Allocation Board (SAB) and the Office of Public School Construction (OPSC)—assess requests for project funding units. Eligibility for new construction is based on five-year projected enrollment. If projected enrollment exceeds the capacity of existing building stock, the district is eligible for new construction funds. Modernization funds are available for buildings at least 25 years old (20 years if leased space) (California Department of General Services, 2002).

Until recently, the SAB funded projects in the order in which they were received, a procedure that favored districts with more staff and better organization. Lawsuits placed on behalf of Los Angeles Unified School District, which did not receive SAB funds proportionate to its enrollment, revealed this method to be discriminatory. As a result of the ruling, the SAB has developed new criteria for processing applications that utilize a "priority point" system and consider enrollment levels. Once eligibility has been established, districts must obtain approval for specific project plans from the California Department of Education's School Facilities Planning Division and the state architect. Districts submit these plans to OPSC, which seeks approval from SAB; once approval is granted, OPSC can release state matching funds to the district. After construction, districts submit expenses to OPSC for audit.

The entire capital outlay process from initial planning through completion usually takes two to four years. For this reason, schools often make use of portable or temporary classrooms, which are authorized and funded under the State Relocatable Classroom Program. Portable classrooms can be completed in nine to 15 months (California Department of General Services, 2002).

SB 50 funds deferred maintenance conditional on the preparation of a five-year plan. After the plan is approved, districts receive a fund based on 0.5 percent of total district general funds besides capital outlay and debt service. Uncertainties in funding, however, have resulted in a backlog of deferred maintenance projects. In 1998, the California Department of Education estimated \$2.6 billion in deferred maintenance needs through 2003 and an additional \$9 billion for modernization, including seismic upgrades and technological improvements (California Department of Education, 1998b).

Higher Education

Higher education is governed by the state's Master Plan for Higher Education, first issued in 1960 and updated twice since then. Among other things, the original Master Plan defined the respective roles of the UC, CSU, and CCC systems. The Coordinating Council for Higher Education (now the California Postsecondary Education Commission) was established to review budget and capital outlay requests, manage growth, and interpret the Master Plan. Under that plan, UC continued to be governed by the regents, CSU gained a body of trustees modeled after the regents, and the community colleges formed district boards that were guided by statewide standards from the Board of Education (Liaison

Committee of the State Board of Education and The Regents of the University of California, 1960, p. 29).

The Master Plan suggested that no tuition be charged to California residents, although it recommended fees for access to ancillary facilities, such as laboratories. It also suggested that capital outlay funds be raised through bonds instead of pay-as-you-go financing to spread expenses over several years. Not all of the Master Plan's recommendations were embraced, however. Bond financing has been split equally among the three segments of higher education according to a "gentleman's agreement," despite the fact that the original Master Plan and subsequent reviews in 1972 and 1987 suggested that CCC receive as much as 45 percent of the total capital outlay (Liaison Committee of the State Board of Education and The Regents of the University of California, 1960, p. 171).

California Community Colleges. We turn now to a discussion of each segment and its capital outlay practices. The CCC system, which served over 1,558,500 full-time-equivalent (FTE) students in 2000, is spread across 72 districts, which consist of 109 campuses, more than 50 off-campus centers, and 20 district offices (California Department of Finance, 2001a). Its capital outlay process, described in the CCC *Facilities Planning Manual,* is more complex than those of the other higher education systems (Figure 3.2).

Two principal divisions of the CCC Chancellor's Office oversee the capital outlay process: the Building and Facilities Planning and Utilization Unit, which provides capital outlay assistance to campuses and centers; and Fiscal Services, which allocates state funds and sets forth accounting reporting requirements. Both are part of the Fiscal Policy Division of the Chancellor's Office. Partly because local districts oversee community colleges, the Chancellor's Office has done relatively little centralized planning for the system as a whole. At the campus level, college Master Plans, which are recommended but not required, show how facilities will fit into an overall educational plan and how goals will be financed. Five-Year Construction Plans list proposed projects in order of priority, inventory current space in terms of capacity and load, and describe how space needs will change if proposed projects are approved.

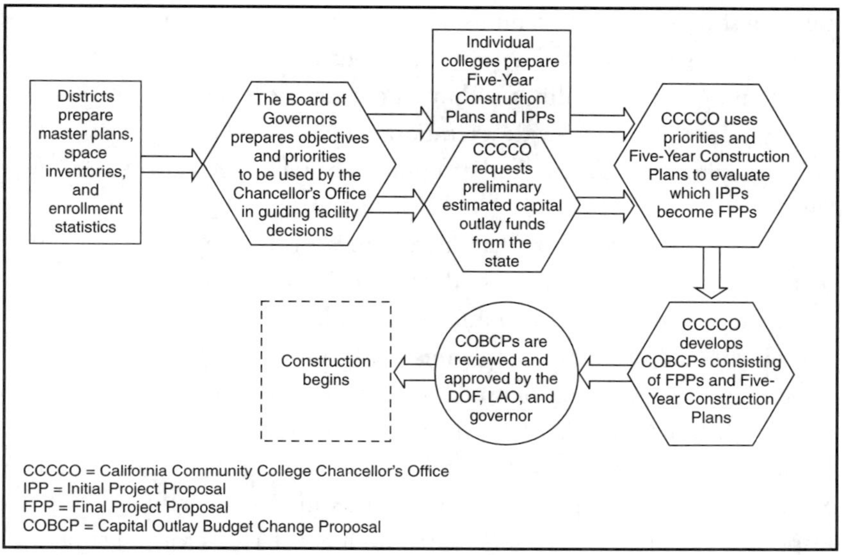

SOURCE: California Community Colleges (2002).

Figure 3.2—California Community College Capital Outlay Process

The CCC Chancellor's Office keeps copies of the college's Five-Year Construction Plans and maintains a space inventory of all CCC-owned buildings.

The Chancellor's Office reviews Initial Project Proposals from each campus based on the following ranked criteria: health and safety (with toxicity ranking above seismic upgrades), growth, modernization, campus completion, and instructional support (California Community Colleges, 1999). Historically, the Chancellor's Office has assessed proposed projects based on costs per square foot, but the system is moving toward a measure of cost per FTE served. No uniform standards exist for modernization costs. Instead, the review process ranks modernization projects according to how much less it would cost to modernize a structure than to build a new one.

The system has a large backlog of approved but unfunded capital projects (California Community Colleges, 2000). The "gentleman's agreement" has been hard on CCC—a system that has many more campuses to complete and maintain than other sectors. Because of funding shortages, many campuses have begun to depend on leased buildings outside the CCC system. Campuses may use state funds for maintaining leased buildings, although not for the lease itself. Although leasing is intended to provide a temporary option, the duration of lease occupancy for each district and campus is not monitored at the state level.

CCC's capital outlay and approval process is lengthy; it can take up to seven years from the time a building is proposed to the time of occupancy. Although leased buildings can fill temporary need while permanent facilities are being planned and constructed, buildings used for student occupancy (as opposed to administrative functions) must comply with the Field Act. The Field Act contains strict engineering and construction standards, intended to protect students in the event of an earthquake. Among other things, this act requires state architect inspection during construction—a requirement that has the effect of limiting qualifying facilities for CCC occupancy largely to K–12 schools. The Baldwin Act allows the Division of the State Architect to certify other types of buildings, such as vacant commercial buildings targeted for lease, as Field Act compliant, but the Division of the State Architect (DSA) at present has a large backlog and has not been able to certify any facilities.

Many CCC buildings are at least 40 years old; in addition, the state architect has identified 86 buildings in need of immediate seismic retrofit. CCC's revised funding priorities are designed to increase the rate of building modernization.

California State University. CSU consists of 23 campuses and seven off-campus centers, including the recently added Monterey Bay, Maritime Academy, and Channel Islands facilities, and served almost 367,400 FTEs in 2000 (California Postsecondary Education Commission, 2002). In theory, CSU serves the top third of California high school students. The Chancellor's Office estimates enrollment using information provided by the campuses. Current enrollment includes estimated summer-term students, whose numbers CSU hopes to increase through expansion of year-round education.

Although the system includes 22.5 million assignable square feet (ASF), (California State University, 1996), CSU is currently close to exceeding capacity if it has not done so already. Starting with the current budget cycle, CSU is shifting to a new method of calculating space needs that straightforwardly assesses ASF available per FTE. Campus officials are enthusiastic about this system, which replaces an older model based on station occupancy, although it is probably too early to assess true gains in efficiency. Space inventories are maintained by each campus and include a number of factors such as ASF, number of floors, and current use. This inventory is designed to guide campuses in estimating capital outlay needs. According to the new model, each campus is required to update this inventory every five years.

CSU is more centralized than CCC or UC. Within the Chancellor's Office, Capital Planning, Design, and Construction (CPDC) assists campuses in acquiring and budgeting needed physical facilities. CSU is the only one of the four educational sectors that explicitly requires that capital outlay expenditures be justified by a strategic plan. CSU conducts centralized strategic planning through its *Cornerstones Report*, issued in 1998, which defines the system's goals. In place of the *State Administrative Manual*, CSU makes use of its own contract and labor code, the *State University Administrative Manual*. CSU hired an outside firm to specify systemwide materials and unit costs, making the construction bidding process less expensive and more predictable. In addition, CSU is instituting a web-based system to track capital outlay project management and monitor costs.

In recent years, CSU has been delegating more authority to individual campuses. Since 1997, the authority to manage projects from design through occupancy has been assumed by individual campus presidents. The Chancellor's Office maintains oversight through quarterly status reports, expenditure projections, required compliance letters after drawings have been prepared, and a post-project review at completion. The capital outlay process recently devolved further to the campuses as a result of the findings of a Coopers & Lybrand report, which aimed to make the process shorter and more efficient. The new process is detailed in Figure 3.3.

Under this new system, CPDC consults, coordinates systemwide capital outlay, acts as advocate in Sacramento, and provides capital outlay management services for the three campuses—Los Angeles, Monterey

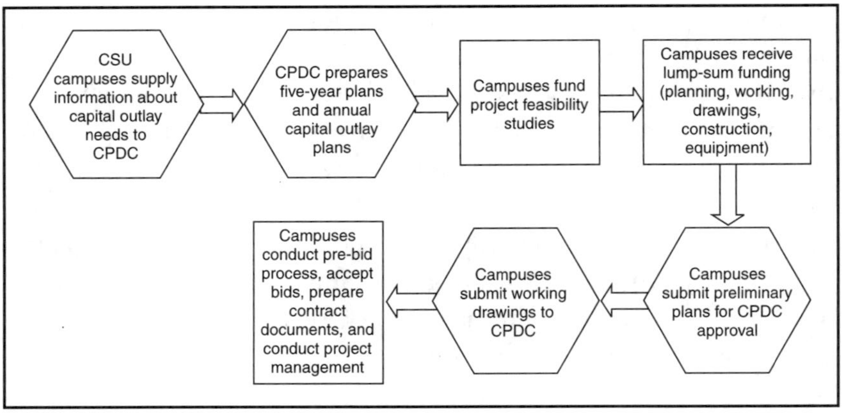

SOURCE: California State University (1996).

Figure 3.3—California State University Capital Outlay Process

Bay, and Maritime Academy—that are not certified to do so. Historically, the capital planning and outlay process has taken several years, but some CSU officials believe that the new system has shaved two years off the process.

A systemwide set of Academic Master Plans, adopted in 1963, is supposed to guide capital outlay decisions. Each campus is required to have a Physical Master Plan and a Five-Year Plan, compiled by CPDC into Five-Year Capital Outlay Plans. Like the CCC Chancellor's Office, CPDC has a priority system, funding projects with systemwide benefits first, then renovations, then new growth. Within the first two categories, projects that address life safety or telecommunications improvements have priority. Campuses can submit one project per budget year (excluding equipment, seismic upgrades, and telecommunications infrastructure) and three projects per year for the four planning years.

According to a 1998 CSU survey, 35 percent of CSU's buildings are more than 38 years old, and 73 percent are more than 18 years old (California State University, 1998b). Campuses are required to annually audit maintenance needs, develop a work order system for maintenance tasks, and keep a five-year prioritized list of maintenance projects. In addition, campuses are supposed to estimate deferred maintenance and equipment replacement needs.

University of California. UC's nine campuses had an overall FTE of 183,400 in 2000 (California Postsecondary Education Commission, 2002). As of 1998, UC maintained 5,015 buildings and 53 million ASF (California Postsecondary Education Commission, 1999). The UC Office of the President (UCOP) projects enrollments based on demographic factors, eligibility, and expected economic changes. These projections approximate those of the Department of Finance, although they are calculated by a different system. UC was originally designed to serve the top 12.5 percent of California high school students. In reality, the figure in recent years has been closer to 15 percent. In addition to ordinary enrollment growth, the California Postsecondary Education Commission (CPEC) projects that the number of community college transfers into UC will increase 5 percent annually in the next decade. Enrollment increases have already resulted in a slight capacity shortfall. CPEC predicts a 50,000 FTE capacity shortfall by 2010 if current trends continue.

As with the other sectors, UC's capital improvement has focused recently on seismic retrofit rather than new construction. The system's need for advanced research facilities has resulted in the construction of modern laboratories and other such facilities as a capital improvement priority. As a result, little new construction for the general student body is projected in the next few years.

Unlike CSU, UC uses a station-occupancy standard of space utilization rather than an ASF/FTE standard. Along with new construction, other solutions to the capacity shortfall include increased use of the summer term, more efficient use of existing classrooms (e.g., scheduling them for longer portions of the day), expanded use of off-campus centers, increased use of technology to facilitate distance learning, and shared-use facilities (e.g., with community colleges).

UC's 53.2 million ASF are 63 percent controlled by the state (California Postsecondary Education Commission, 2000). The state's responsibilities to the UC system are clearly delineated; the state funds infrastructure and basic research facilities, and UC funds housing, parking, recreation, hospitals, and, lately, research facilities that the state cannot afford to fund. In general, the state funds operations and maintenance for some UC as well as state-funded buildings.

Individual campuses conduct long-range planning; however, UCOP provides planning and oversight to campuses with less-experienced planning offices. After individual campuses decide their needs, UCOP provides feedback based on the expectations of the regents and the state. UCOP allocates state money to each campus based on projected enrollment, budget size, seismic and modernization needs, geographical variations in construction costs, and other funding considerations (e.g., alumni donations). Campuses have the authority to prioritize projects based on the funding targets they are given from UCOP.

Figure 3.4 shows the steps in the capital outlay process. The entire process, from conception and planning through occupancy, takes two to five years. UCOP helps each campus fund detailed project planning studies on facility requirements for upcoming projects in the next fiscal year. Campuses compile the studies into Five-Year Capital Plans—or, as of 2000, Ten-Year Plans—which are approved by the regents and sent to the state. Individual campuses must fund cost overruns from these projections. In addition to producing the Five-Year Plans, campus planning offices are responsible for the preparation of

- Long-term space plans detailing the projected uses of buildings,
- Long-range development plans integrating academic and physical development,

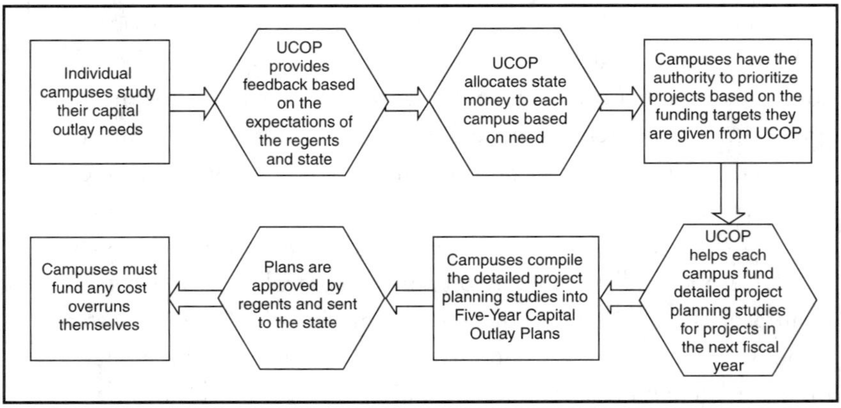

SOURCE: University of California (2002).

Figure 3.4—University of California Capital Outlay Process

- Ancillary planning, including leased properties, area plans, and income production areas,
- Predesign after funding is secured, and
- A Capital Improvement Program dealing with issues of growth, renewal, life safety, and environmental concerns (University of California, 2002).

Individual campuses oversee the construction process; completed construction documents are reviewed by the DSA, state fire marshal, and other applicable agencies such as the Office of Statewide Health Planning and Development (for health facilities) or the Coastal Commission.

Like the other sectors of higher education, UC has urgent maintenance and building replacement needs. This urgency is compounded by insufficient funds for operations and maintenance. Since 1970, UCOP has been required to submit an annual report to the legislature on deferred maintenance; since 1984, it has also had to audit, inspect, and prioritize deferred maintenance projects. The UCOP Budget Office compiles funded and unfunded deferred maintenance lists based on information submitted by the individual campuses. Another category of modernization, called "renewal," is distinguished from deferred maintenance and defined as comprehensive upgrading or replacement of facilities, systems, and infrastructure. Although these are included in the Facility Audit, they are considered to be included in the Capital Improvement Program and not in deferred maintenance. In practice, however, the distinctions may be less clear-cut.

Transportation

Compared to public education, the transportation sector and its organizational structure is monolithic. Transportation management is conducted by a single statewide entity that sees itself as the trustee of the state's highway system. That entity, California's Department of Transportation (or Caltrans), has undertaken and managed almost every major transportation project in the state.

State involvement in transportation began in 1895 with the formation of the Bureau of Highways, the precursor to Caltrans, and grew with the popularity of the automobile. In 1923, the state levied its first gasoline tax; during the Great Depression, it took over toll bridges and joined federal efforts in road building (California Department of Transportation, 2001b). In 1956, a nationwide gasoline tax was passed; in 1959, plans for a 12,240-mile California Freeway System were completed (Federal Highway Administration, 1996). Almost three-quarters of the state's highways were built in the next 15 years (California Department of Transportation, 1998a, p. 19). Demand for road construction continued to rise in subsequent years, but state and federal funding slowed and interest in public transit increased. In the late 1980s and early 1990s, the effects of two major earthquakes further diverted transportation funds to seismic retrofits and rehabilitation.

As of 2000, the state highway system encompassed 15,251 centerline miles (Table 3.2), which, when split into lanes, comes to some 51,000 lane miles. About 925 lane miles are high occupancy vehicle (HOV) lanes, which are restricted to vehicles with two or more (sometimes three or more) occupants during peak travel hours. The system also includes about 80 miles of toll lanes in Southern California that charge variable

Table 3.2

State Road Transportation Network, 2000

Type	Description	Miles
State highways	Centerline miles	15,251
	Lane miles	50,519
	Two-lane conventional roadway in centerline miles	8,492
	Multilane conventional roadway in centerline miles	885
	Expressway in centerline miles	1,638
	Freeway in centerline miles	4,188
HOV lanes[a]	HOV lane miles	925
Toll lanes[a]	Toll lane miles	80
Maintained roads	Total centerline miles of public roads (state highways included)	168,132
	Cities' total centerline miles	70,273
	Counties' total centerline miles	66,131

SOURCE: California Department of Transportation (2002); and Legislative Analyst's Office (2000b).

[a]HOV and toll lanes as of 1998.

tolls based on congestion levels. The state supports the construction and maintenance of 66,131 centerline miles of county roads and 70,273 centerline miles of city streets—a total of about 381,000 lane miles (California Department of Transportation, 2002; California Department of Finance, 2001a; Legislative Analyst's Office, 2000b).

From 1988 to 1998, the state's population increased 18 percent, vehicle registration 7 percent, licensed drivers 9.5 percent, and vehicle miles traveled 21 percent. Since 1990, however, the supply of freeway lane miles has increased by about 1 percent, or about 70 new miles of highway with 1,300 new lane miles. Demand is unevenly distributed, contributing to mounting delays on urban freeways (Legislative Analyst's Office, 2000b).

The State's Transit System

The state also plays a major role in supporting California's 209 public transit operators. The majority of these are bus operators, but commuter and urban rail systems, ferry boats, demand response vehicles, and the nation's intercity rail system—maintained by Amtrak—are also included in this figure. In all, about 1.16 trillion riders use nine modes of service annually throughout the state (see Table 3.3) (California Department of Transportation, 1999a).

Like highway VMT, transit is concentrated in large urban areas. Approximately 82 percent of transit ridership occurs in the metropolitan regions of San Francisco and Los Angeles. Unlike VMT, however, transit ridership has remained relatively stable over the last decade (Legislative Analyst's Office, 2000b). However, this steady ridership belies the financial needs of transit. Transit tends to serve the poorest populations, and historic investment has favored highway expenses. Operating costs for transit seem high relative to those for highways. Farebox revenues often provide less than 50 percent of operating costs, and local subsidies of transit operations are often under threat.[3]

---

[3]Operating costs typically include labor for operations and maintenance and the capital cost of maintenance and rehabilitation. Popular perception holds that transit operations are set apart from highways by farebox revenues, which are used to cover operational costs. In reality, highways and transit are both subsidized.

Table 3.3

The State Transit System, 1998

Metropolitan Area	Agencies	Annual Ridership
Los Angeles and vicinity	Los Angeles Metro Rail	377,237,475
	Orange County Transit	48,594,433
	Long Beach Public Transit	24,041,288
	Santa Monica Transit	19,321,060
	Foothill Transit Zone	15,249,854
	Montebello Transit	5,802,802
	Southern California Regional Rail	5,497,704
	Six others with 1–5 million riders each	20,250,278
	Total annual ridership	*515,994,894*
San Francisco Bay	San Francisco MUNI	217,629,795
	Bay Area Rapid Transit	82,899,655
	Alameda–Contra Costa Transit	62,879,364
	Santa Clara Transit	53,330,866
	San Mateo Transit	18,652,256
	Golden Gate	11,124,740
	Peninsula Corridor	7,040,034
	Six others with 1–5 million riders each	13,309,574
	Total annual ridership	*466,866,280*
San Diego	San Diego Transit	33,266,035
	San Diego Trolley	18,286,616
	Northern San Diego County Transit	12,809,832
	San Diego Metro Transit	7,499,747
	Three others with 1–5 million riders each	8,433,304
	Total annual ridership	*80,295,534*
Sacramento	Sacramento Regional Transit	26,700,405
	One other with 1–5 million riders	2,101,302
	Total annual ridership	*28,801,707*
San Bernardino-Riverside	Omni Trans	11,078,698
	Riverside Transit	6,391,632
	Two others with 1–5 million riders each	5,007,957
	Total annual ridership	*22,478,287*
San Joaquin	Fresno Transit	9,632,078
	Golden Empire Transit	5,133,487
	Three others with 1–5 million riders each	7,022,258
	Total annual ridership	*21,787,823*

Table 3.3 (continued)

Metropolitan Area	Agencies	Annual Ridership
Santa Barbara	Santa Barbara Transit	6,846,029
	One other with 1–5 million riders	3,125,286
	Total annual ridership	*9,971,315*
Monterey	One agency with 1–5 million riders	3,816,002
	Total annual ridership	*10,506,534*

SOURCE: California Department of Transportation (1999a) .

NOTE: Details shown for 44 transit operators, known to carry 98 percent of the state's ridership. The remaining 2 percent of riders are carried by 165 operators spread throughout the state in small urban and rural areas. Figures are for fiscal year 1997–1998.

Management of the System

The design, operation, and maintenance of this vast transportation network is the responsibility of state headquarters, three engineering service centers, and 12 district offices of Caltrans. Caltrans works with the California Transportation Commission (CTC) and 43 Regional Transportation Planning Agencies (RTPAs).[4] RTPAs, in turn, work with county governments and other regional or local entities, such as Transit Agencies and Congestion Management Agencies. Although Caltrans recognizes itself as "the unit of state government responsible for the state highway system (or as a 'trustee' on behalf of the citizens of the state)" (California Department of Transportation, 1998c), it is primarily responsible for interregional transportation planning. The interregional road system was identified by statute in 1989 and now includes 87 of the state highway system's 249 routes. Planning for all others is the domain of the RTPAs.

The CTC consists of nine members appointed by the governor for staggered four-year terms. Each house of the legislature includes a transportation committee, and the chairs of these committees commonly serve as nonvoting members on the CTC; the chairs of the legislature's budget committees are ex-officio members. The CTC has been

[4]RTPAs in urban areas are commonly known by their federal term, Metropolitan Planning Organizations.

operating as a banker for proposed and ongoing projects. The CTC may also recommend policy and funding priorities to the legislature.

The state uses the State Transportation Improvement Project (STIP) to select projects for funding, to schedule those projects, and to decide when to allocate funds (Figure 3.5). A new STIP, which is essentially a list of new projects added to ongoing ones, is prepared in even-numbered years. The 1998 STIP included new projects slated to begin development over a six-year horizon; in 2000, that horizon changed to four years.[5] At any one time, there may be 2,000 to 3,000 projects active or listed and awaiting completion in the STIP. Caltrans conducts 20-year needs assessments, based on conceptual studies of transportation

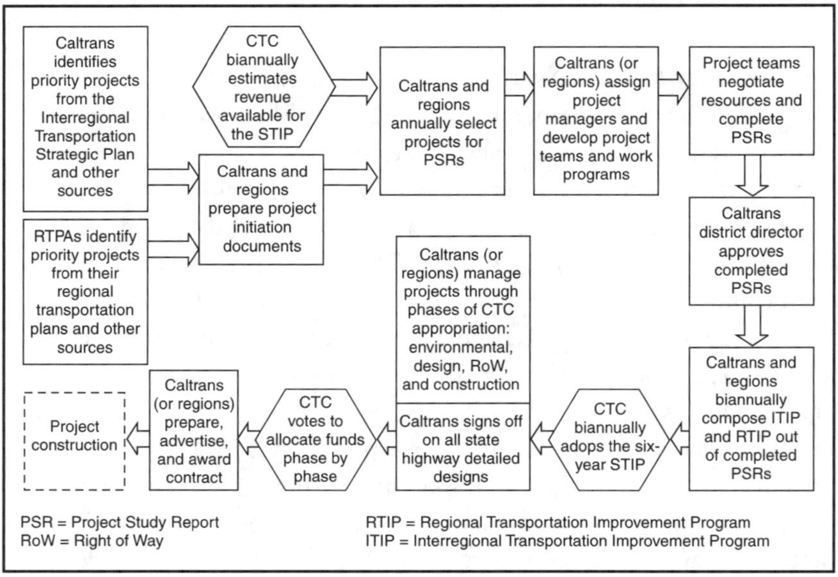

SOURCE: California Department of Transportation (1998b), Legislative Analyst's Office (2000b), and personal interviews.

Figure 3.5—Caltrans and California Transportation Commission STIP Process

---

[5]Proposals abound to change the time horizon for the STIP, with the intention that projects listed in each STIP should be fully funded and completed by the end of that period.

corridors, the Transportation System Development Program, and Caltrans District System Management Plans. Most interregional projects that emerge from long-range planning are identified in Caltrans Interregional Transportation Strategic Plan (California Department of Transportation, 1998b). RTPAs vary in their planning methods but look generally toward a 20-year horizon for the preparation of Regional Transportation Plans.

Projects are advanced to the STIP by Caltrans district managers and regional agencies. Project initiation includes analyses of engineering feasibility and financing, railroad and utility involvement, traffic operations, transportation management plans, environmental questions, and identification of individuals and institutions likely to be affected. After screening the project initiation documents, Caltrans and regional agencies select projects for continued study every year. Large projects require Project Study Reports, and small projects—categorically exempt from National Environmental Policy Act and California Environmental Quality Act review—require Project Scope and Summary Reports (California Department of Transportation, 1998c). Even though regional agencies plan for a vast majority of state highway routes, new projects will not advance to the STIP for funding without the signature of a Caltrans district manager on the project report. Caltrans staff prefer to conduct all engineering tasks in-house, including the conceptual engineering for Project Study Reports. In doing so, they call attention to the constitutional requirement that Caltrans sign off on every state highway design.

Project selection depends in part on the amount of funds anticipated from the next STIP; the CTC therefore approves revenue estimates generated by Caltrans every two years for the upcoming STIP. Caltrans prepares estimates from projections of funding sources for the State Highway Account. The estimates are prepared by placing available funds in order of priority as follows: revenues are forecasted; inflation is added; overhead costs, such as Caltrans administrative costs, are subtracted; funds required for maintenance and rehabilitation of state highways are subtracted; funds for local assistance are subtracted; funds are then devoted to previous STIP projects; and any remaining funds are divided 75 percent to new regional projects and 25 percent to new interregional projects. STIP funds for new regional projects are distributed according to statutorily defined formulas to county governments, based on a north-south split, the number of centerline highway miles in the county, and population. Fifty-eight counties and the Tahoe region receive STIP funds, and these organizations work with the RTPAs to identify projects.

All projects funded 50 percent or more by the state are assigned a Caltrans project manager. Project managers select a team of experts and define the work program for each project. These project managers and their teams are responsible for re-evaluating preliminary engineering and systems planning data, ensuring design quality and constructability, assessing the need for advisory committees and additional studies, recommending the appropriate environmental document, initiating community involvement, and various other tasks. Project teams may include individuals from outside agencies, experts in various fields, and representatives from community groups. Theoretically, project managers and their teams stay with their projects from the Project Study Report stage through construction. In reality, turnover is common, and the agency has difficulty hiring in high-demand regions such as Los Angeles. When regions are responsible for project management, they may call on Caltrans for local assistance; indeed, a sizable portion of Caltrans operating budget is devoted to this category. They may also hire Caltrans to perform tasks.

Projects are selected during odd-numbered years and submitted to CTC in September. The CTC holds hearings in October and November and adopts the STIP in December of the same year. In approving projects for the STIP, the CTC can accept or reject only the entire list nominated by each county.[6] By adopting the STIP, the CTC promises to make a certain set of funds available to Caltrans and the counties for the projects listed therein. Each project has its own schedule and budget, outlined in the Project Study Report (PSR). Project managers then request funds from CTC, which votes to distribute the

---

[6]Although counties control STIP funds for regional projects, and therefore approach the CTC for STIP funds, the RTPAs develop the regional lists of projects. All projects nominated for the STIP in a region must fit within the funding available to the counties in that region. Needs are often greater than available funds, and how these regional lists are finalized varies from region to region.

funds in six phases: environmental review, detailed design, right-of-way acquisition capital costs and support, and construction capital costs and support.

Although funds may be requested from CTC at any time during the calendar year, projects may not request funds until they are ready to engage in the next phase of work. If funds are programmed for that year and are not requested within a three-year window, they revert back to CTC for other uses. As schedules slip, however, project managers and sponsoring agencies may request up to 20-month extensions for access to programmed funds. The extension request must specify the cascading effect any delay will have on subsequent requests for funding. Extensions are allowed once per project phase. As costs increase, Caltrans and counties or the sponsoring agency may simply request augmentations for the same project in the next STIP cycle. In cases where projects are completed ahead of schedule, sponsoring agencies may go on to the next project with remaining funds.

It is important to note that the allocation of STIP funds to projects is restricted by source of funds. The California State Constitution restricts the use of state gas tax revenues to the planning, construction, maintenance, and operation of public streets and highways, and to the planning, construction, and maintenance of mass transit tracks or related fixed facilities, such as transit stations. The Public Transportation Account funds projects that are ineligible for State Highway Account funds, such as transit rolling stock and operations. In accordance with SB 45, the allocation of State Transit Assistance funds has been folded into the STIP. Nevertheless, highways have consistently received more funding than transit projects. The Legislative Analyst's Office (2000b) estimated that mass transportation constituted 9 percent of the total state transportation expenditures in 2000–2001. Only a handful of RTPAs evaluate the mass transit sector along with highways in their travel-demand models; as a result, regional forecasts of demand for transit and highways are separate, making prioritization between transit and highway projects difficult.

The entire process can take as little as three years, although projects that have multiple jurisdictions, potentially large environmental impacts, and substantial federal funding frequently take ten or more years to implement. Some projects have been on the books for as long as 30 years. New measures have begun to address the timing of project delivery. One of the most promising is a pilot project in design sequencing pursuant to Assembly Bill (AB) 405 (Chapter 378, Statutes of 1999), which allows construction to begin for portions of projects as soon as design is complete.[7]

The STIP is not the only method by which transportation projects receive funding. SB 1435 (1992) redirected about $600 million per year in federal transportation funding to regional agencies, counties, and cities outside the STIP process (California Transportation Commission, 1999a). Local funds—such as state gas tax subventions, local sales taxes, general funds, bond proceeds, and road taxes—also dedicate a significant amount of revenue to transportation purposes. Many projects in the Governor's Traffic Congestion Relief Plan (AB 2928) were not developed using the planning processes of the STIP, and these new funds and projects create pressure at the local level to re-prioritize regional plans.

Maintenance

Caltrans plans and implements state highway maintenance through the State Highway Operations and Protection Program (SHOPP). The Streets and Highways Code mandates that the operation, maintenance, and rehabilitation of the state highway system is the first priority for highway account funds (California Department of Transportation, 1998a). As a result, SHOPP funds are approved very early in the STIP process.

Unlike highways, no mandate exists for prioritizing maintenance and operations within the mass transit sector. Transit systems typically carry an operating shortfall of 60 percent or greater, which has generally been

---

[7]AB 1012 (Chapter 783, Statutes of 1999), which created the State Highway Account Loan Program, also attempts to expedite project delivery. County-level allocations of Federal Surface Transportation Program and Congestion Mitigation and Air Quality funds can be redirected by CTC if a region fails to obligate those funds within three fiscal years. The measure allows local governments with qualifying projects to apply for use of these unobligated funds on a first-come, first-served basis. It also authorizes CTC to make loans available for local projects and adds an "advance project development element" to allow environmental review and project development work to proceed earlier than usual.

met by local sales tax revenues—which are scheduled to sunset over the next 11 years in 15 out of 21 counties—and a small portion of federal and state funds. Federal law eliminated transit operation subsidies for urban areas with populations greater than 200,000, although preventive maintenance has emerged as a new category of transit funding.

Water Supply

On average, about 200 million acre-feet (MAF) of snow and rain fall annually in California.[8] About 40 percent of this precipitation occurs in the North Coast region, and about 32 percent falls in the Sacramento River region (California Department of Water Resources, 1999a). Most of the state's residents, however, live in the arid southern part of the state. This fact, coupled with the variability of the state's annual precipitation, has driven the gradual buildup of water regulation, management, storage, and conveyance through most of California's history.

In 1887, the legislature enacted the Wright Irrigation District Act, one of many acts allowing the formation of local water districts. By 1914, the Water Commission Act took effect, establishing a system of state-issued permits and licenses to appropriate water; this function is carried out today by the State Water Resources Control Board (SWRCB) (California Department of Water Resources, 1994; Littleworth and Garner, 1995). The state's largest municipalities used their financial and political wherewithal to obtain rights to water in the Sierra Nevada and to develop elaborate conveyance systems for importing that water. The scale of these projects increased the state and federal involvement in water supply. The two largest water supply systems operating in California today are the Central Valley Project, which is directed by the U.S. Bureau of Reclamation (USBR), and the State Water Project, which falls under the auspices of the California Department of Water Resources (DWR). These vast developments are at the heart of California's water supply system.

[8]An acre-foot is the amount of water that would cover a one-acre area to a depth of one foot, or 325,850 gallons. Water planners typically estimate that one acre-foot is sufficient to supply a family of four for a year. In agricultural usage, an acre of crops requires between two and seven acre-feet per year. In both sectors, climate and other factors affect consumption.

In an effort to make use of the 71 MAF of surface water flowing annually through the state, California has built 47 MAF of storage capacity. Most of this capacity was added between 1935 and 1979, when nearly 39 MAF of reservoir capacity was constructed. Since 1980, less than 1.8 MAF of storage capacity has been added. The USBR controls about half of the state's surface water storage, including California's annual entitlement to 4.4 MAF behind Hoover Dam. The state is directly responsible for 5.6 MAF of storage (including facilities shared with the USBR) through the DWR. The remaining storage is controlled by a variety of national, regional, and local entities (Table 3.4.)

The largest of these agencies, USBR and DWR, act as state-level wholesale suppliers. In addition to storing the most surface water, these agencies manage the most significant conveyance systems (Table 3.5).

Table 3.4

California's Surface Water Storage Capacity, by Agency with Greater Than 250,000 Acre-Feet of Storage Capacity

Agency	Acre-Feet of Storage	Percentage of Storage
U.S. Bureau of Reclamation	21,318,981	45
California Department of Water Resources	5,668,223	12
U.S. Army Corps of Engineers	3,788,516	8
Pacific Gas and Electric Company	2,493,597	5.3
Turlock Irrigation District	2,077,060	4.4
Metropolitan Water District of Southern California	1,087,715	2.3
Merced Irrigation District	1,049,030	2.2
Yuba County Water Agency	971,897	2.1
City and County of San Francisco	896,357	1.9
East Bay Municipal Utility District	796,172	1.7
Monterey County Water Resource Agency	700,000	1.5
Southern California Edison Company	637,936	1.3
Yolo County Flood Control and Water Conservation District	615,000	1.3
City of Los Angeles Department of Water and Power	435,046	.9
San Diego County Water Authority	430,869	.9
Sacramento Municipal Utility District	371,975	.8
Placer County Water Authority	348,491	.7
Nevada Irrigation District	262,344	.6
Subtotal	43,949,191	92.8
1,008 other facilities	3,389,987	7.2
Total	47,339,178	100

SOURCE: California Department of Water Resources, Division of Dam Safety.

Table 3.5

Major Conveyance, by Agency

Agency	Miles of Conveyance[a]
U.S. Bureau of Reclamation[b]	889
California Department of Water Resources[b]	662
Metropolitan Water District of Southern California	294
City of Los Angeles Department of Water and Power	244
San Diego County Water Authority	164
City and County of San Francisco	152
East Bay Municipal Utility District	90
Kern County Water Agency	20
Mojave Water Agency	71
Total	2,586

SOURCE: California Department of Water Resources (1987).

[a]Greater than 200 cubic feet per second flow capacity.

[b]USBR and DWR figures include the 165-mile San Luis Canal, which is shared by both agencies.

USBR and DWR supplement water furnished by thousands of water wholesalers and retailers at the regional and local levels. A total of 2,850 water districts, agencies, or other entities in California provide supply functions (Table 3.6). Several agricultural and municipal agencies function as wholesalers at the regional level, transporting water directly from source basins, rivers, or USBR and DWR facilities to smaller distributors or consumers in their own service areas.

This system of reservoirs, aqueducts, pipelines, and pumping stations is intended to smooth out the peaks and troughs that occur in the natural hydrologic cycle. Yet the state's water system is not integrated along the lines of the highway system or electricity grid. Instead, each component has been added incrementally to meet specific demands.

Beneath this latticework of dams and aqueducts, groundwater serves as the next largest source of water supply in the state. In an average year, about 14.5 MAF, or 30 percent of the state's annual water consumption, are supplied with groundwater (California Department of Water Resources, 1999a). The total storage capacity of California's groundwater basins is estimated at one billion acre-feet. The largest of

Table 3.6

Local Water Supply Agencies in California

Type	Ownership	Number
County Service Area	Public	880
Mutual Water Company	Private	801
Community Services District	Public	309
Investor-Owned Water Utility	Private	195
County Water District	Public	178
Water District	Public	157
Irrigation District	Public	97
Public Utility District	Public	52
Flood Control and Water Conservation District	Public	41
County Water Works District	Public	40
Municipal Water District	Public	40
Water Agency or Water Authority	Public	31
Water Conservation District	Public	13
Water Storage District	Public	8
Municipal Utility District	Public	5
Water Replenishment District	Public	2
Metropolitan Water District	Public	1
Total		2,850

SOURCE: California Department of Water Resources (1999a, Table 4A-1).

NOTE: Water supply may also be provided by local agencies having other purposes (e.g., reclamation districts).

these basins are in the alluvial plains of the Central Valley. Of the total groundwater supply, the State Water Resources Control Board estimates that about 250 MAF are usable with today's pumping technology.

As a method of storage, groundwater has some advantages over surface water. It does not evaporate, the basins do not require continual maintenance and repair, and a certain amount of groundwater can be extracted regularly without seriously depleting the aquifer. DWR has estimated, however, that California's groundwater supply is being overdrawn by an average of 1.5 MAF per year. Although groundwater concerns are left largely to local entities, the ties between surface water and groundwater are inescapable. State involvement in groundwater management has, for the most part, been limited to the adjudicating function of the SWRCB, as refined over time through court cases.

On the demand side of the equation, there are three general categories for water demand in California: urban, agricultural, and environmental. The urban category comprises residential, commercial, industrial, and institutional uses of water. In 1995, about 8.8 MAF were used in the urban sector. Agricultural water use accounts for the water consumed through the irrigation of over nine million acres of crops, located primarily in the Central Valley. Irrigated agricultural acreage has decreased slightly since 1980 without a discernible decrease in the demand for irrigation water. In 1995, about 33.8 MAF were consumed in agriculture. Court cases and a series of federal and state laws directed at restoring and maintaining water quality, protecting species and habitat, and preventing environmental degradation have brought about the recognition of environmental demands for water. In 1995, these uses accounted for about 36.9 MAF.

California's projections of water demand for 2020 depict a 36 percent increase in urban use, about a 7 percent reduction in agricultural use, and an increase in environmental use of less than 1 percent. These projections leave California consuming approximately 2.5 MAF more, in an average year, than is supplied annually. In drought years the deficit is estimated at 6.2 MAF.

The traditional response to such shortfalls has been the development of more surface water infrastructure. At this point, however, the promising surface water supply projects have either been built or excluded through increasingly protective regulations and laws. Smaller, costlier projects are being pursued by local agencies, which have become the primary constructor of water projects over the last 20 years. The desire for a cooperative solution to the state's water problems led to the 1994 formation of CALFED, whose features are discussed in the following section.

The U.S. Bureau of Reclamation

We turn now to the major institutions and projects of California's water supply system, beginning with the largest water wholesaler in the nation. The USBR's jurisdiction extends across 17 western states. Within these states are five administrative regions, delimited largely by watersheds as opposed to political boundaries (Figure 3.6). As one of eight bureaus housed in the Department of the Interior, the USBR was founded to provide irrigation water to homesteads and family farms.

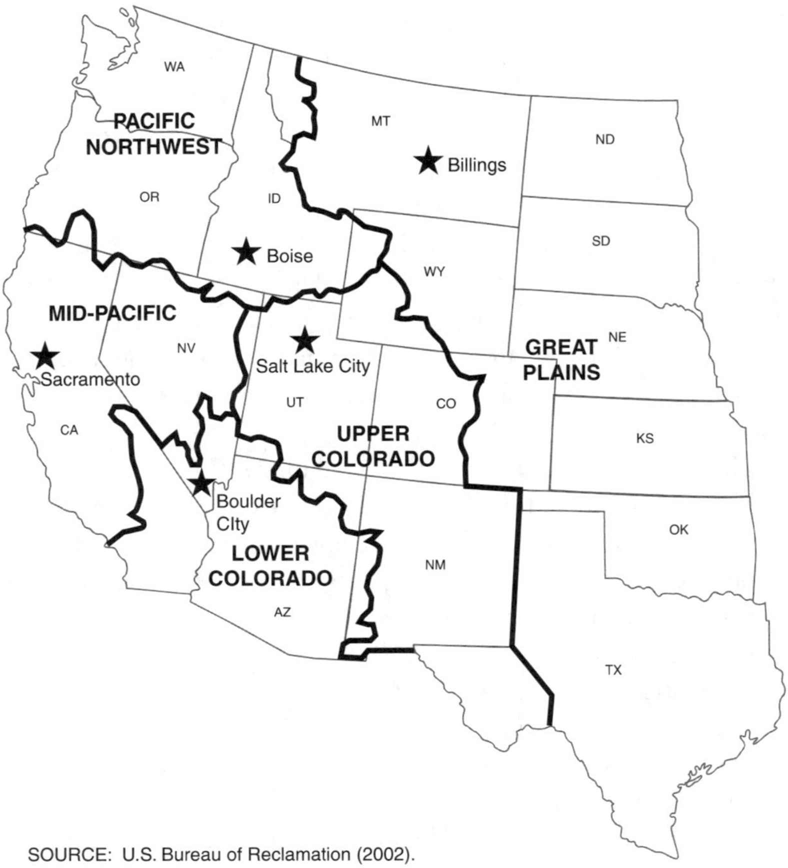

SOURCE: U.S. Bureau of Reclamation (2002).

Figure 3.6—Regional Offices of the U.S. Bureau of Reclamation

Over the years, the USBR expanded its services to include municipal and industrial users, Native American tribes, fish and wildlife, and recreational users of water. Its primary role is to "deliver water to customers to provide social, economic and environmental benefits, as authorized by Congress" (U.S. Bureau of Reclamation, 2001a, p. 23). Historically, this role emphasized impounding and diverting waters with new dams and conveyance facilities.

The Reclamation Act of 1902 required that the USBR conform to state laws relating to the control, appropriation, distribution, and use of water. Water rights settlements, local regulations, and legal mandates are beyond USBR control, and they have gradually placed pressure on the USBR to discontinue development plans. Today, USBR's primary role is reflected in the long-term goal of increasing water use efficiency and recycling. These goals are carried toward the USBR's management of water for California from the Lower Colorado River and the Central Valley Project (U.S. Bureau of Reclamation, 2001a).

The Lower Colorado River. As one of seven states entitled to Colorado River water, California began diverting water in 1914. The state's use has gradually grown over time, from an initial 1.7 MAF in 1914 to 5.2 MAF in 1999 (U.S. Bureau of Reclamation, 1996). Its rights are governed by a complex set of compacts, laws, court cases, treaties, and contracts developed over the past 75 years. The last 688 miles of the Colorado River—the portion of the river accessible to California users—is managed by the USBR's Lower Colorado Region, which apportions water to Nevada, Arizona, and a handful of Southern California water districts (see Figure 3.7). The USBR's Lower Colorado Region is directly accountable to the Secretary of the Interior because of the interstate nature of the Colorado River.

The Colorado River system of reservoirs is built to sustain several years of drought, with a ratio of storage to flows of about 4:1. Yet the demand for water has continued to grow unabated, gradually limiting the window of drought that these facilities may sustain. California's excess use of Colorado River water—beyond the initial allotment of 4.4 MAF—has occurred because the other basin states or users have not yet developed the capacity to use their water. Even so, pressure will continue for California to reduce its overall consumption of Colorado River water (Johnson, n.d.).

The Central Valley Project. Although the Lower Colorado Region offers promise for California in critical drought years with its high storage-to-flow ratio, California's dominant source of water comes from the USBR's Mid-Pacific Region. The Mid-Pacific Region, with a staff of about 700, is the owner-operator of the Central Valley Project (CVP), and a participating agency in CALFED (U.S. Bureau of Reclamation, 2000). The CVP includes 22 reservoirs, capable of storing over 12 MAF, and over 600 miles of canals and aqueducts. Facilities are at the northern extreme of the Sacramento Valley and along the western valley floor of

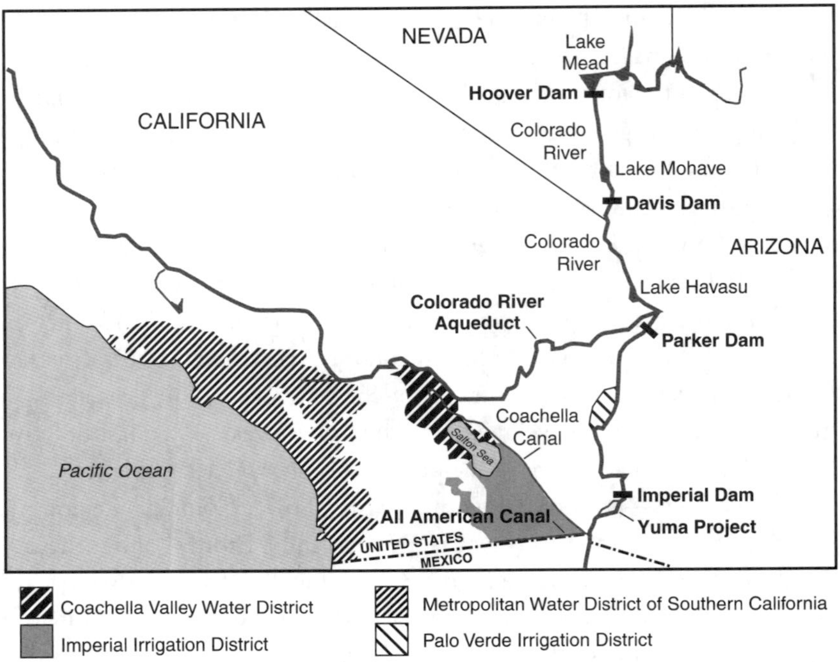

SOURCE: Metropolitan Water District of Southern California (2001).

Figure 3.7—California Service Areas for Colorado River Water

the Sierra Nevada as far south as Bakersfield in Kern County. The CVP provides nearly 90 percent of its water to agriculture.[9] In a year of normal precipitation, it delivers 6.2 MAF to 2.6 million acres of farmland, 500,000 acre-feet to nearly three million urban customers, and 300,000 acre-feet to wildlife refuges (California Department of Water Resources, 1999a). The CVP is also California's largest generator of electricity, producing an average of 5.1 billion kilowatt hours.

The CVP suffers from overallocation. According to DWR estimates, the more than 250 water contracts governing CVP deliveries call for a maximum annual delivery of 9.3 MAF. Of this total, 4.5 MAF are

[9]Although CVP service to agricultural users is supposed to be limited to family farms of 160 acres or less, this requirement has never been enforced, and many agricultural users have by-passed this requirement by administering their service through local water districts.

assigned to individuals and organizations that held water rights before the CVP was constructed, and 4.8 MAF were assigned and granted water rights commensurate with CVP construction. However, the CVP typically delivers only 60 to 70 percent of this amount to its users. These contractual obligations place the CVP in a precarious position, leaving little room for weathering drought. The ratio between storage and allocations is slightly over 1:1.

As with most USBR projects, power revenues were intended to subsidize the provision of water, municipal and industrial rates were intended to cover interest, irrigation rates were intended to cover remaining costs, and flood control and other uses were to be paid for with federal subsidies. However, initial water rates were set very low and extended over 40 years. Although most of the costs were supposed to be borne by irrigation users, a 1989 study of project costs from the Interior Department's economist Richard Wahl suggested that taxpayers and other project beneficiaries were actually paying for approximately 86 percent of the CVP's costs (Water Education Foundation, 1998).

Long-term water contracts established for the CVP began to reach their date of expiration in the late 1980s, and this discovery of the federal taxpayer's cost burden prompted changes in the rate structure for CVP water. In addition, the Mid-Pacific Region has been under increasing pressure to set aside additional water for environmental use pursuant to the Endangered Species Act and to meet the federal trust responsibilities to protect the resources of Native American tribes. These issues have culminated in the passage of the Reclamation Projects Authorization and Adjustment Act of 1992 (Public Law 102-575), which included Title 34, the Central Valley Project Improvement Act (CVPIA). This measure

- Mandates firm water supplies for Central Valley wildlife refuges,
- Calls for reasonable efforts to boost anadromous fish populations by 2002 to twice the population levels of 1967–1991,
- Creates a restoration fund financed by water and power users,
- Authorizes water transfers outside the CVP service area,
- Reduces the duration of water supply contracts from 40 to 25 years,

- Prices water to encourage conservation and meet the full cost of CVP facilities, and
- Retires lands from willing sellers using funds provided by the CVPIA, beginning in the San Joaquin Valley (U.S. Bureau of Reclamation and U.S. Fish and Wildlife Service, 2001b, p. 1).

The CVPIA has significantly changed USBR's operations. Contract renewals are proceeding at a brisk pace. Pricing is tiered in an 80-10-10 hierarchy, where the first 80 percent of allocated water consumed is priced to cover the cost of service, the next 10 percent is higher, and the final 10 percent is the highest, intended to cover interest on project capital costs. All contractors' water systems are being equipped with water measurement devices.

To guide its activities, the USBR relies on strategic planning as well as congressional mandates. Every three years, the USBR publishes a five-year Strategic Plan. Pursuant to the Government Performance and Results Act of 1993, the USBR publishes Annual Performance Plans and Reports. USBR's regional offices identify projects and programs for their annual budgets. Individual projects spanning multiple years are also assigned Capital Asset Plans (U.S. Bureau of Reclamation, 1999, 2001b). These plans and performance indicators facilitate the flow of top-down directives including mission goals, long-term goals, annual goals, and performance goals measured through project plans and outcomes. On a quarterly basis, reports also flow bottom-up from those responsible for projects and programs, area office coordinators, regional office coordinators, regional management, agencywide coordinators, and USBR's Director of Operations and Commissioner.

USBR uses the concept of risk management to prioritize facility reviews and rehabilitation. Dams with high and significant hazards must be reviewed once every three years for structural integrity and operational reliability. Approximately 50 percent of the USBR's projects were built between the years 1900 and 1950. Only 10 percent of them were built according to current state-of-the-art design and construction practices. As a result, at least 358 of the USBR's 457 dams and dikes are considered significant hazards, where failure would place downstream populations at risk. Modifications are identified on a long-term and annual basis through the budget and strategic planning processes.

The California Department of Water Resources

California's Department of Water Resources was created by the legislature in 1956 to plan and guide the development of the state's water resources. DWR's mission is to "manage the water resources of California in cooperation with other agencies, to benefit the State's people, and to protect, restore, and enhance the natural and human environments" (California Department of Water Resources, 1997).

The water resources mentioned in this passage refer primarily to the State Water Project (SWP) as conceived in the 1957 *California Water Plan* (Bulletin No. 3). SWP programs are funded through continuous appropriations provided for in the Burns-Porter Act of 1960 and the State Central Valley Project Act of 1933 and are not subject to annual review by the legislature. The SWP currently consists of 32 dams, lakes, and reservoirs extending from high elevations in Plumas County to lower elevations in northern Los Angeles County and through about 660 miles of open canals and pipelines. The SWP's California Aqueduct is the only conveyance system linking water-rich Northern California with water-scarce Southern California. The pumps used to move water south and over the Tehachapi range make the SWP the single largest user of electrical energy in the state (5.7 billion kilowatt hours in 1997) (California Department of Water Resources, 1999c).

Like the CVP, the SWP was designed as a series of reservoirs, aqueducts, and pumping and power plants. Unlike the CVP, the SWP has a decidedly urban focus. Although it provides only about 7 percent of California's consumable water supply, the areas it serves rely heavily on SWP deliveries. With the onset of environmental regulation, facility construction slowed significantly in the 1970s. Voter discontent with the transfer of water from north to south brought construction to an abrupt halt in 1982, when California voters overwhelmingly rejected Proposition 9 (SB 200) and thereby prevented construction of the Peripheral Canal along the eastern edge of the San Joaquin Delta.

Also like the CVP, the SWP is overallocated. It was planned to supply 4.2 MAF of water per year to 29 regional and local contractors, but these plans were based on the inclusion of the Peripheral Canal and numerous facilities that have yet to be approved. As a result, the SWP conveys only about 2.3 MAF per year. The ability of the SWP to deliver to its contractors depends on rainfall, snow-pack, runoff, carryover storage from the preceding year, pumping capacity from the Delta, environmental constraints, and, more recently, flows required for power generation (California Department of Water Resources, 1999c). Operation plans are refined as seasonal conditions arise. With environmental and water quality regulation, the uncertainty of pumping through the Delta has increased, narrowing the scheduling of water operations to as little as three days in advance.

Since its inception in 1956, DWR's focus has expanded. Today it maintains a full-time staff of 2,300 who plan, design, construct, operate, and maintain the SWP. The DWR's other major responsibilities include

- Preparing and updating the California Water Plan to guide development and management of the state's water resources,
- Protecting and restoring the Sacramento-San Joaquin Delta,
- Regulating dams, providing flood protection, and assisting in emergency management to safeguard life and property,
- Educating the public about water use and collecting, analyzing, and distributing information to the scientific, technical, educational, and water management communities, and
- Serving local water needs by providing technical assistance, supporting watershed and river restoration programs, encouraging water conservation, exploring conjunctive use of ground and surface water, facilitating voluntary water transfers, and operating a state drought water bank when necessary (California Department of Water Resources, 2000).

The DWR's goals are defined and placed against quantified performance measures in its Strategic Plan, the most recent of which was published in 1997. DWR also publishes summary assessments of water supply planning every five years in the California Water Plan (Bulletin 160). Bulletin 160 provides the most comprehensive picture of water conditions at the scale of the state. In terms of maintenance, DWR conducts inspections of over 1,200 dams statewide.[10] To help promote efficient use of irrigation water, the department also operates the California Irrigation Management Information System, a repository of climatological data collected at more than 100 computerized weather stations. DWR also works closely with the USBR (California Department of Water Resources, 1998b). In 1987, after more than 25 years of negotiations and after receiving congressional approval, the two agencies signed a Coordinated Operation Agreement (U.S. Bureau of Reclamation and California Department of Water Resources, 1986).

Groundwater Supply

Groundwater may be monitored by local agencies, but most of California's production is not managed or quantified. DWR monitors about 20,000 wells in groundwater basins throughout California and maintains a file of well completion reports, which must be submitted whenever a driller works on a well. The SWRCB, which is responsible for water quality, provides limited regulatory oversight of groundwater; but California is one of the last western states that does not regulate groundwater. After receiving pressure from the U.S. Environmental Protection Agency, the state legislature enacted the Groundwater Management Act in 1992 (California Water Code, Section 10750, et seq), authorizing assessments to fund local agencies with critically overdrafted basins for the development of groundwater management plans. These plans are undertaken on a voluntary basis and are not submitted to the state for review or record-keeping purposes. As of 1998, about 150 local agencies, many of which were located in the Central Valley, had adopted AB 3030 plans (California Department of Water Resources, 1999a).

Groundwater is easily contaminated and, once contaminated, practically impossible to clean up. Until the 1970s, conventional wisdom and legal practice supported the notion that all contaminants, including chemicals, were removed by percolation through the soil and sediment. Only since then have Californians discovered the extent of

---

[10]To be included, a dam must exceed 25 feet in height or hold more than five acre-feet of water and pose a potential danger.

contamination in the state's groundwater basins (California Department of Water Resources, 1993).

When water users turn to the courts to settle disputes over water, these groundwater basins become known as "adjudicated" basins. The courts set up a system of governance for each basin, define its safe yield, and appoint various individuals or agencies to be the "watermasters" of the basin. The court may delegate these responsibilities to the SWRCB. As of 1996, there were 16 adjudicated basins in California, all but one located in Southern California (California Department of Water Resources, 1996a).

CALFED

CALFED is made up of agencies collaborating to manage the water resources of the Sacramento-San Joaquin Delta, a 1,153 square mile area of rivers, sloughs, and islands. Water flows through these natural waterways and man-made channels as they narrow into Suisun Bay, through the Carquinez Straits, and into San Francisco Bay and the Pacific Ocean. Both the SWP and CVP divert these flows into enormous pumping systems, which distribute the water to southern and Central Valley locations. As freshwater flows have been diverted, salt water has moved further up into the Delta. Combined with the 1987–1992 drought, this saltwater advance is believed to have increased populations of nonnative fish species and reduced indigenous fish populations. It also created water quality problems for Delta water users. CALFED was largely formed to deal with these problems.

CALFED itself does not directly control or manage any of California's water supply or other water-related structural projects. Rather, the organizations that make up CALFED use it as a forum to reach agreements on activities affecting the water quality and quantity flowing through the Delta. These agreements are then carried out by member agencies and are overseen by CALFED.

CALFED's member agencies are shown in Table 3.7. These state and federal agencies are led by the governor and the U.S. Secretary of the Interior; they are advised by numerous interagency teams, consultants, and the Bay-Delta Advisory Commission, which is responsible for coordinating public participation.

Table 3.7

State and Federal Agencies of CALFED

California	United States
The Resources Agency	Department of the Interior
Department of Water Resources	Bureau of Reclamation
Department of Fish and Game	Fish and Wildlife Service
The Reclamation Board	Geological Survey
Delta Protection Commission	Bureau of Land Management
Department of Conservation	Environmental Protection Agency
San Francisco Bay Conservation and Development Commission	Army Corps of Engineers
	Department of Agriculture
California Environmental Protection Agency	Natural Resources Conservation Service
State Water Resources Control Board	Forest Service
	Department of Commerce
Department of Health Services	National Marine Fisheries Service
Department of Food and Agriculture	Western Area Power Administration

SOURCE: CALFED (2001).

CALFED's formative document is the 1994 Framework Agreement (CALFED, 2000a), which directs the state and federal agencies to work together in three areas of management. The first of these areas—water quality standards—was already in the hands of the SWRCB and the U.S. Environmental Protection Agency (EPA). The EPA published its final rule for Delta water quality standards in January 1995 and followed up with a Final Environmental Impact Report, which was released in November 1999 (California State Water Resources Control Board, 1995 and 1999). The second area of management is the coordination of water supply operations. Since 1986, the USBR and DWR had been operating the CVP and SWP under a coordination agreement, seeking to maximize benefits and limit damage to water users and the environment.

The third area was the search for a long-term solution to the Delta's problems. CALFED's membership divided this search into three phases. In Phase I, the program identified the problems facing the Delta, created its mission statements and guiding principles, and distilled hundreds of possible actions into three alternative strategies for resolving the conflicts. Phase I concluded with the release of a report in September 1996. Phase II involved obtaining compliance with the California Environmental Quality Act and the National Environmental Policy Act with the completion of a programmatic Environmental Impact Statement/Report (CALFED, 2000b). CALFED released a Record of Decision, concluding programmatic environmental review in August 2000 (CALFED, 2000c). Phase III entails project implementation, which began in 2000 and will continue through 2007. Approved projects are limited to CALFED's "common program elements"—water conservation measures, ecosystem restoration, and levee improvements. Controversial conveyance and storage decisions have been deferred to a later date. The overall planning and development horizon for CALFED extends 30 years. Recent state legislation (SB 1653, 2002) marks the first step in establishing a governance structure to continue through the life of the program to ensure implementation of objectives and to carry out program elements that do not easily fall within the jurisdiction of an existing agency or department.

CALFED initially operated on a shared-cost basis among the state and federal participants. Since its inception, two state bond initiatives and federal appropriations have funded continued study, staffing, and limited restoration activities. For the long term, CALFED plans support the notion that users who benefit from CALFED's efforts will pay in proportion to the benefits they receive. In California, Proposition 204 (1996) and Proposition 213 (2000) authorize nearly $3 billion in bonds to finance improved water supply and quality, levee rehabilitation, watershed management, ecosystem restoration, and other environmental protection projects. These propositions were paralleled with congressional approval in June 2002 of the CALFED Bay-Delta Authorization Act (S 1768), to provide federal funds amounting to $1.6 billion over three years. These funds are dispersed in large part through the CALFED program and are likely to be augmented with other federal and state agency funds.

4. Is California Prepared for the Future?

Introduction

To supplement our survey of the state's organizational structures in education, transportation, and water supply, we interviewed over 100 managers in those sectors on the effectiveness and efficiency of these systems. We also reviewed reports and databases and attended meetings that revealed the impressions of local, regional, state, and private managers. These sources indicated that these three sectors experience problems that could prevent the effective use of state resources. All of them, however, may in some way be relieved by wider application of the principles presented in later chapters.

K–12 Education

Our interviews corroborated the problems underscored by the state's Little Hoover Commission report of February 8, 2000, *To Build a Better School* (California Little Hoover Commission, 2000a). In general, uncertainty from reliance on bonds and rapidly fluctuating regulations combine with a lack of state oversight to leave lawmakers without the information and analyses they need to improve the effectiveness of state spending.

Unstable and Insufficient Financing

The education sector's reliance on bonds, especially for K–12 facilities, creates planning problems. As one state K–12 manager explained,

> The bottom line is school facilities are funded by bonds in the state of California, and it doesn't provide a permanent funding stream, so that does create issues. When the economy turns sour, what happens? The voters

> tighten up . . . the purse strings and they don't want to pass bonds. The reality, though, is that there is a burgeoning enrollment increase and every year it goes up two to three percent.

This handicap is well known, but the state has yet to act to counterbalance its effects. The same manager notes,

> There is a facility need, obviously, and it's driven by the rapid growth of California. How are you going to address that need? It's been addressed historically with bonds. In the past years, prior to Proposition 13, there was an assessed valuation on property, and that is how locals raised money. . . . That was a permanent revenue source. Proposition 13 did away with all that . . . and . . . the state had to get more involved in the financing of schools. Since then, there has been a back and forth. Is the state [responsible]? Is it the locals? We've been seesawing, because I think the state as a whole has realized that this is a huge juggernaut here, we can't afford to pay for this infrastructure either, we really need help from the locals. So, it has been that tug of war and finding that balance for the last 20 years, roughly, maybe longer than that, since 1978.

Indeed, the state has yet to generate enough money to address K–12 infrastructure needs. Much of the funding authorized by Proposition 1A (1998) was exhausted by the year 2000, although state lawmakers expected the funds to last through 2002. Recent state legislation (AB 16, 2002) authorizes an additional $21.4 billion in general obligation bonds, pending voter approval in two elections. Voters approved the first segment, for $11.4 billion, on November 5, 2002 (Proposition 47). The second, for $10 billion, will be placed on the 2004 ballot. With a local match, these funds are designed to allow completion of projects currently approved but unfunded. Still, the Department of Finance acknowledges that these funds may fall short of K–12 facility needs over the next five years (California Department of Finance, 2002).

Lack of Planning and Record-Keeping

The early draining of Proposition 1A funds suggests that the state's need estimates were inadequate. Unlike other sectors, school district capital needs are recurring and forecasted with demographic projections, facts that would seem to make the determination of need a fairly simple exercise. State agencies diverge in their perspectives, however, leaving managers, lawmakers, and other organizations without a clear sense of capital funding needs. The K–12 managers we interviewed questioned

Department of Finance estimates of future enrollment, which they maintained were purposefully low to make the budget balance, especially in times of recession. The Department of Education stopped generating statewide demographic projections several years ago. Instead, it has set up a cohort survival model that local districts use on the web to calculate their future enrollment on an ad hoc basis.

That being said, demographics mark the first step in determining needs. Demand is weighed against the capacity of existing facilities. The Little Hoover Commission suggests that the state has difficulty assessing its existing education infrastructure as well as its future needs.

> As local districts lost their ability to finance construction, the State assumed the need for assessing existing facilities and forecasting needs. The State, however, has never developed that ability. While it has approved and financed the construction of thousands of schools in recent years, it does not have a comprehensive inventory of what exists, or even what it has paid for. . . . While there is no inventory and no formal planning process, policy makers are given projections of future financial needs. A number of entities make projections. None of the projections are based on what actually exists, or take into consideration where the growth is occurring, and so do not assess how the current infrastructure could be used to meet future needs. The Department of Education has estimated that 60 percent of the State's schools are more than 30 years old, but there is no database or assessment of school condition. The State's projections are based primarily on how many children are expected to show up for school multiplied by a cost variable (California Little Hoover Commission, 2000a, pp. 47, 50).

In spite of an allocation of $600,000 in the mid-1980s to develop a statewide inventory, no such inventory exists. Instead of tackling this deficit of data, the state seems to have withdrawn from the task.

One state manager noted that eligibility requirements are based on past enrollment and can fall short of actual demand, especially in areas of new growth and development. To deal with this issue, the Department of Education and Office of Public School Construction have been approving school site development based on site sizes called for in local district Master Plans. However, with the implementation of Proposition 1A and SB 50, the state Department of Education stopped requiring that local districts submit master plans when they apply for state funding.

> There is no state law that requires a master plan. . . . That went away when SB 50 came into being. . . . Now that one tool that encourage[s] planning is gone

> away, but we still encourage it. We recommend that a facility—a five, ten, 15-year facility master plan be done (California Little Hoover Commission, 2000a, p. 48).

Only new schools asking for state funds receive an onsite review from the Department of Education, and those districts with the skills and foresight to submit detailed plans benefit from plan review. For all others the state, in effect, waits until the California Teachers Association or some other entity files suit against a district for noncompliance with space standards.

The Little Hoover Commission described the need for a statewide inventory including the age, size, capacity, condition, available technology, and environmental equipment of all schools. That inventory could also specify such critical information as the availability of closed or underused facilities that could be used by neighboring districts (California Little Hoover Commission, 2000a, p. vii). Without such an inventory and Five-Year Plans, it is practically impossible to know how demands statewide may be efficiently fulfilled.

Shifting Regulations

Regulations governing the state's support of K–12 education change dramatically and rapidly. With each bond, new regulations governing the distribution of funds and state oversight are created, which are then modified by the many players involved in K–12 management. As one state manager noted,

> SB 50 (Proposition 1A) was a politically motivated bill; that was a Republican bill. . . . Local control, too much state intrusion . . . that's what it was . . . there have been three or four legislative changes. . . . We had a nice, simple, down-and-dirty program that has been tweaked. . . . You have LA [Los Angeles Unified School District] suing us, they want their little tweak. In this office we have a tough job because we have a lot of different people that we report to and the reality is we have a lot of beatings from the people out there who don't understand what is going on, and . . . these bills we are trying to implement [are] having to go through the Board [State Allocation Board] and it's getting tweaked through different mechanisms, and it just happens that way due to these processes, because of different vested interests. We always try to take the feasible, the reasonable, the logical approach to things, but sometimes when politics get involved, it doesn't make sense.

In fact, changes to the implementing regulations for Proposition 1A have been numerous. There were 41 regulatory changes to the school facility program itemized for the year 2000, and an additional 28 changes either proposed or approved through September of 2001 (California Department of General Services, 2001).

Lack of State Oversight

Proposition 1A and SB 50 streamlined bond fund allocations. The Department of Finance estimates that most projects can be reviewed and approved by the State Allocation Board in 90 days (California Department of Finance, 1999). In streamlining the process, however, the state may have impaired its ability to judge program effectiveness. The Little Hoover Commission and our research suggest that local districts often lack the skills appropriate to manage construction contracts, that savvy districts out-game the others for access to state funds, and that the state lacks both the resources and authority to prevent mismanagement. Serious misappropriations of funds can and sometimes do result. With only 11 employees surveying new sites across the entire state, the Department of Education is ill-equipped to correct local incompetence, much less police errant behavior.

As one state manager notes,

> The growing urban districts probably have a real good handle on master planning. But the vast majority of the 1,000 districts in the state are small districts and they really lack facility planning. They have a superintendent and some of them have a business manager. . . . If he wants anything done he has to hire consultants because he doesn't understand . . . [that regulatory compliance] usually falls on the architect. He wants the job to design the school and build the school, [so] he is involved in the master plan, he is involved in the site approval. And if it is a big enough district, there might be money for other consultants.

Before Proposition 1A and SB 50, the state used to oversee the process of development to prevent against cooptation by consultants in the form of excessive fees. As another manager noted, "There is less intrusion in terms of us checking this and why you are spending this much on your architect and your construction manager and you're only getting this allowance. We don't do good approvals anymore, anyway." The Little Hoover Commission noted the districts' inability to manage construction programs, which is compounded by the fact that they operate independently, repeating mistakes and isolating innovation. Concerning state regulations, the commission noted, "the regulations are not always effective at preventing bad decisions as intended: Districts that want to skirt the rules often figure out a way to do so" (California Little Hoover Commission, 2000a, p. 23).

Instead of oversight, Proposition 1A and SB 50 rely on incentives. Local districts pocket savings from new construction and bear the burden of cost overruns. However, such incentives can lead to skimping on materials or cause local districts to scale down construction plans submitted to the state. Since funds are allocated on a set per-pupil basis, some districts scale down construction to a cost below the amount allocated by the state, which allows them to pocket and spend the difference at their own discretion. This last observation prompted action on the part of the State Allocation Board with a "New Construction Commensurate Requirement" proposed at their June 23, 1999, meeting. Even so, this new requirement stipulates that only 60 percent of the costs covered by state and local funds show in submitted plans (California Department of General Services, Office of Public School Construction, 1999).

Our interviewees were aware that some districts were able to gain disproportionate access to state funds. Proposition 1A and other funds are divided into three categories: new schools, modernization, and deferred maintenance. The state paid out much larger shares of modernization costs than it did for new schools or maintenance. Ambiguity in the definitions of these terms allowed sophisticated districts to acquire modernization funds, which were the first to run out.

The State Architect Bottleneck

Countering this tendency toward quicker allocation and construction is the Field Act—a set of seismic safety and structural regulations for K–14 facilities administered by the Division of the State Architect. Backlogs for plan review at DSA can leave drawings on the shelf for months, even years. Part of this problem is that consultants for local districts have been known to submit any plan they have lying around—even shopping mall designs—to get their application in early for review and funding. The review process is further delayed as state architects painstakingly manage local architects through the creation of new designs.

Portable buildings require significantly less review from the DSA, which reviews only the structural soundness of the foundation when the portable designs are familiar. Whereas other new construction can take two to four years, portable construction can be completed within nine to 15 months (California Department of General Services, Office of Public School Construction, 2002). The fact that portables—designed for up to 20 years of use—have been in use for as long as 30 to 40 years is an indication of problems in processing as well as in funding.

Another indication of processing problems emerged at a recent meeting of the SAB's Implementation Committee. Projects with cost estimates under $100,000 do not require DSA approval. Apparently, local districts have been splitting their development into as many as six applications that result in one big project.

On the surface, issues over DSA review for the Field Act would seem isolated to design review. However, all aspects of project development are interconnected. The long-standing presence of this design review bottleneck has led DSA staff to de-emphasize other critical aspects of review, such as the Field Act requirement that DSA representatives perform ongoing construction inspection. DSA is the only link the state has to oversight of project delivery. Meetings with DSA staff, who are distributed among four regional offices across the state, revealed a tendency to visit construction sites close to their homes or offices. The DSA under new leadership has since been working to expand its certified staff statewide and improve its fieldwork.

In short, state efforts to reduce intrusion on local decisionmaking processes have left the state compromised when it comes to ensuring the efficient and effective use of state dollars. The use of incentives rewards districts that already have skilled facilities departments or that use cookie-cutter designs to reduce costs; but it also rewards districts striving to skirt regulations and has had the unintended effect of drawing valuable state resources into design review and away from site inspection. These problems are exacerbated by the uncertainty surrounding bond approval and the state's difficulties with projecting statewide needs.

Higher Education

CPEC has been outspoken about the new tidal wave of enrollment anticipated and severe shortages in capital outlay funds. In a flurry of planning efforts, it formed the Capital Outlay Planning Advisory Committee, collected long-range plans and facilities data for all three sectors of higher education, and published a series of reports examining enrollment demands, existing physical capacity, space utilization standards, costs for maintenance and expansion, the need for new facilities, existing funding sources, and potential alternative funding sources (California Postsecondary Education Commission, 1987, 1990, 1992a, 1992b, 1995a, 1995b, 2000).

Until the late 1990s, CPEC maintained a steady if somewhat grim position on the condition of the state's higher educational system. Enrollments were going to be higher than those forecasted by the Department of Finance, the data used to determine capacity posed problems, the three sisters were underinvesting in maintenance and renovation, existing capacity would soon be overtaken by new enrollment, and the state would be hard-pressed to provide badly needed funds. Our interviews affirmed CPEC's analysis and demonstrated the persistence of these problems.

Projections and Planning

CPEC takes a bottom-up approach to planning, collecting data from the system's 137 campuses and three head offices. In contrast, the Department of Finance generates its estimates in more of a top-down fashion. Enrollment has matched CPEC projections since 1995, but estimating existing capacity has proven to be a more significant challenge.

Estimates of capacity are based on age, condition, and utilization rates. Age and condition of facilities aside, CPEC created temporary standards for classroom and laboratory space utilization in the early 1970s. These standards assume, for example, that classrooms, lecture halls, and seminar rooms require 15 assignable (usable) square feet per student, known as a student "station." Student stations are utilized to the extent that a student in a scheduled course occupies them for a number of hours each week, where the workweek extends from 8 am to 10 pm, Monday through Friday. This standard for student stations is a minimum of 35 hours per week of occupancy.

CPEC studied these standards more thoroughly in the 1980s and 1990s and recommended significant changes. Perhaps the most egregious problem now is a lack of standards for the use of supporting facilities such as libraries, research laboratories, administrative offices, food service, or athletic facilities. Such facilities constitute 55.5 percent of CCC space, 76.5 percent of CSU space, and 94.1 percent of UC space (California Postsecondary Education Commission, 1995a). CSU is testing new standards that may prove more effective in determining the overall need for space for its campuses. These standards suggest that campuses should provide 75 assignable square feet, as measured across the entire campus, including off-campus leased space, per FTE. This measure gives departments an incentive to share space, which, CSU managers note, creates more efficient rates of occupancy. CPEC notes that the new standard may provide more flexibility to campus planners designing facilities, while checking overly ambitious designs. CCC and UC continue to use the outdated standards.

Inadequate Data and Estimates of Need

Lacking data on facility condition, CPEC could provide only ballpark estimates of maintenance needs. CPEC acknowledged the problem in a 1999 report.

> Unfortunately, there is no detailed analysis available of the condition of higher education's physical plant. While local administrators and planners have a general idea of the individual campus renovation or replacement needs, there is no systematic, statewide compilation that can inform the estimate in this report (California Postsecondary Education Commission, 1999, p. 91).

For all three sisters, deferred maintenance has compounded problems with capacity and added to overall expenses. In 1995, CPEC estimates of capacity for all 137 campuses were reduced by 10 percent owing to the notion that some buildings were kept in such poor condition that they were rendered unusable. In 1995, CPEC estimates of demand were $1 billion annually; a year later, the Department of Finance increased this estimate to $1.4 billion (California Department of Finance, 1996).

Since then, the three sisters have continued to underinvest and defer maintenance. By 2000, CPEC estimates were at $1.5 billion per year. In the words of the CPEC, deferred maintenance is a "dilemma" (California Postsecondary Education Commission, 1995b, 2000). As a result of AB 1473 (Chapter 606, Statutes of 1999), however, greater attention to maintenance seems to have been attached to estimates of future infrastructure need for the UC system. UC's recently designed Facilities Renewal Resources Model estimates ongoing maintenance and modernization needs at $190 million per year, with an additional $78 million per year to address a backlog of deferred maintenance (California Department of Finance, 2002).

State Funding Shortfalls

State funds for higher education have been under stresses similar to those experienced by K–12. After relying on general obligation bonds for over 80 percent of all state funding since 1965, bond issues in 1990 and 1994 did not receive voter approval. In the wake of these disappointments, CPEC wrote,

> [T]he continuation of bond financing for higher education facilities should be examined carefully, from the points of view of both political viability and fiscal prudence. Whether or not the people of California will approve general obligation bond issues in the future is uncertain, but if the State decides to propose them, it should at least be confident that the proposal itself is a fiscally responsible act. . . . The principle . . . that debt should be used for capital construction on the grounds that it can be retired during the life of the facility is normally sound fiscally, but trouble can ensue if the need to construct facilities becomes a permanent obligation over a long period of time. In such a circumstance, retired debt is simply replaced by a larger debt (California Postsecondary Education Commission, 1995b, pp. 188–120).

CPEC estimated that, at best, the state would be able to provide about half of the annual capital outlay needed for higher education. Proposition 1A, passed by voters in 1998, subsequently provided a total of $2.5 billion to higher education over a four-year period (California Postsecondary Education Commission, 1995b, 2000). Proposition 47 (2002) will add another $1.7 billion in funds (California Department of Finance, 2002).

A UC manager described the paucity of funds as having driven a change in mindset, as, he said, "We were no longer a state-supported institution, we were a state-assisted institution." UC is able to raise considerable private funds—amounts that climbed from $300 million in the early 1990s to $1.2 billion by 1999–2000 (Obra et al., 2001). UC has also devoted tuition from foreign students to deferred maintenance to make up for the lack of state funds. The CSU and CCC systems are not so well endowed and have considerable difficulty raising necessary funds.

Although the CCC will be taking in most of the new enrollments, it will receive only one-third of every state bond issue. As one manager described it, this one-third split for CCC is

> [M]utually assured destruction. . . . There is the feeling that UC has the political muscle to get whatever they want. My belief, and I think others' beliefs, is that community colleges are a sleeping giant because there are facilities in every member's district. . . . CSU is worried that they're going to get pinched. . . . I just finished an analysis from the '92 bond act, the '96 bond act and of course so far the '98 bond act. We haven't got our third. We have gotten less than 30 percent.

The CPEC has recommended local bond issues to help close the gap. Until the passage of Proposition 39 in November 2000 reduced the voting requirement (for K–12 and CCC alike) from a two-thirds majority to 55 percent, the passage of local bond issues was virtually impossible, and the CCC backlog of deferred maintenance and renovation needs ballooned.

Inadequate Data Collection for CCC

Data collection problems for the CCC resemble those of the K–12 sector. The state lacks the capacity to collect the data needed to oversee district space utilization and expenditures, districts often lack the ability to manage projects effectively, and both of these factors prevent CCC from achieving a shorter, less-expensive review process than other state agencies, such as the DSA and Public Works Board.

CCC managers have been wary of space utilization studies and lack the resources to conduct their own. One manager said, "I have problems with utilization analysis because of the way it has been misused, and also

I don't have the capability to do utilization analysis. It is a big job . . . you're talking about a major Herculean effort to push a database system through."

Similarly, the Chancellor's Office does not collect the data needed to oversee projects, and districts vary considerably in their ability to manage them. A manager at the state level estimates that at least 80 percent of CCC projects run over budget and all local projects use up contingency funds built into the bidding process. Districts are reluctant to report these cost overruns, however, as that information would trigger a delay of about 75 days in review by the Public Works Board. Also, many CCC campuses have been engaging numerous off-campus leases, which exacerbate problems of statewide measurement; data on leased space are not provided for in the plans submitted by each CCC district to the Chancellor's Office.

CCC managers would like to improve their data-gathering capacity and streamline the project approval system. Some of their problems arise from the governance system set up in the Master Plan for Higher Education (Liaison Committee of the State Board of Education and The Regents of the University of California, 1960), which established local control at the expense of state oversight on the part of the Chancellors Office of CCC. Some of these issues are recognized by CPEC in its 1998 Master Plan and a study devoted to CCC governance (California Postsecondary Education Commission, 1998). In 1997, the legislature granted UC and CSU a streamlined project approval process, where projects could be allocated state funds in a lump sum instead of across consecutive project phases. CCC suspects that such streamlining could shave two to three years off its project delivery process (Neuman and Whittington, 2000). (Currently, it takes anywhere from six to ten years to build a CCC project.) CCC managers feel that they are caught in a "Catch-22." The Chancellor's Office needs additional resources to collect data and provide oversight, yet without data and oversight, the state is reluctant to grant CCC relief from its extensive review process.

In sum, both K–12 and higher education face serious challenges in data collection, financing, and service delivery. Although guided by the historic Master Plan, higher education suffers from data gaps that prevent adequate assessment of the most persistent, growing need: deferred maintenance. Also, outdated standards for space utilization remain in spite of the best efforts of CPEC to foster change. Higher education has amassed enough research to render some solutions possible. Many of these solutions have been developed under the auspices of CSU. As later chapters make clear, practically everything that CSU has initiated would be of greater value if applied to other sectors.

Transportation

Funds for transportation are more reliable than those for education. The gasoline tax, truck weight fees, local sales taxes, federal funds, and occasional bond funds provide copious resources for transportation services. In fiscal year 1998–1999, for example, the state spent $2.1 billion on transportation projects of all kinds (Legislative Analyst's Office, 2000a, p. A-44). Also, the governance in this sector has remained relatively stable over time. Even so, the sector faces persistent problems.

Slow and Expensive Project Delivery

CTC officials say that one of the major frustrations of the administration and local governments is the length of time it takes to deliver a project. The LAO estimates that from initial planning to ribbon cutting, Caltrans takes anywhere from five to 11 years to deliver a STIP (such as adding High Occupancy Vehicle lanes to an existing freeway) and from about three to nine years to deliver a SHOPP project. Some projects have been on STIP lists for as long as 30 years. These figures would not appear so alarming if companies in the private sector—working largely for counties spending local sales taxes—had not demonstrated their ability to cut these times and the cost of projects in half, with comparable or improved service quality. This disparity will be discussed further in a subsequent chapter.

The LAO, CTC, and upper-level managers at Caltrans present the same set of explanations for untimely and costly delivery. Caltrans cannot seem to hire enough people to do the work, project managers are overloaded with work, local agencies lag behind in their spending of federal funds, state and federal funds are tied to different and complex requirements, and the process of environmental review—especially for the National Environmental Policy Act—is onerous. To address some of these problems, the legislature established a "use-it-or-lose-it" approach to federal funds available to local agencies (Chapter 783, Statutes of 1999); directed Caltrans to negotiate interagency agreements hiring additional staff in various natural resources agencies to review their projects; and initiated a pilot program allowing selected projects to proceed in phases, beginning construction as soon as design is completed for each phase (Chapter 378, Statutes of 1999) (Legislative Analyst's Office, 2000a, pp. A-46, 47).

The concerns articulated by high-level managers and others are valid, and the legislative measures should offer substantial improvement. Our interviews, however, revealed an entirely different set of problems contributing to cost and schedule delays, beginning with planning and extending to cost estimating, project management, and maintenance.

Lack of Approved Plans

Caltrans has devised lengthy processes by which projects are studied, planned, and executed. Up to the mid-1980s, this process was fairly regimented. The plans were keyed into deadlines that fit within the two-year cycle established by the STIP. However, several of our interviewees noted that the planning process lay fallow through the 1990s, leaving Caltrans without a stock of reliable plans. Transportation corridor or "concept" studies now tend to be ten or more years out of date. As one planner noted,

> A lot of those system planning documents are out of date now, with the recession in the early 90s we . . . just did away with [planning], or it went by the wayside. The economy is good now, we're staffed up, [and] starting up that again. That's the good news . . . the bad news is that means we don't really have a good shelf of projects. We haven't been doing the preliminary planning work. . . . We need to really accelerate and start doing some of these analyses of . . . projects.

Although district plans are the first and in many ways the most important part of the planning process, planners in Sacramento believe that districts often lack the staff or expertise to create system plans, which involve considerable coordination with regional and local entities. The passage of SB 45, which gives regional entities more authority over STIP fund allocation, means that Caltrans district staff now have to "go to the [regions] and sell them on projects for locals to recognize Caltrans priorities," according to one planner. If true, this claim suggests a dramatic shift in roles for Caltrans planners and managers from technocrats to salespeople.

Planners in Caltrans Sacramento offices have attempted to support the process by hiring consultants to put together a statewide Geographic Information System that displays socioeconomic, land-use, and demographic data associated with routes of the state highway system. As one planner suggests,

> One thing that everybody needs to do . . . is to look at all these projects and how they all fit together. What we're trying to [do] is . . . take all of the projects in the [regions] and all the Caltrans projects and just [ask] "Are all these connected?"

If transportation concept plans and district plans are out of date or lacking in substance, then Caltrans will naturally have difficulty generating the analyses necessary to produce adequate project study reports (PSRs).

In the eyes of Caltrans district managers, plans serve little purpose next to the list of projects up for STIP funding. Managers in the districts prioritize their own work according to the accumulation of funds around certain projects, as negotiated through the creation of the PSR. In fact, we were told that managers within the districts build their reputations around their ability to obtain the funding commitments necessary to advance PSRs. Because major projects usually include state funding sources, Caltrans uses the PSR to maintain its leverage over project prioritization. As one interviewee said,

> Funding comes from regional, local, federal, and state funds for most major projects. It's rare that urban projects are funded from just one source. This gives Caltrans sort of a "veto authority" over many regional projects.

Although Caltrans has fallen behind in the development of PSRs, and their quality of analysis may have diminished, many managers were adamant about not contracting out with other agencies or firms to write them. "Caltrans is responsible for actually doing the PSRs, we can't contract them out, or have regional agencies do [them]," said one planner, echoing many statements we heard in our interviews. Not all Caltrans employees resisted the notion, however. Said one manager,

> You can only contract out in an extremely limited [circumstance]: if you can prove that . . . no one in state government has the skills or ability or experience to do the job, then you can contract out, at least for engineering and design. . . . The theory of contracting out makes a lot of sense. . . .

Regional and local managers find the situation infuriating. If there are not enough PSRs from a county for CTC to program its share of STIP funds, the allocation is placed in "reserve." With recent legislation, that county's funds may even be placed up for grabs by other agencies that have more projects with approved PSRs. As one explains,

> That has actually been a real sticking point because [Caltrans doesn't] have the staff to prepare the PSRs, and we can't program the money until the PSRs are ready. So, for instance, we have this $100 million that's coming to us within the next few months to program, but the counties are all saying, "We don't have any projects with PSRs. We have projects we want to do, but we don't have any projects that we can put on the books because the PSR is not done."

Cost-Estimating

Caltrans districts also vary considerably in their approach to cost-estimating. When planning is lacking, the total estimated project cost—one number—becomes the most critical piece of information used to prioritize projects. We found that one district known for attention to detail had increases as high as 39 percent between the PSR phase and final engineering. This gap threatened the district's credibility with local partners, making it more difficult to agree on future transportation needs and issues.

Part of the problem has been Caltrans overall process of programming funds. Although the National Environmental Policy Act and California Environmental Quality Act have been in place for over 30 years, the department has not changed its STIP programming process to accommodate the process of environmental review. If environmental review is conducted properly, there will be several alternative alignments to a highway project. Regardless of the variation in cost of these alignments, they must be given equal weight in analysis; each alignment should have an equal starting chance of becoming the "preferred alternative." Before environmental review begins and without any knowledge of alternative alignments, Caltrans programs (allocates) the total amount of funds estimated for the project from the STIP. This creates the perception that Caltrans has a biased view from the start and has selected the preferred alternative before environmental review has even begun.

The district was aware that increasing cost estimates resulted in significant costs to the region, the counties, and the public. In a draft internal study, it wrote:

> [A]n apparent lack of focus and/or urgency toward cost estimating leads to the belief among externals that the District:
>
> - Does not believe that cost is important. "It costs what it costs."
> - Purposely underestimates preferred alternative so that it is programmed.
> - Others could do it better.
> - Develops estimates in a "Black Box" with little basis (California Department of Transportation, 2001a, p. 3).

The study team recommended a number of improvements that could be made, including scaling construction costs to expected inflation rates and sharing information among groups within and outside the district. This district also found that cost estimates could be improved if experts from functional areas, such as environmental, applied themselves to the cost-estimating process early on and throughout project development. Instead of relying on preset contingencies for a total project cost (25 percent for the PSR stage, 5 percent after final engineering), contingencies would be calculated by each functional group for its portion of the overall project cost.

These recommendations, although sensible, may not reach far outside the district's jurisdiction. Our interviews suggest that Caltrans districts suffer the same sense of isolation as K–12 or CCC districts, so innovations are rarely shared between them. District managers, with their control over district plans that prioritize projects and the approval of PSRs, hold considerable power within Caltrans. They are thought by managers in Sacramento to lead their districts as they see fit, each with a particular management style and sense of values. Thus, some districts produce higher-quality PSRs than others and one district shines above when it comes to cost-estimating.

Caltrans, the CTC, and others in a position to oversee project costs may not confront inaccurate cost estimates. These estimates are divided between soft costs (the cost of management and staff support) and hard costs (the cost of construction, including materials, usually in the form of the anticipated bid price of the construction contract). Generally speaking, soft costs are for people and hard costs are for projects. Caltrans personnel costs are taken off the top of transportation funds, completely separate from the STIP. Even CTC staff describe the system as "strange" because it puts soft costs through the annual budget process for approval by the Department of Finance and legislature, whereas hard costs are approved by the CTC with the STIP on even years and move to the legislature only for broad programmatic approval. Thus, totally different methodologies are used for budgeting soft and hard costs.

This bifurcation hinders accurate cost-estimating because no records are kept on the amount of time people in districts spend on each project. Thus, Caltrans employees have no records with which to estimate the costs of engineering, environmental review, and project management, and they have little incentive to deliver preconstruction engineering or any other preconstruction task on time or within budget. It is impossible to know with any accuracy how much money Caltrans needs every year from the General Fund to support the STIP. Finally, funding sources are separated into "pots," which makes improved accountability more complicated. One Caltrans manager says,

> Caltrans needs to be able to estimate how much it costs to generate a set of plans, and Caltrans can't seem to quickly report back on actual expenditures. There's a six week turnaround, and they have to link to funding types, pots, earmarks, etc. For every two pots consolidated, more are generated.

One-Hat Project Management and STIP Incentives

Caltrans remains largely organized around the functional categories allotted by the six or so phases of STIP funding. As projects progress toward construction, they are handed off from an environmental project manager to a design project manager to a construction project manager, and so on. According to one interviewee, about ten years ago Caltrans leadership wanted to enact organizational changes to denote one person as a single project manager. As this manager says, "Now they want one person working on projects from cradle to grave. This is a big transition."

Private sector firms have long given the autonomy, authority, and resources needed to complete the project on time and within budget to a single project manager, who is held accountable for the project's performance. This fact is not lost on the LAO.

> Project management, a style of managing projects in which one individual is held accountable for the project from start to finish, is widely recognized both in the private and public sectors as the preferred way of delivering transportation projects. The key ingredient is accountability; typically, a single manager is held accountable for the cost and schedule of a project.

In our research, we were consistently told to visit the one district where we could actually find this form of project management in action under the title "one-hat" project management. Otherwise, our interviewees cautioned, we would find projects still traded off to new managers many times during the cycle of development.

We discovered eight project managers who were taking one-hat jobs. They were widely thought to be the best managers, and the director of the district works directly with these managers on their projects. These project managers undergo outside training for as long as seven weeks and are introduced to such popular private sector management tools as Primavera scheduling software. Project managers take their positions seriously. As a one-hat project manager explained, "It's a huge motivating factor to have the responsibility to deal directly with a multimillion dollar job. A $150 million job, with one person accountable." He notes, however, that there is no feedback loop in the organization to learn from project failures.

But although the creation of one-hat project management seems to mark a watershed in improving project delivery, its success is hampered by the district's inability to give its project managers enough authority over functional groups to form and maintain project teams. The LAO acknowledges that Caltrans project managers typically do not have authority over the staff conducting work on various critical aspects of projects, such as environmental reviews or the acquisition of rights of way (Legislative Analyst's Office, 2000a, p. A-50). One interviewee explained,

> Caltrans has a long history of operating as a line agency, where your responsibility was to your area and not to a project. This has made project

> accountability more difficult to implement. Your main obligation is to fulfill your line function, so project responsibilities take a back seat. People are largely rewarded and promoted on the former, not the latter. Projects are for "spare time," and people serve their functional group. There is no leadership from the top.

Furthermore, these managers are inundated with work. One suggested that each project manager is responsible for as many as 30 active projects. They have about three hours each week to review each project. They have no choice but to "manage by exception, to try to catch projects that are falling behind." The LAO recommends that one-hat project managers reduce their load to as few as three to five projects.

Outside this district, Caltrans incentives for performance are fashioned de facto by the STIP process, which is not designed to deliver projects on time or within budget. Caltrans can get one extension to the project schedule of up to 20 months for each of the six project stages. Years can be added on to a project schedule without penalty. As one Caltrans manager notes, "You can do as many amendments to the schedule as you want." Even in the district with one-hat project management, interviewees referred back to the "traditional" way of doing business, where, if you encountered a problem, you could just "wait and the problem will go away . . . delay the project for a year." Also, Caltrans can seek as many augmentations to a project's budget as it likes.

The legislature has a standing rule to appropriate transportation funds in broad programmatic categories. Even if it wished to track cost overruns, it would be practically impossible to do so. As one Caltrans manager explains,

> [W]hen cost overruns occur, there are no records kept. The augmentation simply spills over into the next STIP cycle. Prior to SB 45, there was not even fiscal accountability in the sense that cost overruns came out of your future county shares.

Caltrans simply requests changes to the project schedule and augmentations to the budget, and they are granted by the CTC. Regional managers describe what they see as a double standard concerning CTC approvals. "The CTC lets Caltrans get away with dragging out projects and submitting cost increases, while local agencies get run through the wringer whenever they propose small changes."

Their observations are echoed in the opinions of Caltrans managers. In the words of one manager, "It's harder to go to locals for cost increases than it is to go to CTC. Locals want to be sure costs don't escalate."

As Caltrans proceeds easily through CTC approval for project delays and cost increases, the effects of these delays are borne by the counties.

> You get your county share, and a small county has to wait five STIPs to accumulate enough money to do this project that has been designed. Meanwhile those five have gone by, cost increases, inflation, then [engineers] discover certain other things or new technologies. Then it has to be somewhat redesigned, which takes another couple of years and maybe more money, and in the meantime you have to wait another couple of cycles to gather enough money to do that next.

The STIP process could be altered or managed in such a way as to be more effective in preventing cost and schedule overruns. Promotions could be tied to project performance. The project manager could become a spokesperson for the project, accessible to the legislature in its capacity to oversee Caltrans. Yet according to one regional manager, the current culture does not stress schedules and budgets. One regional manager describes the situation this way,

> So these project managers . . . have a certain culture at Caltrans that is very engineering focused. And often when they hire these project managers, they are looking for people who have those same skills, and it is very different from what I think might be needed for project managers.

Yet another regional manager describes a typical dialogue between locals and Caltrans. Locals say, "Yes, we want these projects, but we also have these other priorities," while Caltrans engineers say, "Oh, this would be a neat thing, let's design this," or "There is a really cool structure that I learned about somewhere, I read an article about it, it is really great." All the time the locals are saying, "No. No, we have this amount of money that can be delivered in this amount of time."

It remains to be seen how much Caltrans will benefit from one-hat project management. When one regional manager, located far from the one district with that approach, was asked about its possibilities, he replied, "I have no idea. It is complicated. They are organized for projects. They call their 'one-hat' project manager . . . I still don't know what 'one-hat' means."

Maintenance

> Standing atop eight lanes of grooved pavement and pristine yellow stripes in the kind of distant Los Angeles suburb made possible by endless highway construction, Gov. Gray Davis today dedicated the latest section of freeway to be built in California and declared that the project would be the last (Sterngold, 2001).

Governor Davis's declaration rings true, at least for upper management in Caltrans. As one manager suggests, "We haven't been meaningfully in the highway construction business for a long time." Taking first priority over dedicated revenue streams such as the gasoline tax, the funding of maintenance through SHOPP is relatively insured and positively stable compared to maintenance funding in education.

However, this priority has created tension between Caltrans and the regions. Every dollar allocated off the top for SHOPP funding, which Caltrans controls exclusively, is one dollar that the regions will not receive through the STIP. Those speaking for the regions suggest that this situation creates an incentive for Caltrans to take advantage of blurred distinctions between SHOPP projects and STIP. One regional interviewee thought that as much as 80 percent of State Highway Account funds have been going to Caltrans for administration and the SHOPP. Regions feel that Caltrans is "empire-building." They cite the large number of "auxiliary lanes" (lanes that run parallel to the freeway and connect exit ramps) in SHOPP plans as an example. As new lane miles, such projects should be considered new construction and placed in the STIP. At the same time, Caltrans has been under negotiations with local agencies to change the classification of some roadways from the state highway system to a local designation. In the minds of local or regional managers, Caltrans is shedding responsibility for maintenance,

> [I]t's a functional classification, they are turning it into a local road and then therefore not having the responsibility for maintaining that. And every year there will be a completely random list. . . . The issue was, are you giving us the money at the same time? You are shedding the responsibility, but you are not giving us our equal share of what it costs you to maintain that piece of roadway.

Our interviews suggest that the separation of pots of funding into the SHOPP and STIP has created an organizational barrier between project development and maintenance. Information is not exchanged between the programs. Cost estimates do not extend beyond construction and therefore do not include maintenance costs. For decades now, there have been no records kept on the materials or thickness of the pavement used for construction, and no feedback from maintenance into design. As a result, contractors hired for rehabilitation work, or even basic repaving projects, go in blind. They literally tear up the pavement to see what is there. SHOPP projects suffer from escalating costs that could be even greater than those in the STIP. As one interviewee noted, "In particular, retrofit or rehabilitation projects are more likely to have higher costs that weren't anticipated at the planning stage."

Structural and Cultural Barriers

Other barriers to improvement are more structural or cultural in nature. For example, Caltrans has increased its number of employees from 14,000 to 22,000 in recent years. Several interviewees suggested that as many as 40 percent of Caltrans employees may have less than four years of experience.

> Many workers who are older and experienced are currently retiring. New workers receive a minimum salary, but it takes two years to get your professional license, so many join, get their license, and quit and then go work for a city at a pay rate of 25 to 30 percent more. Creates a tremendous morale issue.

In effect, Caltrans is spending a lot of money to train engineers for others. In places where these engineers are most needed, such as Los Angeles and San Francisco, the LAO notes that Caltrans has trouble hiring because of the high cost of living (Legislative Analyst's Office, 2000a). District managers focus on the fact that high turnover means that it is hard to find experienced project managers, and there are not enough middle managers to oversee new project managers. As one suggests, "Upper management thinks it's about hiring more people. It's really about paying the people they have more adequately so they can hang on to experienced personnel."

Cultural problems also form systemic barriers to change. Speaking of the organizational culture of Caltrans, one manager explained, "Caltrans suffers from a classic mix of arrogance and ignorance."

> The "not invented here" syndrome is a key barrier to change and innovation. Because Caltrans was considered the premier agency 30 to 40 years ago when they were simply building highways, they have tended to rest on their laurels. The attitude is changing as they have slowly realized just how far behind they are.

In one particularly candid interview, a manager summed up the situation by saying, "A lot of people think we're still on the cutting edge. Hell, we're not on the sword."

Water

Water can be priced and sold more readily and consistently than education or transportation services. For this reason, problems in the water sector rarely stem from a lack of funding or financing. Instead, our research suggests that water supply problems stem from political inaction on the part of the state, or a lack of cohesiveness between state and local water supply entities. This condition is readily apparent when we consider the need for future supplies and begin looking at issues surrounding groundwater management.

We approached our research with the notion that California water is a scarce commodity. In fact, inexpensive surface water is scarce. The State Water Project, Central Valley Project, and Lower Colorado River are oversubscribed, and CALFED's focus is largely on the preservation of existing assets. As an interviewee confirmed, "The state and federal governments have pretty much focused on preserving what they have, if you will, and maintaining the CALFED process." In their defense, CALFED officials described state and federal agencies as "entrenched bureaucracies"; for CALFED officials, getting these agencies to think beyond the current year was "like pushing a rock uphill."

For about 20 years, only local agencies—usually serving urban populations—have been able to proceed with surface water development, sometimes doing so by politically by-passing environmental restrictions. One state-level interviewee summed up the situation.

> It basically is a local agency ballgame now that the state and federal projects are really not significant players. . . . They may be doing a fair amount of restoration work, but they are not building infrastructure in the sense of facility type stuff. . . . So the ball is really in the local agencies court right now.

Our interviews suggest that local districts are combining forces, through Joint Powers Associations and other means, to lobby the state and float bonds for local development of supplies, whether in the form of new dams or water recycling projects. The trend is especially pronounced among urban districts south of the Sacramento-San Joaquin Delta, as agencies are using their desire to wean themselves from inadequately serviced state supplies as leverage in obtaining state funds for their own projects.

"Groundwater Is Akin to the Right of Free Speech"

Groundwater is much less scarce than inexpensive surface water. The State Water Resources Control Board estimates that 250 MAF are available with today's pumping technology. The DWR suggests that, excluding basins already suffering from overdraft, there is an estimated "usable storage capacity" of about 143 MAF—about three times the amount of surface water stored across the state (California Department of Water Resources, 1975). CALFED's plans for expanding water supply depend on anywhere from 500,000 to one million acre-feet in groundwater storage projects—as much as half of all anticipated future supplies. Similarly, Proposition 13, a CALFED-backed bond passed in 2000, included $200 million for groundwater storage projects—nearly one-third of the total bonds to be issued (CALFED Bay-Delta Program, 2000c, pp. 41, 43). That report clearly spelled out the benefits of and need for efficient groundwater management.

> Effective groundwater management programs are essential to the success of groundwater and conjunctive use projects, as well as to other CALFED programs such as water transfers and water quality. Currently, groundwater is managed in some areas of the State through adjudicated basins and by local water districts and agencies. While many of these districts and agencies have developed effective local groundwater programs, most groundwater management basins in California are not managed to obtain the benefits that could be gained through conjunctive management of both groundwater and surface water. These benefits can include increased local water supply reliability, water quality protection, reduced subsidence, and mitigation of overdraft (p. 46).

The conjunctive use of groundwater was recommended as an essential part of the California Water Plan as early as 1957.

> Storage of water underground through artificial recharge has been widely practiced in California since 1895. . . . Under conjunctive operation, ground water pumping units would be distributed more uniformly over the underground basins, in comparison to the present over-concentration of wells in regions that derive their entire supply from underground sources. . . . [T]he utilization of the groundwater storage capacity of the Central Valley is essential to the full ultimate development of the water resources of the State (California Department of Water Resources, 1957, pp. 208, 209).

To this end, the plan urged the state to take up a constitutional amendment and accompanying statutes creating procedures for using groundwater basins and the adjustment of conflicts with existing water rights. The plan also suggested the requirement of permits and licenses for the appropriation of groundwater and control and supervision of depleted groundwater basins. Unfortunately, these suggestions were not embraced with the same enthusiasm as those regarding surface water projects (California Department of Water Resources, 1996b).

Today, the State Water Resources Control Board and DWR share responsibility for groundwater, but both are so limited in their authority that neither can effectively manage the resource. DWR is responsible for statewide water planning, which naturally includes attention to groundwater demand and supply. There are no statewide requirements leading to the quantification of groundwater. It may be monitored by local agencies, but most of the state's production is neither managed nor quantified (California Department of Water Resources, 1999a, pp. 3–48). Even so, DWR has no authority to collect the information that does exist from local agencies. When asked by the legislature in 1997 (SB 1245) to report on groundwater management in the state, DWR published the following findings:

> The Water Code does not require local agencies to submit their groundwater management plans to DWR. Information about groundwater management was compiled from telephone calls, e-mail, letters, three surveys conducted by the Association of California Water Agencies, and a questionnaire from DWR. The questionnaire was mailed to over 1,000 water agencies; DWR received 650 responses. . . . Not every water agency contacted has provided information concerning their management of groundwater. The information that has been submitted indicates that about 267 agencies have a groundwater management plan and 93 of those agencies have entered into some type of coordinating agreement with other agencies (California Department of Water Resources, 1999a, p. ix).

This level of information would not allow DWR to construct a map showing the actual acreage supported by groundwater planning. The DWR recommended that the legislature require local agencies to submit groundwater management plans to the Department, though no action has been taken in this regard (California Department of Water Resources, 1999b).

State and federal officials have attempted to develop groundwater projects but have backed away. While preparing plans for the Peripheral Canal, the DWR tried to tie the canal to a package of more efficient water storage programs, including conjunctive use. When agricultural interests objected to the package, it was removed. Governor Jerry Brown pressed on with the DWR to find optimal storage sites and to establish groundwater management. They studied Kern County but dropped the project when agricultural interests in the area objected to anything that might have led to formalized accounting of groundwater. These concerns were overcome by Kern County Water Agency and the City of Bakersfield, when the drought of 1976–1977 underscored the need for more efficient storage (Gottlieb and Fitzsimmons, 1991, pp. 201, 202).

The Madera Water Bank is another example of a failed project—one that was pursued by CALFED interests only to be picked up by a subsidiary of the Enron Corporation. The U.S. Bureau of Reclamation lobbied for funds to purchase Madera and develop the site for groundwater storage, but local lawmakers suggested that the project would, among other things, increase water pumping costs, contaminate local groundwater, kill farm crops, and lower property values (Orr, 1999). In the words of one federal official, rural counties "go bananas" about these proposals. At the time of our interviews, roadways in the Madera area were lined with homemade billboards telling Enron to go away. Local suspicions over groundwater management extend beyond Kern and Madera. The Regional Council of Rural Counties is suing to block CALFED proposals and helping the north Sacramento Valley counties develop local regulations that would prohibit the export of groundwater.

The only consistent arena of state involvement is entirely reactive: determined by case law through the system of rights administered by the SWRCB. The SWRCB's permitting authority applies to surface water and subterranean streams—a form of groundwater confined to a known and defined subsurface channel. However, their are few subterranean streams. All other forms of groundwater may be pumped without notice or permit.

For groundwater issues to end up in court is not surprising. Water disputes that end up in court may be delegated to the SWRCB for resolution. In these cases, the courts and SWRCB appoint an individual or organization to manage the basin, known as a "watermaster." There are about 450 water basins in the state, but only 16 have this form of management (California Department of Water Resources, 1999b, p. 5). In terms of water supply, however, adjudication does not necessarily lead to the conjunctive use of groundwater. Absent specific plans for conjunctive use, local water users were found to pump groundwater up to the court-enforced level each year and to turn to imported sources such as the State Water Project after their annual allotment of groundwater had been exhausted. Conjunctive use involves purchasing imported water during times of surface water surplus and storing it underground so that imports are not needed. So, although the SWRCB engages in a form of management, this form does not optimize groundwater resources.

One state manager summed up the state's role in groundwater management as follows:

> The state only gets involved if they absolutely have to to save a strategic resource . . . because water rights in the state for groundwater are different than surface water, and it's largely left open to anyone who wants to pump. . . . Groundwater is akin to the right of free speech. The legal aspects of water in the west are so complex and messy that the state does not want to touch it unless it has to, and then, they do so reactively. This compounds the water problem.

Part of the problem may be cultural. Several interviewees—inside and outside of the DWR—described the department as focusing exclusively on the State Water Project. Others felt that the legislature needs to redirect DWR toward the broader needs of the state. In fact, the State Water Project plans (1957) had a comprehensive system of groundwater management in mind, and DWR pressed for additional oversight of groundwater in its report to the legislature pursuant to SB 1245 (1999b).

Not all DWR employees think it preferable to shy away from groundwater management, but the department has made few inroads along these lines. Even CALFED, with its extensive commitment to groundwater as a source of future water supplies, is careful to assure every reader that groundwater will remain locally controlled.

> CALFED Agencies will facilitate and fund locally supported, managed and controlled groundwater and conjunctive use projects. . . . Groundwater/ conjunctive use projects will be implemented through locally supported and managed projects or through partnerships with local and regional interests. It is CALFED's intent to support voluntary, locally controlled groundwater projects which are designed to address local water needs first, before considering regional or statewide benefits (CALFED, 2000c, p. 46).

Instead of requiring local agencies to report to the state, CALFED suggests financial incentives for that sort of reporting.

> CALFED will work with local governments and affected stakeholders to develop legislation to strengthen AB 3030 and provide technical and financial incentives to encourage more effective basin-wide groundwater management plans, in part by conditioning future State funding for water programs on the development of local groundwater management plans by 2004 (CALFED, 2000c, p. 47).

Local Agencies and State Oversight

In a study released in May 2000, the Little Hoover Commission found "virtually no oversight by the State or other local governments of the investment policies and practices of special districts" (California Little Hoover Commission, 2000b, p. ix). These findings echoed a 1991 study by Gottlieb and Fitzsimmons, which looked into the history and governance of the Metropolitan Water District of Southern California (MWD) and five other influential local water districts in California. That study found governance structures that allowed for the appointment of board members in perpetuity—accountable to no one except perhaps the governing body creating the statute that allowed for the initial formation of the district. Board members established their own perquisites and reached unanimous conclusions outside public arenas to avoid dissent during public meetings.

> As water wholesalers or "pass-through" agencies, MWD and [San Diego County Water Authority] had been further removed from any direct

> accountability or oversight. Their clients are not individual customers but member agencies, municipalities as well as smaller water districts in turn made up of municipalities or other retailers. According to the charters of both MWD and San Diego, the water districts and the municipal member agencies each appoint representatives . . . nearly all make appointments to the larger board from among their own directors. These "wholesaler" boards are thus quite removed from direct public oversight, though it is here that major regional policy choices are made (Gottlieb and Fitzsimmons, 1991, p. 115).

As the Little Hoover Commission (LHC) explains, districts are required to submit minimal financial reports—difficult to decipher—to the state controller's office. The state controller does not audit these agencies. County auditors routinely check the numbers provided by districts but do not scrutinize investment decisions and, more important, do not pass on the information to local policymakers.

Many districts also operate independently of cities and counties. As Gottlieb and Fitzsimmons suggest, the jurisdiction of a water district may encompass many cities or counties, leaving no local government with the unique obligation of overseeing water district activities. For example, the scandal that brought special districts to LHC's attention involved a groundwater district, the Water Replenishment District of Southern California, serving 43 cities pumping groundwater from basins in the Los Angeles region. The state auditor found that the district consistently overestimated the amount of water it would need, thereby inflating the costs of groundwater replenishment. After purchasing less water than it had estimated, it did not pass the savings on to customers or lower future rates. Four lawsuits were filed by member cities.

California voters passed Proposition 218 in 1996 partly to ensure that fees for water not exceed the cost to provide the service. The LHC found that water districts are maintaining the largest financial reserves of all types of special districts—$11.8 billion in retained earnings. At the same time, 271 districts continue to collect $181 million a year in local property taxes. For example, Santa Clara Valley Water retained earnings of $391 million, with gross revenues of $102 million, while collecting an additional $17 million in property taxes. San Bernardino Valley Municipal Water retained earnings of $193 million, with gross revenues of $23 million, while collecting over $4 million in property taxes

(California Little Hoover Commission, 2000b, pp. xi, 57). The LHC also noted that local districts were in a position to issue bonds, charge fees, and maintain reserves even as they paid lobbyists to promote the passage of statewide bonds to be paid out of the state's general fund. The state, perhaps unaware of the districts' assets, is unable to consider them when making its own decisions. Proposition 13 (2000) commits the state to annual payments of about $135 million out of the General Fund for 25 years for district projects. Our interviews with state administrators confirmed that a district's assets do not play a part in determining whether the district qualifies for grants and loans out of state bond sales.

By way of oversight, the legislature has asked that the state serve as an informational "clearinghouse" for water transfers. Managers in state offices indicated, however, that a more hands-on approach will be required. As one state manager remarked,

> [T]he Legislature is trying to pass laws now that make it easier to do water transfers. In these cases, you almost have to regulate who controls the pipes, because they're the ones that can jack up the price . . . as in the case of San Diego County Water Authority wanting to buy water from the Imperial Irrigation District where it had to flow through the Metropolitan Water District's pipes.

The last comment refers to a deal between the San Diego County Water Authority (SDCWA), MWD's largest customer, and the Imperial Irrigation District, a large beneficiary of Colorado River water. By lining its aging canals, the irrigation district would conserve water, which it would then sell to SDCWA. But MWD, which owns and maintains the Colorado River Aqueduct, could not be persuaded to "wheel" the water to SDCWA at an acceptable price. Talks broke down and SDCWA took the MWD to court. In our interviews, SDCWA officials described their ideas for using $2.5 million in funds from Proposition 204, $3 million in Proposition 13 funds, and about $500,000 from their own accounts to build an entirely new canal from Imperial Irrigation District through Mexico to San Diego users. If this idea is realized, the state's inability to ensure an equitable wheeling charge may leave the state paying for over 100 miles of entirely new and redundant aqueduct.

Dam Safety

A less-controversial issue, but one that threatens the system of supply we already have, is that of dam safety. The 1976 failure of the Teton Dam in the Pacific Northwest region exposed the hazards of dam construction. In California, the USBR had already had a brush with disaster, when in 1975 an earthquake measuring 5.7 on the Richter scale occurred near the Oroville Dam, about 50 miles northwest of the site of the Auburn Dam. Although Auburn was not damaged, the Association of Engineering Geologists, Seismic Hazards Committee, issued a report stating that a moderate earthquake similar to the one in Oroville would cause the Auburn Dam to fail (U.S. Bureau of Reclamation, 1994).

Congress reacted in 1978 with the Reclamation Safety of Dams Act, amended in 1984, authorizing funding for dam safety improvements. High and significant hazard dams must be reviewed once every three years for structural integrity and operational reliability. By 2005, USBR intends to reduce risk at 25 facilities, through structural modifications or operational restrictions. In 2002, USBR planned to complete structural modifications at six dams. However, the costs to modify one facility have proven to be much higher than anticipated, and at least four of these facility upgrades have been deferred to 2003. The ability to meet these goals seems increasingly contingent on Congress's willingness to increase the budget of the Dam Safety Program (U.S. Bureau of Reclamation, 2001a).

Although DWR is responsible for the oversight of all dams that are not federally managed, its safety efforts are not supported by continuous appropriations from the legislature or by fees from the State Water Project. Instead, these activities are paid for each year with revenue from the General Fund. In their Strategic Business Plan of 1997, the DWR noted that its dam safety and flood management programs had been underfunded since 1988 (California Department of Water Resources, 1997, p. 20).

Water Policy and Politics

Gottlieb and Fitzsimmons suggest that water managers—even at the local level—know of the benefits to be gained from the conjunctive use of surface water and groundwater but that they are too focused on building their own district assets to pay attention to the greater needs of the public. LHC's research underscores this point, as does the case between SDCWA and MWD. For its part, the state has made little effort to understand the shortcomings of local water management or to take into account the local ability to pay when considering state bond measures or procedures for distributing grants for water supply. This nearly complete lack of attention to local assets seems unique to water, as the state actually endeavors to understand the resources already available to locals for education and transportation.

The only consistent role for the state in groundwater management has been played out through the courts; yet adjudication is widely understood to be long, arduous, costly, and inefficient. Drawing its own conclusions from a recent case in the Mojave Desert, an editorial in the *Sacramento Bee* (August 24, 2000) characterized the case as a call to California policymakers.

> The case involved the arid Mojave Desert, some long-standing farm operations and some growing communities such as Barstow. . . . The pumping was unsustainable. Something had to be done. The question was whether the laws gave the courts the ability to maximize the public good in apportioning this water by balancing interests—regardless of who started pumping when. The ruling is in. . . . So long as a longtime pumper is putting that water to beneficial use, that priority must be honored, rather than be balanced against some new, perhaps more important public purpose.

Thus a farmer raising trout in the desert cannot be forced to reconcile this practice with the needs of urban users. As early as 1957, the writers of the California Water Plan warned of the day when water resources would become scarce enough to have to rely on the state's messy system of water rights. Today the state continues to rely on this system, knowing that new regulations and conjunctive use could serve the greater public good by providing more efficient, balanced use of water.

If groundwater seems too politically hot to touch, then dam safety is too politically boring to capture anyone's interests. Given the dire consequences of dam failure, the underfunding of dam safety inspection, rehabilitation, and maintenance cannot be explained.

Conclusion

Our research indicates that the state's most highly prized infrastructure systems face persistent and related problems. In K–12 education and water supply, the state allocates funds in the absence of basic information about demand and capacity. In the case of groundwater management, the state knows so little that estimates of actual dependence on groundwater from the DWR and the State Water Resources Control Board differ by as much as eight million acre-feet—almost twice the amount of water allocated to California from the Colorado River, and four times the amount of additional water expected to be gained from CALFED's development plans. Critical functions, such as K–12 education and higher education, rely on unpredictable bond funding. Higher education and the local development of water facilities are supported with state grants, although both the University of California and the Metropolitan Water District have their own bonding capacity and the ability to charge user fees.

Once funds are allocated, the state has considerable difficulty ensuring their efficient management through project delivery. In the transportation sector, the state itself is known for the slow and costly delivery of services. Although our research turned up a number of bright spots, including one-hat project management at Caltrans, we also encountered efforts that are best described as empire-building or enforcement of the status quo. Districts independent of state departments, such as local water districts and school districts, have fortified themselves against state oversight. The use of incentives does not ensure effectiveness, as demonstrated by efforts to reduce the cost of K–12 project delivery and to implement groundwater management plans.

Perhaps the most persistent of all problems is the state's inattention to maintenance. All three sectors lack systematic record-keeping for maintenance, and none has adopted a lifecycle approach to infrastructure costing and maintenance. In too many cases, such maintenance has been deferred or provided on an ad hoc basis.

The next chapters of this report explore solutions to these persistent problems.

5. Planning for the Future

California's postwar infrastructure investments carried the state through the 20th century. It is now time for a new round of investments in the state's core infrastructure. How effectively the state plans, finances, delivers, and maintains these new core investments will greatly determine California's economic future and quality of life for the next generation. This process is inherently long-term, as infrastructure is the ultimate capital good. It is highly durable and expensive and it takes time to plan and build—five to ten years for new educational facilities and ten to 20 years for highways and water supply systems. However, time and expense are not the only challenges the state faces at this juncture, for the institutional ones are equally daunting. As the LAO pointed out in 1998:

> Neither the administration nor the Legislature evaluate statewide infrastructure needs and infrastructure investment as a program in and of itself. . . . Proposals are reviewed in isolation of each functional area—an approach that does not allow examination of how competing proposals fit within a context of overall state infrastructure needs, priorities, and funding capabilities. The result is that capital investment decisions are made more on an ad hoc basis (1998b).

It is not that state agencies have not planned. Most do so as a matter of course, and some plans have proved useful or even prescient. Rather, the problem is that these plans do not consider alternative methods for delivering services, assess the overall quality of these services, or form an overall strategic plan for statewide service delivery. As a result, capital decisionmaking is usually reactive and poorly planned, and too little effort is given to strategic planning as a front-end input to infrastructure investment. The legislative procedures that determine capital outlays have not been based on future demand or existing capacity; indeed, some agencies lack the most basic data on existing facilities. Also, the dollar estimates from needs studies are frequently much higher than budgets realistically permit. The result is not a workable strategic plan so much as a series of wish lists subject to the vagaries of the annual budget process.

Given the gap between the state's infrastructure requirements and its available resources, the state urgently needs to develop a strategic plan for programming and budgeting infrastructure investment. In this chapter, we review how strategic planning can shape capital investment and programming.

California's Capital Budgeting Process

Public and private sector capital investment decisionmaking can be divided into four fairly distinct phases: planning, budgeting, financing, and project management. In California, budgeting drives the process. Proposals for infrastructure capital projects, called COBCPs (capital outlay budget change proposals) are prepared by each state agency and line department. The proposals are made on a one- and five-year basis. These proposals are forwarded to the DOF by February 1 of each year for inclusion in the following year's state budget.

There is virtually no interaction between agencies as they prepare their COBCPs. Furthermore, there is no standard method for determining the scale, scope, or function of each project. Agencies rely on DOF population projections, but few other common criteria are commonly used. Agencies see themselves as providing unique services and as competing with other agencies for budget resources. Using a process prescribed in the *State Administrative Manual,* the DOF reviews capital projects before the governor's office makes its budget decision. In particular, the DOF assesses projects, determines whether they are warranted, and implicitly ranks those that meet the department's criteria. The DOF's statutory responsibility, however, is not to prepare or execute a strategic plan for infrastructure but to ensure the state's "long-term financing needs in a manner which will protect the financial integrity of the state" (Government Code Sec. 13104). As a result, the state's capital investments are driven more by financial considerations than by long-term goals (Neuman and Whittington, 2000).

Over the past decade, the state has started to respond to criticisms of poor capital decisionmaking. Much of the groundwork was established in the Performance and Results Act of 1993 (Section 11800 of the

Government Code), which called for using strategic planning to improve the quality and effectiveness of government services. Reform activities began in 1994–1995, when the Department of Finance developed a performance budgeting pilot project. That project called for the development of agency strategic plans and outcome measures as well as productivity benchmarks to measure progress toward strategic goals. After positive results from the pilot project, the state required that most agencies (but not UC, CSU, Caltrans, or the DWR) prepare strategic plans and use them to justify budget requests (Section 11815).

AB 1473, known as the California Infrastructure Planning Act (Chapter 606, Statutes of 1999), marks a substantial shift toward statewide, long-term capital planning. Administered by DOF, AB 1473 requires that UC, CSU, K–12 education, and Caltrans (for the state highway system) participate in the process. DWR has also attended workshops for AB 1473 and seems to be contributing on a voluntary basis. Starting in 2000–2001, agencies must use their strategic plans to determine infrastructure investment needs. AB 1473 also requires that the governor submit annually to the legislature a proposed Five-Year Infrastructure Plan containing specific information concerning infrastructure needed by state agencies, schools, and postsecondary institutions and a proposal for funding the needed infrastructure. The plan is intended to complement the existing state budget process for appropriating funds for infrastructure by providing a comprehensive guideline for the types of projects to be funded through that process.

With the exception of one statewide plan produced during Jerry Brown's administration (Office of Planning and Research, 1978), these AB 1473 plans will be the first effort in cross-sectoral capital outlay planning attempted in California. They will require the following information:

- All new, rehabilitated, modernized, improved, or renovated infrastructure requested by state agencies as identified in their strategic plans.
- Aggregate funding for transportation as identified in the four-year State Transportation Improvement Program Fund Estimate prepared pursuant to Sections 14524 and 14525.

- Infrastructure needs for K–12 schools necessary to accommodate increased enrollment, class size reduction, and school modernization.
- The instructional and instructional support facilities needs for the University of California, the California State University, and the California Community Colleges.

The plans will also include estimates of the cost of providing the identified infrastructure and proposals for funding it. Funding proposals are required to set priorities for which projects should be developed. The plan must also identify sources of funds used to finance projects, including the General Fund, state special funds, federal funds, general obligation bonds, lease revenue bonds, and installment purchases. If a plan proposes the issuance of new state debt, it must evaluate the effect of that debt on the state's existing overall debt position.

The first plan pursuant to AB 1473 was released in April 2002. In preparation, the DOF pressed departments to determine the factors that drive facility needs—absent budget estimates. Departments were encouraged to share metrics and methodologies. They examined their program goals and operating environments to see whether alternative modes of program delivery could prove more beneficial. The bulk of the plan lays out funding over a five-year period in several programmatic categories, such as critical infrastructure deficiencies, facility modernization, program delivery changes, environmental restoration, and anticipated changes in enrollment, caseload, or population. Although departments did not have to identify actual projects, the precision and specificity called for in the plan posed a daunting challenge, as many had not developed the databases and reporting relationships necessary for long-term planning. As the DOF notes,

> Despite the attempt to be more thorough and specific about both needs and funding, this plan contains gaps . . . it became apparent that many departments have not been doing long-range assessments of their capital outlay needs. Although some agencies with expansive capital investments, such as the University of California and the California State University, have substantial internal systems for monitoring and planning their capital needs, other departments have relatively few or no systems of this type. Some do not even have a complete inventory of their existing facilities and an assessment of the

> functional capabilities and deficiencies of those facilities. Lacking such "base" infrastructure data, it is difficult for a department to calculate its future needs (California Department of Finance, 2002, p. 9).

Still, the DOF urged departments to convey current needs and move toward a more complete picture of future needs.

These reforms are important positive steps toward improving the effectiveness and efficiency of capital infrastructure investments. However, significant gaps remain in linking strategic plans to capital investment decisions. During the making of the state's first Five-Year Plan, the DOF found this aspect of AB 1473 very difficult to implement. Many strategic plans adopted by state agencies still lack performance measurements and constructive self-criticism. Moreover, they have rarely, if ever, attempted to link performance shortfalls with capital and noncapital alternatives. When quantitative measures are provided, they are often convenient numerical counts of activity not clearly connected to the goals and objectives of the organization. In this sense, these efforts still do not rise to the standard of strategic plans.

The Need for Strategic Planning

Strategic planning is best thought of as a process to produce fundamental decisions and actions for guiding an organization. In particular, it is used to

- Clarify goals and missions,
- Establish priorities,
- Make immediate decisions in light of future consequences,
- Develop a coherent and defensible basis for decisionmaking,
- Exercise maximum discretion in areas that are under organization control,
- Make decisions across levels and functions,
- Improve organization performance, and
- Deal effectively with rapidly changing circumstances (Bryson and Einsweiler, 1988).

The typical process of strategic planning for public sector agencies moves through eight discrete steps as described in Table 5.1.

Table 5.1

Typical Strategic Planning Process in the Public Sector

Step 1: Agreeing to Plan
As a starting point, the agency must agree to develop a strategic plan. In some cases, the process is imposed on the agency, as is the case with California's new statute Section 11816, requiring that agencies and developments prepare a strategic plan. The agreement should provide a description of the purpose of the plan: who should participate in the process, what should be accepted as a given, which topics should be covered, and the timing of the process.
Step 2: Defining the Mandates
Next, the agency should review and define its required mandates. What is the agency responsible for? It is especially useful to review these mandates over time and to assess boundary areas where the activities of other agencies overlap.
Step 3: Clarifying the Agency's Mission and Values
The planning process needs to be based on a clear understanding of the perceived mission of the agency. What is its core mission? What are its basic values regarding service delivery? In clarifying the agency's mission, it is very important to consult with both internal and external stakeholders: customers, taxpayers, and other individuals or groups that can lay claim to the agency's resources or outputs or are affected by the agency's actions.
Step 4: Scanning the External Environment
In this step, planners identify and assess the range of external threats and opportunities the agency faces or will face. The scanning process includes assessing demographic and economic trends, shifts in policies or values, and other forces that lie outside the control of the agency. Again, it is important to consult the full range of external stakeholders to gauge potential threats and opportunities. It is also imperative that the agency develop a range of future scenarios. In this way, planners can develop a menu of strategies and tactics for dealing with unforeseen events.
Step 5: Scanning the Internal Environment
In this step, planners assess internal capabilities, strengths, and weaknesses by reviewing budget allocations and resources, assessing staffing levels, and gauging the capacity to produce services. They might benchmark the performance of its services or products against other best-practice agencies and should carefully assess the effectiveness and efficiency of existing procedures and processes. This scanning process should help to identify a range of strengths and weaknesses of the organization.
Step 6: Identifying Strategic Issues
Then, the outputs of the first five steps should be integrated and used to identify key strategic issues. Normally these are fundamental policy issues that center on mandates and mission, resources, external threats, and opportunities. Other strategic issues center on mismatches between mandates and resources. A failure to address strategic issues will nearly always result in an undesirable outcome or result.
Step 7: Developing Strategy
In this phase of the process, planners start by developing practical alternatives for resolving strategic issues. Next they should identify the barriers to implementing the alternatives and assess whether they can be overcome. This step should result in the identification of practical alternatives.

Table 5.1 (continued)

Step 8: Visualizing the Agency in the Future
In this final step, the process imagines or visualizes how the agency will look in the future. How will it function once it has overcome its threats and weaknesses? The vision should provide enough specificity to enable managers and policymakers to evaluate the performance of the agency in the future.

SOURCE: Bryson and Einsweiler (1988).

In California, the Department of Finance has already initiated Step 1 by engaging the state's 64 departments in a series of workshops designed to launch AB 1473. Now agencies should assess and reaffirm their mandates, missions, and core values. What do Californians expect from the agency? Does the agency have the human, physical, and financial resources to adequately meet user and beneficiary demands? Are there critical threats or weaknesses that the agencies should address to meet their mission?

Once these assessments have been completed, managers can identify key issues that affect their performance. What should the agency do to overcome these issues? What role do capital investments play in helping the agency achieve its objectives? Does the agency need to renew facilities? Does it need to expand operations? This process provides a framework for thinking about the role of the agency in society and in determining how it should utilize scarce resources to meet the demands of its customers.

When the planning process is complete, steps must be taken to implement, evaluate, and monitor the strategy. Each agency's strategy should be updated frequently to reflect changing external and internal conditions and to track the performance of the agency as it strives to reach various goals and objectives. Annual performance reports, developed from bottom-up monitoring of performance indicators, should allow agencies to revisit each goal and objective for the next strategic plan and serve as a reporting device on progress for the governor and legislature.

In preparing strategic plans for education, transportation, and water supply, agencies should focus on missions and end users rather than on the physical plant. The mission of these organizations is not to provide stocks of infrastructure investments—campuses, freeways, or reservoirs or canals—but to provide services to customers. Seen in this light, strategic planning should be used as a tool for determining how to best deploy and utilize resources to provide the best quality service at the lowest possible cost. Accordingly, capital investment decisions should be based on focused assessments of service demands rather than on formulaic requests for additional assets.

Linking Capital Budgeting and Strategic Planning

Strategic planning provides a means for more rigorously assessing capital expenditure proposals. Whereas strategic planning addresses the question of whether the agency actually needs the assets, capital budgeting concentrates on achieving more for the money invested. The U.S. General Accounting Office (GAO) (1998) and the Office of Management and Budget (OMB) (1997) have developed an integrated approach to strategic planning and capital budgeting. Their approach, which reflects more than a decade of work to improve the performance of federal agencies under the Government Performance and Results Act (GPRA) of 1993, defines decisionmaking processes for the various phases of capital investment—planning, budgeting, procurement, and management in use (Office of Management and Budget, 1997). In the course of developing management tools for implementing the GPRA, OMB and GAO conducted a best-practice survey of capital decisionmaking based on studies of various state and local governments as well as large corporations. The GAO discovered that these organizations shared many common traits. They all use strategic planning and visioning[1] to drive their capital decisionmaking process. They also ensure that the entire process is informed by and supported with intensive feedback and evaluation mechanisms. Finally, these organizations follow very similar decisionmaking procedures, which can be summarized by the five principles in Figure 5.1.

The GAO found that best-practice organizations begin their capital decisionmaking process by defining their overall mission in

---

[1]Visioning is a term used by strategic planners to refer to the process of defining a preferred future state of affairs or condition that the strategic plan aims toward.

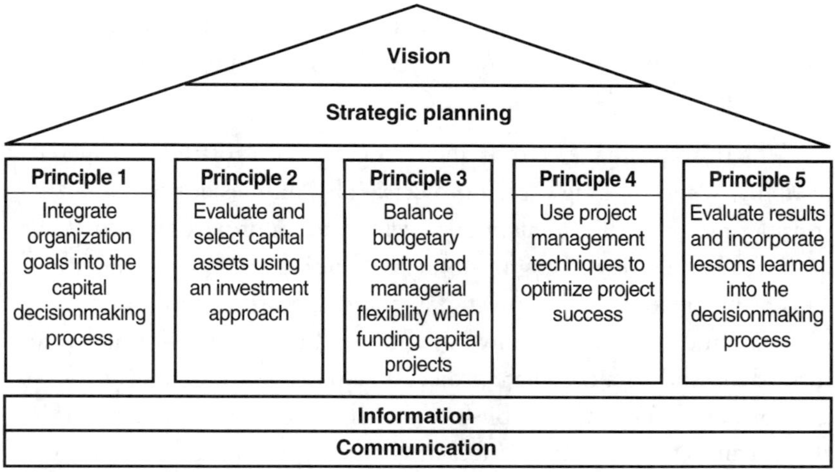

SOURCE: U.S. General Accounting Office (1998).

Figure 5.1—The Capital Decisionmaking Framework

comprehensive terms and by setting results-oriented goals and objectives. This principle leads to three practices:

- Conducting comprehensive needs assessments to meet results-oriented goals and objectives,
- Identifying current capabilities, including the use of an inventory of assets and their condition, and determining whether there are gaps between current and needed capabilities, and
- Identifying and evaluating alternative approaches (including noncapital alternatives) to reducing or eliminating those gaps.

The second principle, which concerns the evaluation and selection of capital assets, also leads to three practices:

- Establishing a review and approval framework supported by proper financial, technical, and risk analyses,
- Ranking and selecting projects based on established criteria such as cost savings, benefit cost ratios, or increased market growth, and

- Developing a long-term capital plan that defines capital asset decisions over a five- to ten-year horizon and updates them annually.

The third principle is to balance budgetary control and managerial flexibility when funding capital projects. This implies not only considering the total capital and lifecycle cost of a project when making decisions but also exercising flexibility in funding and management. This principle leads to two practices: budgeting projects in useful segments and considering innovative approaches to full up-front funding. Instead of funding a complete project on a pay-as-you-go basis, for example, an agency may establish capital accumulation accounts that allow managers to accrue user fees or charges to pay for projects in the future.

The fourth principle is to use project management techniques to optimize project success. The notion here is to more effectively manage capital project delivery so that projects are completed sooner and at lower costs. Two main practices follow from this principle: monitoring project performance, which includes establishing incentives for accountability, and using cross-functional teams to plan and manage projects. Given the complexity of projects, leading organizations have found that diverse teams are better equipped to manage project delivery.

The final principle is to evaluate results and incorporate lessons learned into the decisionmaking process. Two practices issue from this principle: evaluating results against organizational goals and evaluating the decisionmaking process to ensure that goals are met.

With the passage of GPRA and the directives from the OMB and the GAO, many federal agencies have adopted these strategic planning principles. The next section offers an example from the federal government—the U.S. Bureau of Reclamation. The USBR case offers a good example of how a functional infrastructure agency uses the strategic planning process to set goals, targets, service levels, and benchmarks for evaluating achievement. It serves as a useful model for how California infrastructure agencies might approach capital planning in a more strategic and accountable manner.

U.S. Bureau of Reclamation: A Best-Practice Model of Capital Decisionmaking

The USBR, in accordance with GPRA, demonstrates the benefits that can be provided by strategic planning. Although the USBR is a federal agency, its practices are highly relevant to California both as an example of strategic planning and insofar as it manages surface water supplies for the Central Valley Project and Lower Colorado River.

The USBR's mission and goals bear directly on management decisions throughout the organization. Equally important, capital and operating decisions are tied to these goals and tracked in a transparent and fundamentally accountable way. It publishes strategic plans every three years; each uses a five-year time horizon and clearly states the mission and long-term goals. The plan also presents strategies for achieving each long-term goal and the cross-cutting relationships necessary to reach it. For example, USBR's *Strategic Plan 2000–2005*, which includes a long-term goal geared toward the preservation of fish and wildlife habitat, reads as follows:

> By 2005, Reclamation will protect and enhance fish and wildlife habitat by restoring and/or establishing wetlands and instream or riparian habitat affected by Reclamation projects (U.S. Bureau of Reclamation, 1999, p. 14).

Directly under this goal, USBR promises to provide approximately 1.4 MAF of water each year to address the concerns of the Endangered Species Act and commits to a "no net loss of wetlands" policy. Of the five strategies identified for accomplishing the goal, one is the "completion of a multi-species conservation plan for the Lower Colorado River that will guide management of the basin for the next 50 years." Under cross-cutting relationships, the USBR mentions working with four other agencies; the states of California, Arizona, and Nevada; five Native American tribes; and 18 water and hydropower management agencies. The program is evaluated annually and semi-annually in bureauwide meetings.

The USBR's strategic plans are followed up with Annual Performance Plans and Annual Performance Reports, which present USBR's long-term goals from its strategic plan, identify strategies, and measure the resources needed to achieve them. These plans enhance managerial accountability by linking annual goals and resources to the strategic plan and quantifying and tracking performance for each of these goals. In 2002, USBR released its 2000 Annual Performance Report and 2002 Annual Performance Plan in a single, 135-page volume. In this annual plan, the long-term goal of enhancing fish and wildlife habitat was given further detail in the form of a 2002 annual goal of providing 1.1 MAF of water to conserve threatened species, protecting 720 acres of wetlands habitat, and protecting 350 miles of instream or riparian habit (U.S. Bureau of Reclamation, 2001a, p. 49).

The annual plan also lists three performance measures (Table 5.2). Note the quantification of each measure as planned and actually carried out in the year 2000. Each performance measure is quantified and reported on with accompanying discussion when the bureau exceeds or falls short of targets. As a direct result of GPRA, for each performance measure the USBR must validate the data, indicate how the data are verified, indicate the source of data, explain the limitations of the data, and present planned improvements to these measures. For the annual goal of water provided in support of the Endangered Species Act, these additional features are illustrated in Table 5.3.

Table 5.2

Sample of USBR's Annual Performance Measures

Performance Measures	2000 Plan	2000 Actual	2001 Plan	2002 Proposed
Acre-feet of water provided for purposes of the Endangered Species Act (ESA) and other project benefits requiring instream enhancement	1.7 million	1.9 million	900,000	1.1 million
Acres of wetlands protected and maintained, established, restored, or enhanced	1,547	7,187	1,000	720
Miles of instream or riparian habitat protected and maintained, established, restored, or enhanced (this is a new indicator in fiscal year 2001)	—	—	40	350

SOURCE: U.S. Bureau of Reclamation (2001a, p. 50).

Table 5.3

Sample of Additional Features Required by GPRA for the USBR

Data validation (water for ESA)	Management has determined this goal to be an appropriate measure of the ability to address ESA issues affected by USBR projects.
Data verification	To determine acre-feet of water for ESA, Memoranda of Agreement (MOAs) are negotiated with states, local, and federal agencies to set minimum flow requirements and regimens for endangered and other species. Amounts of water verified through operational water records and in some cases water levels are monitored.
Data source	MOAs, operational records, and water level monitoring reports.
Data limitations	Flows of water provided are estimates and subject to the accuracy of monitoring equipment.
Planned improvements	Some offices are improving their tracking of water releases through real-time monitoring systems.

SOURCE: U.S. Bureau of Reclamation (2001a, p. 52).

If California were to pursue AB 1473 with equal rigor, legislators could easily visualize the capital decisions and organizational changes necessary to improve state government performance. Because AB 1473 requires that all COBCPs be linked to strategic plans, state agencies and departments have been busy dusting off their strategic plans from the Wilson era and working closely with the DOF to prepare the first Five-Year Infrastructure Plan. So far, these strategic plans do not compare to those of the USBR in scope or quality.

There are two important steps in reforming California's performance-based infrastructure service delivery. The first is to link agency-related goals and missions with the capital decisionmaking process for infrastructure investment. The second step is to broaden the application of strategic planning across infrastructure sectors. This means developing a statewide vision or strategy for future development and using it to order and set investment priorities. Working across sectors is technically and politically complicated.

Can the application of strategic planning be broadened and used to guide cross-sectoral infrastructure planning? Experience over the past decade suggests that it looks possible. Many states and provinces in the United States, Canada, and Australia have developed strategic plans to help them shape their infrastructure and urban development plans. The next section illustrates how several states have used strategic planning.

State-Level Strategic Plans

Three states provide excellent examples of how strategic planning can be used to guide infrastructure investment decisionmaking: Minnesota, New Jersey, and Washington. In each case, state government has developed a vision of its future and has used it as a compass for setting appropriate investment goals and urban development policies.

Minnesota

Minnesota prepares a Five-Year Strategic Capital Budget Plan. The plan is prepared by the Governor's Office and submitted to the state legislature. The most recent Strategic Capital Budget Plan is for 2001–2006 (Office of the Governor of the State of Minnesota, 2001). The plan recommendations reflect the governor's commitment to the following goals and principles:

- Protecting existing state investments,
- Protecting the life and safety of Minnesota citizens and employees,
- Completing important projects that have been partially funded, and
- Making selective strategic investments consistent with the state's "Big Plan" (its statewide strategic development plan) and smart growth principles.

These four goals serve as the main driver for the governor's Strategic Capital Budget Plan. They are broad and multisectoral, cutting across the state's range of infrastructure mandates—transportation, education, housing, economic development, and environmental protection. The first element centers on the importance of asset management and stewardship. It places priority on ensuring that state facilities will not be in disrepair or endanger users. It also calls for the replacement of facilities that have outlived their useful life. The second principle focuses on ensuring that the health and safety of citizens and state employees are not at risk because of inadequate facilities or the absence of infrastructure to protect health and safety. The third principle affirms the importance and necessity of continued funding of projects that are under development.

The fourth principle is more inclusive. It is based on the governor's Big Plan, which envisions "life is good no matter where you live in Minnesota." The plan promotes healthy, vital communities. It consists of eight initiatives:

- Making Minnesota's K–12 education system the best in the nation,
- Improving the competitive position of rural Minnesota,
- Promoting smart growth,
- Multimodal transportation solutions for people and goods,
- Affordable housing,
- Living human rights and respect,
- Telecommunications and economic development, and
- Reliable energy and consumer choice (Office of the Governor of the State of Minnesota, 2002).

Taken together these principles are used by the Governor's Office to set priorities for prioritizing capital outlays over the 2001–2006 period. The Strategic Plan calls for the allocation of $576 million over the period—$365 million for bricks and mortar to repair and renew educational facilities, roads and bridges, and public facilities, and to expand educational and health facilities, and $211 million for statewide strategic investments in light rail, Minnesota River watershed restoration, and rural mortgage assistance.

The Strategic Capital Budget Plan devotes considerable attention to deferred maintenance, calling it "melting the capital iceberg." The state estimates that the state's deferred maintenance backlog exceeds $1.5 billion. Since 1990, the state has been focusing on how to melt the iceberg, by increasing appropriations for asset renewal.

The plan recommends a range of investments covering five areas:

- Moving Minnesota—providing high-quality environmentally sound and cost-effective transportation,
- Cleaning up the Minnesota River—a massive project covering 37 counties to restore the environmental quality of the river,
- Water Management and Pollution Control, calling for investments in water and wastewater facilities,
- Supporting Agriculture—providing funds to help farmers cut costs and become more competitive, and
- Building Our Economic Future—rebuilding brownfield areas, promoting employment generation, and fostering economic diversification across the state (Office of the Governor of the State of Minnesota, 2001).

Minnesota's integration of basic capital budgeting principles with its statewide strategic plan allows the Governor's Office to effectively and transparently set capital spending priorities. The principles of the Big Plan and the priority given to asset management, health, and safety provide the strategic framework for carrying out multisectoral investment planning.

New Jersey

Urban and regional planning and state-level infrastructure planning and programming are guided by New Jersey's State Development and Redevelopment Plan. The plan has five major elements: a vision statement, goals and strategies, statewide policies, state plan policy map, and monitoring and evaluation programs. The key goals and strategies of the plan call for

- Revitalizing the state's cities and towns,
- Conserving natural resources and systems,
- Promoting economic growth, development, and renewal for all residents,
- Protecting the environment and cleaning up pollution,
- Providing adequate public facilities and services at a reasonable cost,
- Providing adequate housing at a reasonable cost,

- Preserving and enhancing areas with historic, cultural, scenic, open space, and recreational value, and
- Ensuring sound and integrated planning and implementation statewide.

The list details a range of public investment priorities. They are intended to guide how state and local governments make investment decisions by placing higher priority on the following: public health and safety, infrastructure maintenance and repair, support for capacity expansion in urban areas, support for the revitalization of distressed areas, and support for local governments with approved moderate-income housing plans and for projects with higher benefit-cost ratios. In terms of infrastructure, the plan states:

> Provide infrastructure and related services more efficiently by investing in infrastructure to guide growth, managing demand and supply, restoring systems in distressed areas, maintaining existing infrastructure investments, designing multi-use school facilities to serve as centers of community, creating more compact settlement patterns in appropriate locations in suburban and rural areas, and timing and sequencing the maintenance of capital facilities service levels with development throughout the state (New Jersey State Planning Commission, 2001b, p. 35).

As part of the strategic planning process, the state assessed infrastructure needs. It noted that, since the adoption of the state plan in 1992, the rehabilitation, repair, and expansion of infrastructure has been increasingly guided by the policy and program goals of the plan. Strategic plans are now being developed and applied to state agencies to guide public investments in transportation, energy, water supply, higher education, housing, and other areas.

The 2001 statewide assessment identified $75 billion in needed infrastructure investments over the next 20 years (New Jersey State Planning Commission, 2001b). Approximately 60 percent of the total is needed to renew and upgrade existing systems ($46 billion). The remainder, 39 percent, is required to meet additional capacity requirements ($29 billion). New Jersey planners follow a strategic infrastructure investment decisionmaking process. The process is outlined in Figure 5.2.

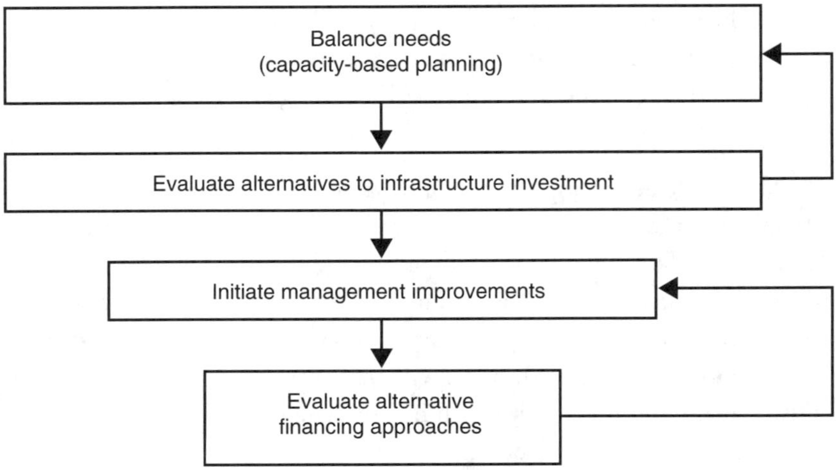

Figure 5.2—New Jersey State Strategic Infrastructure Planning Process

Washington

The Washington State Budget and Accounting Act (RCW 43.88) mandates a long-range approach to capital budget planning. The act requires that state agencies prepare and submit a Ten-Year Capital Spending Plan to the governor each biennium. These long-range plans identify critical future issues and outline a capital program to address them. The capital plan must be consistent with the agency's required strategic plan. Using these submissions, the governor prepares a Ten-Year Capital Plan.

The state's capital planning process outlines the following priorities:

- Protection of people,
- Protection of assets (repair system failures or emergencies),
- Protection of the environment,
- Cost savings (projects that reduce cost of service delivery), and
- Program need or requirement.

Under the state's Growth Management Act, the capital plan must also assess the effects of investments on urban areas. The goal of the act is to

> promote state capital facility expenditures that minimize unplanned or uncoordinated infrastructure and development, minimize unplanned or uncoordinated infrastructure and development costs, support economic and quality of life benefits for existing communities, and support local government planning efforts (Office of Financial Management, 2002, p. 11).

Over the next year, the State of Washington will begin to frame its overall infrastructure capital investment strategy. It will be linked with the state's growth management policies (Washington State Community, 2002).

Although these are but three examples, it seems clear that other states are making progress in linking strategic planning and capital budgeting. Many states require that agencies prepare strategic plans and use them to program capital investment plans over a five- to ten-year horizon. States with more advanced planning processes (such as New Jersey) have articulated urban and regional development plans and begun using them to prioritize and coordinate infrastructure capital investment. California can learn from these other states.

6. Managing the Demand for Infrastructure Services

Strategic infrastructure planning poses a basic question: Are there ways to meet infrastructure needs without investing in new capital equipment? It may be possible, for example, to manage the demand for existing infrastructure in ways that encourage its most efficient use and thereby minimize the need for new investment. This sort of demand management contrasts with traditional planning approaches, which focus almost exclusively on increasing the supply of infrastructure. In its baldest form, supply-oriented planning forecasts infrastructure needs based on per capita estimates of consumption. These per capita estimates, in turn, are based on historical patterns of infrastructure use. Demand management, in contrast, begins with consumers' willingness and ability to pay for services. It recognizes that the demand for infrastructure is dynamic, and it seeks to control the key drivers of that demand to make the most efficient use of existing resources.

To manage the demand for infrastructure effectively, planners must first understand what drives that demand. The eight key drivers are as follows.

Growth and composition of the population: As supply-oriented planners understand, the state's infrastructure must expand as the population increases. However, the composition of the state's population is also an important factor in infrastructure demand. For example, age profiles determine schooling and corrections needs, and the demand for some infrastructure services may vary across ethnic groups.

Level of economic activity: Economic expansion generates increased demand for infrastructure services such as energy, transportation services, and water supply.

Income: As income rises, the demand for infrastructure services tends to increase. A study of urban water demand in California, for example, estimates that the demand for water increases by 2.5 percent for each 10 percent increase in income (Renwick et al., 1998). Similar trends are found for electrical power, recreation, higher education, and vehicle miles traveled.

User fees: Consumers will economize on their use of services as prices increase. In Singapore, a toll of S$3.00 (about U.S. $1.70) reduced inbound traffic to the city by 38 percent (Seik, 1997). Forecasting methods that ignore the potential effects of pricing will routinely overestimate capacity requirements.

Tastes or preferences: The demand for certain services can change as social groups develop new preferences. To date, the demand for higher education among Hispanics has lagged the demand among whites and Asians. If Hispanic participation rates rise to match white and Asian rates, enrollment for UC, CSU, and CCC will increase by 270,000 by 2010 (Park and Lempert, 1998).

Availability of alternative services: Consumers have increasingly sought out alternatives to such public goods as schools, roads, police enforcement, and parks. For example, private schools have proliferated, gated communities have provided their own roads and security services, and new partnerships between park districts and local organizations have formed to improve park management and operations (Blakely and Snyder, 1999; Reason Public Policy Institute, 1999; Walker, 1999). The availability of these alternatives tends to diminish the demand for publicly funded infrastructure.

Technology: Changes in technology are likely to affect the demand for and supply of infrastructure services. The growth of electronic commerce, for example, has altered shopping patterns and may change the future demand for certain kinds of infrastructure. Likewise, distance learning technologies may shift the demand for higher education (Park and Lempert, 1998).

Conservation: Utilities have introduced a range of energy conservation programs that have altered the demand for electricity and other forms of power. More recently, urban water districts have offered incentives for low-flush toilets, drip irrigation systems, and drought-tolerant landscaping. Agricultural water users have also lined canals and sold their surplus water to metropolitan markets.

All eight factors will shape California's infrastructure requirements in the future. Some of them, however, can be managed more productively than others. The following sections describe how demand management can be applied in California's water, education, and transportation sectors.

Managing Water Demand

By 2020, the state's population is expected to grow by 15 million, but the state's water supply is predicted to increase by only 180,000 acre-feet (TAF), or about 0.02 percent (California Department of Water Resources, 1999a). The demand for water in 2020, assuming normal weather conditions, will exceed available supplies by 2.4 MAF. Under drought conditions, the shortage will increase to 6.2 MAF.

To address this projected shortage, DWR and over 200 of the state's water districts have signed a Memorandum of Understanding Regarding Urban Water Conservation in California (see Box 6 .1). This MOU calls for the implementation of 14 best management practices (BMPs) to reduce water consumption among urban users, which currently consume about 11 percent of the state's water. These practices include water audits for residences, rebates for high-efficiency washing machines, and public information programs. The MOU also calls for conservation pricing. A common myth in the water planning and management is that water is not sensitive to price, but there is abundant evidence that water consumption is affected by pricing. DWR's studies of water districts in California suggest that the price elasticity of demand for urban water between 1989 and 1996 was approximately –0.16; that is, a 10 percent increase in water prices will lead to a 1.6 percent decrease in the quantity demanded.[1] This result suggests that price is a significant factor influencing water consumption.

Over the past decade, the Irvine Ranch Water District (IRWD) has been able to reduce its consumption by 12 to 19 percent by shifting from

---

[1]Hanemann's survey indicates a price elasticity ranging from –0.1 to –0.43. For municipal and industrial uses, price elasticities range from –0.1 to –0.7 (Bauman et al., 1998).

Box 6.1

Urban Best Management Practices

BMP 1: Water audit programs for single-family residential and multifamily customers
BMP 2: Residential plumbing retrofit
BMP 3: System water audits, leak detection, and repair
BMP 4: Metering with commodity rates for all new connections and retrofit of existing connections
BMP 5: Large landscape conservation programs and incentives
BMP 6: High-efficiency washing machine rebate program (new)
BMP 7: Public information programs
BMP 8: School education programs
BMP 9: Conservation programs for commercial, industrial, and institutional accounts
BMP 10: Wholesale agency assistance programs (new)
BMP 11: Conservation pricing
BMP 12: Conservation coordinator (formerly BMP 14)
BMP 13: Water waste prohibition
BMP 14: Residential ultra-low-flow toilet (ULFT) replacement programs (formerly BMP 16)

SOURCE: California Department of Water Resources (1999a).

flat rates to block pricing (Wong, 1999, pp. 27–35). Table 6.1 illustrates the IRWD block-price structure. For residential uses, blocks are based on estimates of persons per dwelling unit, landscaped areas, and monthly evapotranspiration rates.

Other user blocks are based on prior patterns and information about best practices by sector. In 1997, the base rate was \$0.64 per 100 cubic feet (748 gallons). If a residential customer had a base allocation of 2,000 cubic feet and used 5,900 cubic feet, the total block rate charges would be \$147.20 (Table 6.2). This approach, although not without complaints, has worked to promote water conservation throughout the district. This conservation, in turn, generated \$17.4 million in net benefits to the district between 1991 and 1998 (Haasz, 1999).

Table 6.1

Block Prices for the Irvine Ranch Water District

Pricing Tier	Residential Water Use (as a % of Base Allocation)	CII and L/A Water Use[a] (as a % of Base Allocation)	Price per Unit Used in Each Tier
Low-volume discount[b]	0–40	0–40	0.75 base rate
Conservation base rate	41–100	41–100	1.0 base rate
Inefficient	101–150	101–110	2 × base rate
Excessive	151–200	111–120	4 × base rate
Wasteful	201 and above	121 and above	8 × base rate

SOURCE: Irvine Ranch Water District (1998).

[a]Commercial, industrial and institutional, and landscape/agricultural (L/A).

[b]The low-volume discount rate applies to nonresidential landscape customers only. Others are charged at the conservation rate for water use up to 100 percent of their base allocation.

Table 6.2

Sample Rates for Irvine Ranch Water District Residential Customers

Tier	Block Time Rate	Charge ($)
Low-volume discount	8 × $0.48	3.84
Conservation base rate	12 × $0.64	7.68
Inefficient	10 × $1.28	12.80
Excessive	10 × $2.56	25.60
Wasteful	19 × $5.12	97.28
Total Block Charges		147.20
Fixed charges		10.80
Total water bill		158.00

SOURCE: Irvine Ranch Water District (1998).

NOTE: Assumes base allocation of 2,000 cubic feet and consumption of 5,900 cubic feet.

Another example of managing water demand began in 1992 with the Marin Municipal Water District (MMWD) and its Integrated Resource Management Plan. The core of the plan is the Conservation Master Plan, which calls for the reduction of water demand by 22 to 32 percent over 1987 levels (Owens-Viani, 1999). An ordinance passed in 1991 requires that customers applying for new or increased services implement a range of indoor and outdoor conservation measures, including ULFTs and low-flow showerheads and faucets. The landscaping policy limits the use of lawns and swimming pools and requires the use of native and other plants that require little extra water. New nonresidential users in MMWD are assigned a water entitlement and budget. The entitlement level is the amount of water that MMWD is committed to providing; the budget is less than the entitlement and is based on MMWD's determination of how much water a client needs. The annual budget is set for the year and then divided into six parts. As long as the customer's consumption during a two-month billing period is at the one-sixth level, they are charged at the first-tier block rate, which reflects the cost of delivering reservoir water; if consumption increases, higher rates are charged. (Tier 2 prices reflect the cost of delivering Russian River water, and Tier 3 prices are linked to the cost of delivering recycled water. In 1998, the rates per acre-foot were $963, $1,779, and $3,410, respectively.) If customers exceed their entitlement three years in a row, they are required to purchase additional entitlements from other users.

Between 1987 and 1998, water use in the district declined from approximately 170 gallons per capita per day to 143 gallons—a reduction of 16 percent. Perhaps the most significant feature of MMWD's conservation program is its cost-effectiveness. The district spends between $1.1 million and $1.9 million annually on its conservation efforts, amounting to approximately 4 percent of its operating budget. Three of the conservation measures—ULFT, single-family audits, and landscaping audits—cost between $191 and $722 for every acre-foot of water *not* delivered because of their implementation. If the district engaged in no conservation and built new capacity, it would need to spend between $1,224 and $1,316 per acre-foot to build new supply—far more than the cost of conservation.

Statewide, demand management strategies reduced urban water requirements by an estimated 11 percent between 1995 and 2020. However, the urban sector at present accounts for a relatively small portion—about 11 percent—of the state's total water use. As a result, these reductions represent only 1.2 percent of total water consumption. The biggest opportunity for managing water demand in California is in agriculture, which accounted for 43 percent of state water use in 1995.

For various reasons, that portion is expected to drop over the next two decades. According to DWR estimates, urbanization will reduce the amount of cropland in California by 325,000 acres between 1995 and 2020, and CALFED has called for the conversion of up to 240,000 additional acres of irrigated cropland to habitat and environmental uses.

Much of the reduction in agricultural water use, however, will also come from demand management programs. Studies indicate that the agricultural demand for water is sensitive to price. A 10 percent increase in water charges, for example, will reduce the demand for agricultural water anywhere from 1.8 percent in the short run to 3.2 percent in the long run. This price sensitivity depends greatly on crop type and whether growers have access to groundwater. Irrigation practices also affect the demand for water. To promote irrigation efficiency, the DWR has entered into an MOU with 31 irrigation districts covering about one-third of the state's total irrigated land (see Box 6.2). The endorsed practices include designating a water conservation coordinator, lining or piping ditches and canals, optimizing the conjunctive use of surface water and groundwater, and facilitating water transfers, alternative land use, and the use of recycled water (California Department of Water Resources, 1999a).

There are also signs that California's farmers are implementing water conservation methods. Drip irrigation use increased from 2.2 percent of total irrigated lands in 1979 to 12.9 percent in 1994 (California Department of Water Resources, 1999a). By 1991, nearly 42 percent of all grape cultivation and 12 percent of orchard farms used drip irrigation. Moreover, the benefits of drip irrigation sometimes go beyond reductions in water use. For example, Underwood Ranches, a vegetable producer in Ventura County, switched to drip irrigation for the cultivation of peppers and reduced its water consumption by 25 percent. However, it also increased its yield per acre by 50 percent in the first year, largely because overirrigation of peppers contributes to damaging fungus on the pepper plant. As a result, Underwood Ranches increased its net profit by $2,000 per acre. In Gilroy, High Rise Farms also made the shift to drip irrigation. Its water use declined 15 percent, its yield per acre increased 81 percent, and its net profit per acre increased by $1,106 (Fidell et al., 1999).

Box 6.2

Efficient Water Management Practices for California Agricultural Suppliers

List A: Generally Applicable EWMPs

1. Prepare and adopt a water management plan
2. Designate a water conservation coordinator
3. Support the availability of water management services to water users
4. Improve communication and cooperation among water suppliers, water users, and other agencies
5. Evaluate the need, if any, for changes in institutional policies to which the water supplier is subject
6. Evaluate and improve efficiencies of the water supplier's pumps

List B: Conditionally Applicable EWMPs

1. Facilitate alternative land use
2. Facilitate using available recycled water that otherwise would not be used beneficially, meets all health and safety criteria, and does not cause harm to crops or soil
3. Facilitate financing capital improvements for on-farm irrigation systems
4. Facilitate voluntary water transfers that do not unreasonably affect the water user, water supplier, the environment, or third parties
5. Line or pipe ditches and canals
6. Increase flexibility in water ordering by, and delivery to, water users within operational limits
7. Construct and operate water supplier spill and tailwater recovery systems
8. Optimize conjunctive use of surface and groundwater
9. Automate canal structures

List C: Other EWMPs

1. Water measurement and water use reporting
2. Pricing or other incentives

SOURCE: California Department of Water Resources (1999a).

Another method for managing water demand is the development of the California Irrigation Management Information System (CIMIS), which consists of 100 computerized weather stations located across the state. The stations gather and report weather information to the DWR, which issues real-time reports so that farmers and other water users can efficiently irrigate their properties. About 370,000 acres of farmland are now benefiting from CIMIS reports. Use of CIMIS is estimated to reduce water application by 13 percent. According to a cost-benefit study carried out in 1996, CIMIS cost approximately $850,000 per year to run and saved over $30 million in water application costs (Parker et al., 1996).

These examples suggest that water conservation and demand management can be applied productively to agriculture. However, water pricing may be the direct incentive for promoting conservation. When the Broadview Water District shifted to block pricing in the 1980s, the acreage planted in alfalfa, melons, wheat, and cotton (all relatively water-intensive crops) dropped. Furthermore, the amount of water applied to these crops declined. For example, cotton acreage dropped 7 percent, and the amount of water used per acre declined by 30 percent (Gleick et al., 1995). In light of these experiences and pressure on water supplies, more districts are starting to apply some form of block pricing. The U.S. Bureau of Reclamation has also initiated large-scale efforts to convert Central Valley Project pricing to block tariffs and achieve full cost recovery. The development of water markets, which will allow owners of water rights to sell surplus water to other users, will also promote more efficient use of water. We will review this development in Chapter 8.

Demand Management in Education

Projections prepared by CPEC indicate that between 1998 and 2010, statewide enrollment in public higher education will increase by almost 715,000 students, or 36 percent. Most of these new students—about 74 percent—will enter the California Community Colleges. The CSU system will attract 18 percent of the total, and the UC system will absorb the remaining 8 percent (California Postsecondary Education Commission, 2000). Using classroom utilization to determine total capacity, CPEC estimated an unused capacity of 86,868 full-time-equivalent students. Most of this excess capacity was in the CCC, with little remaining capacity at CSU and negative capacity (overcrowding) at UC (Table 6.3).

Comparing estimates of projected 2010 enrollment with current capacity provides a rough first-cut estimate of additional capacity needs (Table 6.4). CPEC calculations suggest that higher educational facilities need to expand by approximately 375,000 FTE students.

To estimate the capital costs of meeting this enrollment growth, CPEC multiplied the number of new students by two other factors: assignable square feet standards per student and the typical cost of capital construction (Table 6.5). By this measure, the state will have to pay nearly $10 billion to expand its infrastructure for higher education. This

Table 6.3

Estimated Surplus FTE Student Capacity, 1998–1999

System	Capacity
University of California	–386
California State University	13,982
California Community Colleges	73,272
Total	86,868

SOURCE: CPEC staff analysis, 1999.

Table 6.4

Estimated Surplus FTE Student Capacity and Projected Need

System	1998 Surplus Capacity	2010 Growth	Additional Capacity Required, 1998–2010
University of California	–386	54,009	54,395
California State University	13,982	94,607	80,715
California Community Colleges	73,272	313,077	239,805
Total	86,868	347,263	374,915

SOURCE: CPEC staff analysis, 1999.

Table 6.5

Estimated Capital Costs of Meeting Higher Education Enrollment Growth

System	FTE Growth	ASF/ FTE	Cost/ ASF ($)	Total Capital Cost ($ 000)	Cost of Adding 1 FTE of Capacity ($)
University of California	54,395	140	525	4,002,162	73,576
California State University	80,715	75	384	2,329,537	28,861
California Community Colleges	239,805	42	350	3,525,134	14,700
Total/average	374,915	63	383	9,856,832	26,291

SOURCE: California Postsecondary Education Commission (2000).

method exemplifies a traditional, supply-oriented approach to infrastructure planning insofar as it bases its calculations on the cost of supplying new infrastructure according to existing costs and standards.

At the same time, the Legislative Analyst's Office was considering alternative approaches to accommodating new growth (Legislative Analyst's Office, 1999). One such alternative was to use current facilities more intensively during the summer. The LAO estimates that UC's enrollment capacity could increase by 30,846 FTEs if it operated year-round (Legislative Analyst's Office, 1999). Similar calculations for the CSU system suggest that an additional capacity of 35,883 FTEs could be realized if the system adopted year-round operation. The potential savings of $3.3 billion reflects about one-third of the total capital cost of expanded enrollment for higher education and approximately 52 percent of the UC and CSU capital costs (Table 6.6).

Year-round operation would generate new costs, of course, including increased budgets for salaries and financial aid as well as higher operating, maintenance, utility, and overhead costs. However, these costs would be generated even if the campuses stayed on the academic year calendar.

Efficiencies can also be realized in the area of classroom and laboratory scheduling. Campuses in the UC system, for example, maintain a pool of general assignment classrooms scheduled by campus

Table 6.6

Estimated Capital Cost Savings from Year-Round Operation

	FTE Increased Capacity	ASF/FTE	Cost/ ASF ($)	Capital Cost Savings ($ 000)
University of California	30,846	140	525	2,267,181
California State University	35,883	75	384	1,033,400
Total	66,729	105	471	3,300,581

SOURCE: Legislative Analyst's Office (1999).

registrars. Table 6.7 lists general assignment classrooms and teaching laboratories by campus and tabulates the number of rooms and stations. Additional classrooms and labs controlled by individual departments are not included in these data.

The utilization of classrooms and teaching lab space has recently emerged as an important policy issue between Sacramento and UC. Specifically, analysts in Sacramento argue that some UC campuses do not utilize their classroom space efficiently. The state's utilization measures assume classroom use running from 8 am to 10 pm, Monday through Friday. The state expects classrooms to be used 75 percent of

Table 6.7

University of California General Assignment Classrooms and Teaching Labs

	Classrooms		Teaching Labs	
Campus	Rooms	Stations	Rooms	Stations
Berkeley	253	14,085	123	4,054
Davis	132	8,339	88	2,304
Irvine	129	8,095	29	699
Los Angeles	270	16,051	98	2,542
Riverside	60	4,600	46	1,086
San Diego	101	7,205	56	1,112
Santa Barbara	146	7,232	87	2,262
Santa Cruz	77	4,375	45	887
Total	1,168	69,982	572	14,946

SOURCE: University of California, Office of the President (1997).

the time. It also expects two-thirds of the stations in the class to be occupied (measured on the basis of class enrollment, not actual attendance). Combining these two standards yields a classroom occupancy standard of 35 station hours per week; that is, each station should be occupied 35 hours per week. For teaching labs, the state standard is 22 hours per station per week. If a campus matches the state standard, the utilization rate is 100 percent. Table 6.8 provides campus-by-campus performance data for classroom and teaching lab facilities.

These data indicate that UC's campus facilities are being used at two-thirds to three-quarters of their potential capacity. If UC met its state goals for classroom utilization, it would free up an additional 800,000 station hours of classroom capacity per week and avoid $280 million in new capital costs. In the case of labs, UC Davis and UC Santa Cruz have shown that it is possible to reach 100 percent of the standard. For classrooms, these same two campuses perform much better than the others but reach only 80 percent of the standard. It is therefore worth asking whether the 35 hours per week standard is reasonable.

The UC Berkeley registrar has indicated that improved utilization could be achieved through

- Scheduling classes during nonpeak hours,

Table 6.8

The University of California's Classroom and Teaching Lab Utilization, 1997

	Classrooms		Teaching Labs	
Campus	Average Weekly Station Use (hours)	Utilization as a % of Standard	Average Weekly Station Use (hours)	Utilization as a % of Standard
Berkeley	23.5	67.3	13.9	69.5
Davis	28.9	82.6	19.4	96.9
Irvine	20.0	57.3	16.6	83.0
Los Angeles	19.7	56.2	10.7	53.6
Riverside	23.1	66.1	16.5	82.3
San Diego	27.1	77.4	17.6	88.1
Santa Barbara	24.4	69.6	12.1	60.6
Santa Cruz	28.4	81.1	20.1	100.3
Average	23.6	67.5	14.9	74.5

SOURCE: Space Assignments and Capital Improvements Committee (1997).

- Scheduling more classes on Friday,
- Scheduling classes based on end-of-semester enrollment, not pre-registration levels,
- Equipping rooms with instructional technology to increase utilization,
- Allowing the registrar to schedule departmental classrooms, and
- Improving the database on classroom use.

Another form of demand management that might increase the capacity of California's higher education system is shortening the time to degree. The percentage of entering freshman who graduate within four years is less than 40 percent (Table 6.9), and the percentage of CCC transfers finishing within two years is less than 31 percent (Table 6.10). On this measure, UC compares favorably with other public universities but unfavorably with private schools. According to these data, UC could increase capacity by 20 percent by increasing the four-year graduation rate of freshmen from 37 to 57 percent. Substantial increases could also be generated if more transfer students moved through the system instead

Table 6.9

Percentage Graduation Rates for Freshmen Entering in Fall 1990

	In 4 Years	In 5 Years	In 6 Years
UC systemwide[a]	37.8	69.2	77.1
Average public universities[b]	27.0	63.0	76.0
Average private universities[c]	57.0	77.0	83.0

SOURCES: [a]University of California, Office of the President (1997); [b]UCB Office of Student Research; [c]NCES (1999).

Table 6.10

Percentage Graduation Rates of Community College Transfers in Fall 1992

	In 2 Years	In 3 Years	In 4 Years
UC systemwide	30.7	68.2	78.5

SOURCE: University of California, Office of the President (1997).

of three or four years. One benefit of this acceleration is lower capital costs. According to CPEC, the capital cost of adding one additional FTE of student capacity to the campus is nearly $75,000.

According to 50 undergraduate students we questioned in spring 2001, the factors that slow down time to degree are various. They include

- The need to work while attending university,
- Difficulty enrolling in gateway courses,
- Course workloads that exceed credit hours,
- Physical disabilities that prevent access to classes, and
- Inadequate undergraduate advising leading to "backtracking."

With these factors in mind, what are UC's options? Like the University of North Carolina, it could levy a 25 percent surcharge on educational fees for students taking more than nine semesters of coursework. It could also improve advising and offer more student service infrastructure. Finally, it could offer students scholarships that would offer incentives to work less and study more. In particular, it could link scholarship benefits to progress toward a degree.

Transportation Demand Management

The demand for highways and roads in California will continue to grow at very high rates. Between 1988 and 1998, VMT increased by 21 percent overall and by 30 percent in urban areas. During the same period, however, California expanded its roadway system by less than 1 percent. Since 1990, the state has added only 70 new miles of highway, amounting to 1,300 lane miles of new capacity. The imbalance between the supply of and demand for roads has more than doubled the number of vehicle hours of delay on urban highways from 197,000 hours per day in 1988 to 418,000 hours in 1998. According to Caltrans, the economic costs of these delays are substantial—$7.8 million per day and $2.8 billion per year in lost time and added fuel costs. The California Air Resources Board estimates that traveling ten miles in 30 minutes produces 2.5 times more volatile organic compound emissions than does traveling the same distance in 11 minutes. This congestion dumps an additional 418 tons of pollution into the air each day (Legislative Analyst's Office, 2000b).

Traffic congestion is spreading to more of the state's urban areas. In 1988, approximately 27 percent (1,020 miles) of the state's urban freeways were congested. By 1998, the percentage had increased to 40 percent (1,470 miles). In some areas, such as Los Angeles and San Francisco-Oakland, lane mile increases between 1982 and 1997 actually exceeded population and licensed driver growth. In other metropolitan areas, such as Sacramento, Bakersfield, Riverside-San Bernardino, and San Diego, demand growth has clearly outpaced highway expansion.

Policy analysts recognize two basic options for reducing traffic congestion—increasing supply and managing demand. On the supply side, governments can build more roads and provide more transit. Expanding highway capacity in California's urban areas will be difficult, however, because the social, economic, and environmental effects of widening or double-decking highways are problematic. However, there are viable options for maximizing the capacity of existing facilities. These include coordinated timing of traffic signals on arterials, performing repairs and maintenance work at night to avoid capacity reductions, and monitoring vehicle accidents and breakdowns to maintain traffic flow. Ramp signals to meter access to congested freeways are also very effective. Another option for increasing capacity is to encourage carpooling. HOV lanes offer incentives to drivers of cars with two or more riders. These measures can increase the capacity of existing corridors dramatically. Interstate 5 in the Seattle area, for example, implemented ramp controls, HOV lanes, and park and ride lots; over the six-year project period, average peak-hour driving time decreased by 9.5 minutes, even though peak-hour traffic increased 86 percent northbound and 62 percent southbound (Downs, 1992). The Bay Area has started implementing these measures, but there is still scope for wider application.

Given the persistent rates of traffic growth and limited options for capacity expansion, many transportation policy experts argue that society's interests would be better served if we devoted more attention and resources to demand management. The principal argument for this approach is the fact that investments in new roads and freeways do not solve congestion problems. Rather, they generate a range of short- and long-run demand responses that offset declines in traffic congestion. For example, Downs (1992) notes that creating new capacity will lead to three swift responses. First, travelers who had shifted to less-congested routes (surface arterials instead of freeways) will resume travel on the uncongested route. Second, travelers who shifted the time of their journey to avoid congestion will return to their old schedule. Third, travelers who shifted to another mode (for example, transit) will start driving on the newly expanded route. Downs argues that these behavioral responses will quickly offset the gains generated by the increase in capacity. In the long run, urban development will take place along the route and will generate additional VMT. Therefore, expanding the supply of infrastructure is likely to be ineffective—some would say doomed to fail—if the policy goal is to reduce congestion.

Transportation demand management (TDM) aims to reduce VMT by encouraging travelers to shift to higher occupancy cars or transit or to avoid making a trip. It also seeks to shift travel demand to off-peak times or alternative routes. In the case of increasing the use of preferred modes (e.g., transit), TDM can promote the use of HOV lanes, employer-based carpool and vanpool programs, and the construction of pedestrian friendly environments and bike paths. Economic incentives can also be used to promote use of these facilities—waiving tolls for preferred alternative modes and free parking for HOV and vanpool facilities. Marketing these options is critical as well.

Many cities use parking prices to discourage the use of single-occupancy vehicles in downtown areas. In Portland, Oregon, researchers found that increasing monthly parking fees from $20 to $30 increases transit ridership by 8 percent (Transit Cooperative Research Program, 1998). Using transportation system data from five cities on the West Coast (four of which are in California) and simulating the results of a range of policies, researchers found that a $3 per day fee on each parking space would reduce regional single-occupancy vehicle work trips by an average of 9.3 percent.

Another option for managing travel demand is congestion pricing, which levies a fee on road use based on the amount of congestion cost they generate. The idea of using tolls or charges to control congestion was first proposed by the Nobel Prize–winning economist William

Vickery (1959). Spurred on by growing problems with congestion and declining air quality, congestion pricing for highways has emerged as a possible policy mechanism for improving transportation efficiency and enhancing the urban environment. Proponents argue that congestion pricing allocates scarce resources (road space) efficiently, produces additional revenues to support transportation improvements, and is more effective than regulation to control emissions and reduce congestion (see Brown et al., 1998a; Litman et al., 1998). Furthermore, congestion pricing would reflect the full social costs of driving—including the costs of building and maintaining facilities, delays, and environmental effects. Demand reductions would most likely be manifested in increased vehicle occupancy, but they may also spur greater transit patronage (Association of Commuter Transportation, 1997). Advances in technology, such as electronic toll collection and intelligent highways, suggest that congestion pricing could be very effectively implemented, with prices automatically adjusted in response to varying levels of congestion.

Despite these and other economic arguments for congestion pricing, it is rarely used. Singapore has employed it since 1975, France since 1992 (Gómez-Ibáñez and Small, 1994). More recent examples include SR 91 (1995), Interstate 15 in Southern California (1996), Interstate 10 in Houston (1998), and Route 407 in Toronto. In Singapore, a toll of S$3 (about U.S. $1.70) to enter the Central Business District has reduced traffic congestion by 20 percent (Gómez-Ibáñez and Small, 1994). A similar system has been proposed for the City of London. In France, a congestion-sensitive system of tolls was implemented to reduce peak weekend congestion on a highway linking Paris with Lille. This variable toll system has shifted traffic from highly congested peak periods to off-peak periods, with reductions ranging between 4.4 and 8.2 percent (Gómez-Ibáñez and Small, 1994). The Port Authority of New York and New Jersey recently implemented congestion pricing on the bridges and tunnels connected to New York City.

In the case of Interstate 15, the San Diego Association of Governments has been running a federally funded pricing project for the past three years. The project has implemented a system of tolling on an HOV/express lane in San Diego. Although initially conceived of as real-time dynamic pricing, consumer resistance has forced the project to follow a time-of-day pricing regime. During peak periods, tolls ranging between $0.5 and $4 are imposed on non-HOVs. Demand for participation in the program is strong. All of the initial transponders used to levy the tolls electronically are allocated, and there is a waiting list of over 600 persons. The experiment is viewed positively by most participants (Kawada, 1998).

Experience with SR 91 also suggests that congestion pricing can effectively finance the private construction of toll lanes. In 1989, Caltrans entered an agreement with a private developer to build and operate additional lanes on State Route 91. The private, ten-mile project cost $126 million to construct. Vehicles have the option of using the existing free lanes or shifting to the privately constructed tolled lanes. The tolls on the lanes vary according to congestion. According to a recent study, the tolled lanes were attracting 30,000 vehicles per day, about 15 percent of total traffic volume. The new tolled lanes have added capacity to the corridor and have reduced overall travel times. Most drivers surveyed in the corridor—between 60 and 80 percent—approve of the idea of extra toll-financed lanes. Over time, 60 to 75 percent of drivers have come to approve of time-of-day tolling to reduce congestion levels (Sullivan, 1998).

Researchers have been able to simulate the likely effects of congestion pricing on five West Coast cities, four of which are in California (San Diego, Los Angeles, San Francisco, and Sacramento). They examined the effect of a congestion price of $0.06 per mile on work trips. This fee was estimated to generate a regionwide reduction in work trips of 6.3 percent. The total congestion fee levied per vehicle per day amounted to $1.20. The results indicate that the measure would have the greatest effect in San Francisco, where work trips would fall 11.9 percent. The smallest effect—a 1.6 percent reduction—would be in Sacramento. This difference may reflect the fact that San Francisco has both more transit alternatives and a higher concentration of jobs in the downtown area (Transit Cooperative Research Program, 1998).

Shifting demand from peak to off-peak periods or routes can be implemented with positive and negative incentives. On the positive side, the government can offer businesses reduced taxes if they shift peak trip generation. For example, large institutional users that implement flexible work hours and guaranteed permanent reductions in trip generation rates could receive a tax break or subsidy. Negative incentives include congestion pricing, which would penalize travelers or firms that generate peak period trips.

Another popular means of TDM is the use of employer trip reduction programs. Washington's commute trip reduction (CTR) law was adopted statewide in 1991 and has involved the participation of cities, counties, and approximately 1,100 employers with about 500,000 employees. Transit use increased 23 percent to an aggregate of 11.3 percent of all covered work trips. Carpooling rates increased 10 percent over the baseline rate. By 1999, the percentage of employees driving alone to work decreased from 72 to 67 percent. The program removes 18,500 vehicles per day from the roadways, reducing air pollution by 3,200 tons per year and saving 6.5 million gallons of petroleum annually. Commuters save about $8 million annually in fuel costs alone. Employers spent $4.6 million per year on the program. In addition, cities and counties spent an additional $2.9 million, bringing the total cost of the CTR to $7.5 million per year. Cost per reduced VMT averaged $0.09. Washington estimates the avoided costs of capital investment in the form of new lanes of highway capacity at anywhere from $36 million to $169 million (Washington State Department of Transportation, 2000).

Land-use planning can also foster more transit-friendly environments. Developing transit-oriented town centers, promoting medium-density residential development, and aligning transit corridors to capture both radial and suburb-to-suburb travel can effectively promote the use of transit modes. Land-use planning and urban design policies can also promote the development of pedestrian and bicycle travel. California has implemented mortgage discounts to people choosing to purchase homes near transit, and some suburban developers have been required to post actual commute times to major metropolitan centers on the term sheets of their new houses. These policies have the combined effect of informing and creating incentives for both the homebuyer and developer to build on and live in higher-density, infill development, thereby alleviating some of the pressure on highways caused by jobs and housing imbalance.

As early as 1995, the cost-effectiveness of various TDM alternatives was analyzed in the South Coast Air Quality Management District (Schreffler et al., 1996). The types of projects included

- Carpool projects—remote telephone rideshare matching,
- Shuttle projects—commuter rail feeder shuttles, noontime shuttles, and all-day circulators,
- Bus transit projects—commuter express routes and transit service restructuring,
- Bicycle projects—bike loan program and bikes on buses, and
- Telecommunications—teleconferencing and telecenters.

The evaluation method called for standardized estimates of daily vehicle trip reduction (VTR), vehicle miles traveled reduction (VMTR), pounds of air emissions reduced (ER), total cost per VTR, total cost per VMTR, and total cost per ER. Table 6.11 provides a summary of the results. Cost per reduced trip ranged from $0.43 for the bike loan program to a very expensive $64.52 for the costly teleconferencing center. Cost per reduced VMT also varied considerably, ranging from $0.02 for matching carpool riders to $4.53 for the all-day shuttle bus service.

These experiences, taken together, suggest that the right combination of TDM strategies could reduce single-occupancy vehicles and increase transit modes. If so, the state could avoid congestion spikes over the next five to ten years. Because it will take at least this long to expand the state's highway system, these measures are all the more important. According to Caltrans projections, project approval and construction can take anywhere from seven to 30 years; in contrast, demand management tools can be implemented quickly.

Conclusion

Although all three sectors examined in this chapter could benefit from demand management strategies, the three policy debates differ dramatically. Water pricing to reflect its scarcity is well understood and accepted by urban and agricultural users. In the case of higher education, very little consideration has been given to demand management. Initial reaction to it by higher education policymakers is

Table 6.11

Cost-Effectiveness of TDM Projects in the South Coast Air Quality Management District

Project Category	Project	VTR/ Day	VMTR/ Day	ER/ Year	Cost/ VMT ($)	Cost/ VMTR ($)	Cost/ ER ($)
Carpool	Remote matching	397.8	24,862.0	33,652.5	1.13	0.02	2.09
Shuttles	Rail feeder 1	11.0	174.4	167.2	3.89	0.25	66.80
	Rail feeder 2	23.0	363.4	388.4	11.24	0.71	173.17
	Noon-time	14.7	73.4	120.4	14.15	2.83	449.26
	All-day	17.3	190.6	367.8	49.89	4.53	610.27
Bus transit	Express 1	5.6	88.5	45.3	34.73	2.20	1,117.4
	Express 2	14.0	2,520.0	1,301.4	8.47	0.05	23.69
	Service restructured	70.0	350.0	969.3	20.76	4.15	389.99
Bikes	Loan 1	140.6	421.8	1,600.8	0.43	0.14	5.90
	Loan 2	16.3	48.8	185.4	1.08	0.36	14.84
	Bikes on buses	41.4	645.8	1,124.5	2.47	0.17	26.25
Telecom	Teleconferencing 1	9.4	385.4	546.5	64.52	1.57	288.58
	Teleconferencing 2	7.7	962.5	1,243.6	21.51	0.17	34.63
	Telecenter	0.0	3,236.0	3,981.8	n/a	0.20	43.12

SOURCE: Schreffler et al. (1996).

one of caution—will demand management limit access? In the case of urban highways, transport economists have clearly identified the potential for pricing to manage congestion. Despite its successful application in Singapore and recently New York City, most politicians are very skeptical and resistant—viewing congestion pricing as political suicide. The next chapter explores the implications of pricing in more detail.

7. Recovering Infrastructure Costs: Balancing Efficiency with Equity

As the previous chapter indicates, infrastructure pricing is a key part of demand management. Prices, or tariffs, also play a key role in generating revenues to recover capital, operating, and maintenance costs. Low prices may lead to inefficient resource allocation—socially important infrastructure services may be underprovided and overused and existing facilities may not be adequately maintained. However, if tariffs are too high, critical infrastructure may not be used by society, thereby thwarting education, public health, and economic development goals. High prices are also likely to generate adverse effects on low- and moderate-income households—creating social and economic equity problems.

In theory, efficient tariffs reflect demand as well as supply-side factors, such as the cost of production. They will also tend to settle around the marginal cost of production, which ensures that producers will have an incentive to supply the product and that consumers will not overuse it. Economists have long maintained that such prices serve several vital functions. They allocate scarce resources efficiently, generate revenue to cover costs, provide information to consumers about resource costs, and balance supply and demand.

Three problems can complicate this model. First, prices may not reflect the full social cost of production and consumption. For example, the price of an automobile may not cover the cost of air pollution damage and other negative effects that automobile use causes. Markets can be corrected for these failures if these uncovered costs, which economists called externalities, can be reduced through regulation or included in the costs in the transaction.

Second, the pricing system breaks down when competition is weak or absent. If a single producer can set prices above the marginal costs, fewer consumers will purchase the good than would if prices were competitive. This decreased consumption may result in a net loss of social welfare. This failure can be corrected by certain antitrust measures, most of which encourage or allow new firms to enter the market. Market entry may be impractical, however, in fields that require very high initial capital investments, such as water supply, telecommunications, energy, and transportation. If there is no practical way to foster competition in these markets, the government may choose to regulate them. Nearly all states, including California, have established public utility commissions to regulate such enterprises. Pricing regulation is usually based on some notion of a reasonable return to the provider. The return is predicated on some assessment of the level of capital investment and costs of operation and maintenance. Regulated prices typically reflect a "normal" rate of return on capital invested, usually in the 4 to 8 percent range (Nelson, 1995).

The third problem has to do with social and economic equity. If the profit-maximizing price for an essential good or service excludes large segments of the population from purchasing it, a range of public policy goals may be threatened, prompting the government to intervene. Public utility commissions often address this matter by requiring special rates for low-income customers. For example, Pacific Bell, PG&E, and other utility service providers offer "lifeline rates" for basic service to qualifying customers. These interventions indicate that economic efficiency should be tempered by considerations of equity and opportunity.

For most state-provided services, tariffs and user fees either do not exist or are set well below the marginal cost of supplying the service. As a result, the government must cover the gap between cost and revenues in other ways. First, it can transfer general fund revenues to specific operations to cover shortfalls. Second, it can reduce costs by cutting expenditures for maintenance and facilities renewal or by curtailing services. A third response is to raise additional funds from other private or nonprofit sources to augment state-provided financial support. Finally, the government can raise user fees to offset service costs.

Deciding whether and how to subsidize state-provided services is a critical policy concern. Many argue that tariffs for some public goods should not be based on full cost recovery because the state has an interest in promoting their consumption. For example, requiring households to pay the full cost of polio vaccinations might discourage many families from getting them. Polio vaccinations, however, generate enormous spillover benefits; even people who are not vaccinated against polio will benefit from the vaccination that someone in their community receives. Such spillover benefits from so-called merit goods argue for reduced or zero tariff.

Subsidizing merit goods, however, may generate several problems. Again, if the service is freely provided or offered at a very low price, consumers may overconsume it. This is an unlikely outcome with polio vaccinations, but it may characterize the consumption of other public goods, such as a bridge. If the bridge is not congested, the most efficient bridge toll is zero, which reflects the marginal cost for an additional driver. (We will ignore the bridge's maintenance and operating expenses for the moment.) If a tariff is imposed, some portion of drivers will not use the bridge, and social welfare will decline. When the bridge becomes congested, however, the value derived from using it declines. Each additional user imposes costs on others in the form of delays and increased air pollution. Under these conditions, the state has two basic options: It can charge tolls that reflect the new marginal costs or it can expand capacity. The options are not mutually exclusive, but their time horizons differ dramatically. A bridge may take years to plan and construct, whereas new tolls can be implemented quickly. The equity effects of the two options may also differ, a subject to which we will return.

In this chapter, we examine how pricing and tariffs can be used to improve the efficiency of infrastructure use and how to increase the financial resources for operations, maintenance, and investment. We also outline how adverse equity effects can be addressed through the use of ability-to-pay offsets.

Trends in Cost Recovery

Transportation

As illustrated above, VMT has outstripped highway construction and network expansion. This development is partly the result of declining real fees. Between 1950 and 1997, real state gasoline taxes declined precipitously (Figure 7.1); by 2001, those gasoline taxes were approximately 60 percent of what they were in 1950 (in per gallon terms). The state has not increased the gasoline tax to keep pace with inflation. Moreover, increased fuel efficiency prevented state gasoline tax revenues from keeping pace with VMT.

Beginning in the 1980s, the state authorized 18 counties to impose supplemental sales taxes to fund transportation infrastructure. These general taxes, which are unrelated to highway use, now constitute a substantial part of highway funding. In 1996–1997, they raised $400 million—about 25 percent of the state fuel taxes raised that year. However, they have undermined one of the vital functions performed by

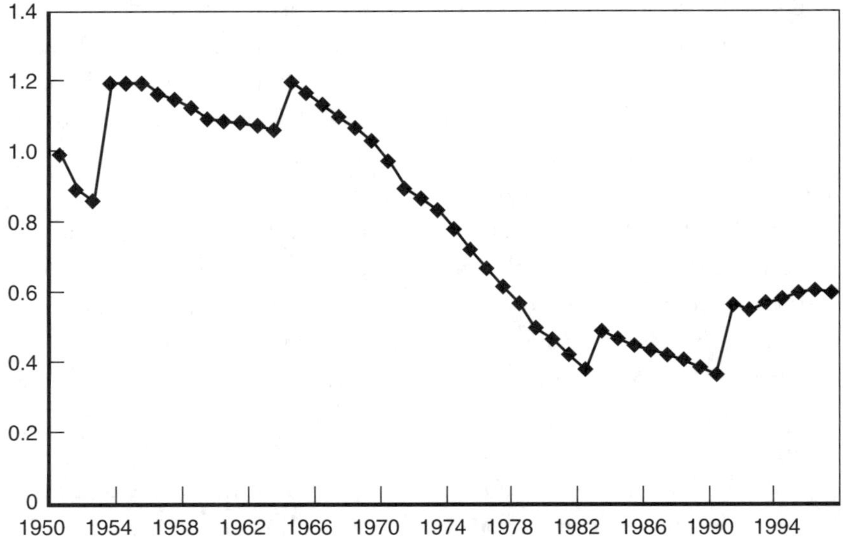

Figure 7.1—California State Gasoline Tax in Real 1997 Dollars (indexed 1950 = 100)

prices insofar as they have disguised the real costs of providing and maintaining roadways.

Water Prices

Long-term trends in real, wholesale water prices differ from those in both higher education and transportation. Real water prices for SWP water declined from 1963 to the late 1970s, falling by 60 percent (Figure 7.2). Since then, the real price of water has been fairly stable, ranging between $170 and $280 per acre-foot.

The SWP charges for bulk water are based on actual costs of production and transportation, including capital, operations, and maintenance costs. Tariffs vary by service area because of cost differentials. In 1999, costs ranged from $31 per acre-foot for the Feather River area to $577 per acre-foot for the Coastal area. The North Bay area tariff was $148 per acre-foot, for Southern California the rate was $230. SWP seeks to recover its capital and operating costs by using an average cost-pricing model to set tariffs. Although this method

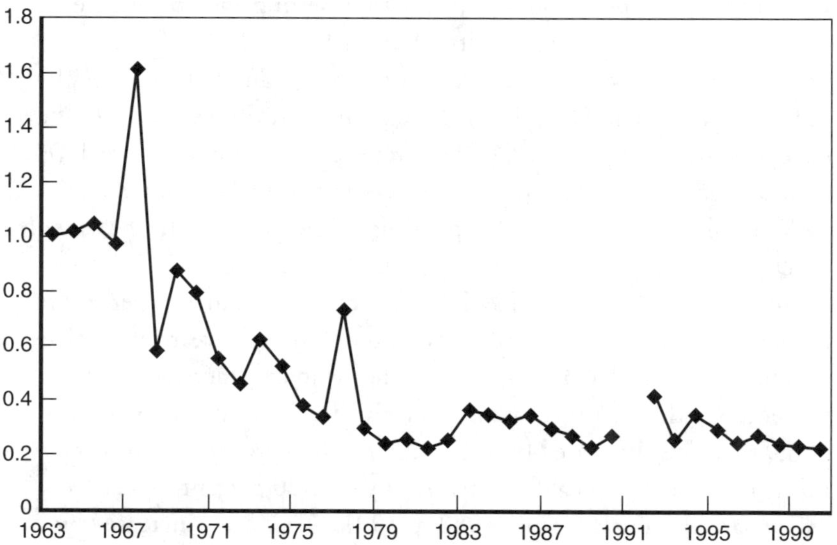

Figure 7.2—Real Wholesale Water Prices from the State Water Project ($/Acre-Foot) (indexed 1963 = 100)

ensures that revenues will cover costs, it does not provide strong incentives to promote conservation. Prices based on marginal (rather than average) costs would better reflect the costs of increasing water supply.

Other agricultural water prices vary across the state. Table 7.1 provides the results of a 1996 survey of agricultural water pricing. As it illustrates, rates range from $10 to $373 per acre-foot on average depending on the region. Minimum rates range from $2 to $131 per acre-foot and maximum rates range from $12 to $604 per acre-foot. The basis for water rates varies as well. As the table illustrates, tariffs are based on (1) acreage, (2) crop and acreage, (3) acre-feet of water used, and (4) acre and acre-feet of water used. Half of the responding irrigation districts stated that their tariffs are based on a combination of acreage and acre-feet of water used.

Higher Education

Most people agree that higher education is a merit good, therefore, full access should be encouraged. Any tariff setting and cost recovery regime needs to carefully assess its effect on access. In California, however, over the last 30 years, resident undergraduate student fees for the CCC, CSU, and UC systems have been erratic and since 1994 they have been declining. For CCC, fees were constant from 1965 to 1993, then they increased by nearly 150 percent in three years. Since 1992, CCC's real fees have declined approximately 30 percent. In the case of CSU, real fees remained relatively constant from 1963 to 1980. Then from 1981 to 1984, CSU's fees increased by more than 100 percent in three years. This rapid increase was followed by eight years of relative stability. Then in 1993, fees began rising again and increased by 60 percent over the next three years. For UC, fees were stable for 1965–1969, then they increased by approximately 60 percent in two years. From 1971 to 1982, real fees declined by over 20 percent. UC's fees were relatively constant from 1982 to 1991. Then they increased by nearly 100 percent over the next four years. Since 1995, UC fees have fallen by over 20 percent (Figure 7.3). The erratic pattern of real fee increases and decreases suggests that little attention has been paid to managing rising educational costs and ensuring access. The process looks

Table 7.1

DWR Survey of Agricultural Surface Water Retail Prices, 1996

Region	Total Deliveries (TAF)	1996 Costs/Acre-Foot			Water Rate Basis by Number of Reporting Agencies				
		Weighted Average	Maximum	Minimum	By Acre	By Crop and Acre	By Acre-Feet Used	By Acre and Acre-Feet Used	Total
North Coast	80	10	12	2	2	0	1	0	3
Central Coast	37	128	533	87	0	0	2	2	4
South Coast	92	373	604	131	0	0	1	7	8
Sacramento River	1,275	12	32	2	1	4	1	2	8
San Joaquin River	1,339	22	238	6	3	0	1	4	7
Tulare Lake	2,672	42	161	9	1	0	4	6	11
South Lahontan	18	61	61	61	0	0	1	0	1
Colorado River	3,403	13	14	8	2	0	0	2	4
Statewide	8,916				8	4	11	23	46

SOURCE: California Department of Water Resources (1999a), p. 4A-5.

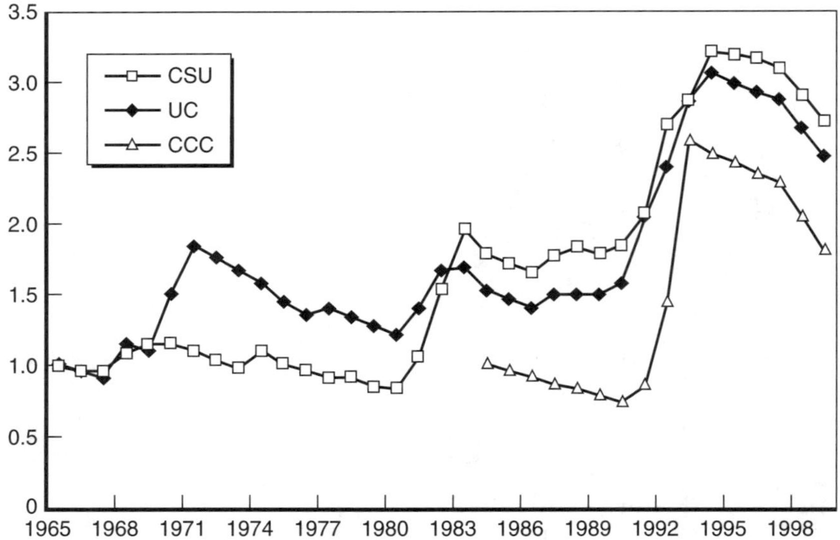

Figure 7.3—Real Resident Undergraduate Student Fees (1999–2000 Dollars) (indexed 1965 = 100 for UC and CSU and 1984 = 100 for CCC)

more like a crisis-response pattern of eroding financial resources, sharp tariff increases and then a protracted period of fixed fees. The pattern serves neither students nor higher education institutions well. Students and their families cannot predict when increases in fees will come or how much they will be. Higher education institutions cannot plan and accurately predict their state support. Instead they must adjust the quality of service to balance budgets.

Over the last seven years, increases in higher education fees have been rejected by Sacramento. In general, however, the ratio of student fees to state support has increased over time for the UC and CSU systems. At UC, student fees as a percentage of fees and state general funds rose from 5.6 percent in 1965 to a high of 24.1 percent in 1994. Since then, the ratio has fallen to 16.7 percent in 2000, as Sacramento continues to buy out fee increases. Much of this increase started in the early 1990s, when UC began to charge higher fees for professional school students and it raised its general fees. There has been virtually no increase in fees since 1995 for either professional fees or general fees, explaining why the ratio of student to total fee and state support declined by nearly 31 percent between 1994 and 2000.

At CSU, students are more heavily subsidized than at UC. Over the period from 1965 to 2001, the ratio of student fees to total fees and state support has been fairly constant—ranging from 6.9 percent in 1965, to 8.3 percent in 1995, to 6.2 percent in 2001. For the state's community colleges, student enrollment continues to be heavily subsidized. In fact, there were no fees up until 1983. In 1985, student fees accounted for 4 percent of total fees and state and local support. By 2000, the ratio had fallen to 2.7 percent. Moreover, the portion of total fees and state and local support provided by local property taxes declined from 62.9 percent in 1965 to 35.8 percent in 2001. Clearly, Proposition 13, which altered the state's approach to property tax, played a decisive role. In 1978, the year Proposition 13 was passed, local property taxes accounted for 60.4 percent of total fees and state and local support. One year later, the portion was cut in half to 29.5 percent.

To offset the decline in real revenues per student, fees could be increased to more closely match the cost of education. One option would be to vary fees according to the level of education, training, and profession. The starting salaries of graduating students vary considerably across disciplines. Teachers earn less than engineers and business majors. For undergraduate degrees, subsidies could vary between schools—education degrees could be more heavily subsidized and engineering, business, and computer science could receive less support. Subsidies could vary between UC and CSU with less subsidies going to UC students than to CSU students.

Financial aid should play a key role in guaranteeing access to higher educational facilities. If fees are raised, more of the revenue can be directed to means-tested scholarship programs. At Berkeley, over 30 percent of undergraduate students come from households with annual incomes above $100,000. Another 30 percent come from low- and moderate-income households with incomes below $35,000. Given such an income distribution, it makes sense to use means-testing and differential pricing. Some commentators might balk at the idea, but it is well accepted in other areas of infrastructure provision, such as energy and water supply. If we follow the examples of PG&E and the East Bay

Municipal Utility District (EBMUD) and incorporate a more aggressive system of financial aid, California's system of higher education could be based more on user and beneficiary charges while remaining accessible through financial aid and stepped tariffs.

Tackling Adverse Equity Effects

Social and economic equity considerations complicate public sector pricing policymaking. To what extent should an individual's income and ability to pay for a good or service be part of the calculus of pricing and tariff setting?

The problem becomes particularly acute when we consider goods and services that are viewed by society as essentials—food, water, shelter, education, health care, and so forth. In such cases, pricing must factor in ability to pay. Unfortunately, most economists sidestep this dilemma by assuming that the distribution of income and wealth in society is fairly allocated and therefore no concern needs to be given to ability to pay.

The situation in California is far from this vision. As Table 7.2 illustrates, the income distribution in California is far from egalitarian and the data suggest that it is becoming more unequal. Between 1975 and 1998, the average real income of all income tax returns for the top 20 percent of the income distribution increased by 66.3 percent. The bottom 20 percent of the distribution decreased by 24.8 percent. Therefore, we cannot sidestep the equity question when considering the pricing of publicly and privately provided infrastructure services.

Table 7.2

Income Distribution Trends of California Single and Joint Return Taxpayers, 1975–1998 (constant 1998 dollars)

Percentile	1975	1980	1985	1990	1995	1998	% Change
0–20	26,248	21,375	20,449	21,494	18,475	19,732	–24.8
21–40	31,903	26,418	25,823	27,620	24,558	26,322	–17.5
41–60	43,535	38,051	38,109	41,133	38,027	40,141	–7.8
61–80	58,714	54,040	55,473	59,035	55,485	58,916	0.3
81–100	109,389	107,685	117,482	146,089	145,908	181,885	66.3

SOURCE: Legislative Analyst's Office (2000c).

In most cases, government-provided necessities are free, some are highly subsidized, and others rely on user or beneficiary charges to cover costs. Over the past ten years, California has relied heavily on personal income and sales taxes to support its budget. For example, the 2001–2002 budget estimated that 83.7 percent of budget revenues would come from income, sales, and other taxes. About 16 percent of budget revenues will come from user fees for highway use, vehicle fees, and other sources. In most cases, publicly provided services are free. This is a common practice because many government services are "public goods." It is difficult to charge fees because people can choose not to pay and still obtain the good (free riders). It is also impractical or inefficient to attempt to levy fees and, in some cases, social welfare is better served by not charging fees for services.

Equity concerns for private utility providers are addressed through public utility regulation. Utilities are required to offer lifeline rates. For example, Pacific Bell, PG&E, and other utility service providers that are under the regulatory authority of the California Public Utilities Commission all offer lifeline rates to qualifying low-income customers. These rates apply to base levels of service (a minimum block of water, power, or telephone service) and individuals applying for the lifeline rate must meet income limits. Some commentators might balk at the idea, but it is well accepted in other areas of infrastructure provision, such as energy and water supply. Boxes 7.1 and 7.2 provide examples of how equity considerations are handled by two major public utilities in the state—PG&E and EBMUD.

When the government provides the service, the pricing and policies about service are left to the public agency. For example, the University of California, the California State University system, and the California Community College system do not have their educational fees approved by the state Public Utilities Commission (PUC). Similarly, the state can increase its gasoline taxes without getting PUC approval. In the course of setting fees for colleges and universities, the discussion over fees is not limited to costs but covers a range of factors—costs, ability to pay, fees at other institutions, past rates of increase, and other factors. The UC system allocates 33 percent of student fee revenue to support means-based scholarships.

Box 7.1
PG&E's CARE Program

PG&E offers CARE (California Alternative Rates for Energy)—a discount program for low-income households and housing facilities. CARE provides a 20 percent discount on monthly PG&E bills and ensures that its CARE customers are not affected by recent surcharges.

CARE Residential Single Family Program is available to single-family, low-income customers with their own accounts. Qualifying households receive a 20 percent discount on PG&E bills.

Households' gross annual income may not exceed these amounts:

No. in Household	Annual Income ($)
1 or 2	22,000
3	25,900
4	31,100
5	36,300
Each additional	5,200

SOURCE: PG&E (2002).

How should adverse equity effects of infrastructure pricing be addressed? One method would be to offer income tax rebates to qualifying low- and moderate-income automobile commuters. Filers could claim a rebate each year. For low-income drivers who do not pay state income taxes, the state could offer a means-tested rebate on vehicle registration. Alternatively, the Metropolitan Transportation Commission (MTC) or other metropolitan transportation planning agencies could administer a voucher or cash rebate system that is based on income, trip patterns, and travel mode. Another option would be to offer low-income residents transit vouchers so that they could avoid driving. Unfortunately, few pilot studies have been designed and carried

Box 7.2
EBMUD's CAP

East Bay Municipal Utility District sponsors a program to pay part of the costs of water service for low-income customers who apply and qualify. The Customer Assistance Program will subsidize, for single-family dwellings, one-half of the standard bimonthly service charge of $13.84 and one-half of home water use in each eligible household, up to a maximum of 1,050 gallons per person per month. To qualify, total gross household income must not exceed:

No. in Household	Annual Income ($)
1 or 2	16,875
3	21,225
4	25,575
5	29,925
6	34,275
Each additional	4,350

SOURCE: East Bay Municipal Utility District (2002).

out to test these proposals. The state should begin designing and testing ability-to-pay offsets. If they prove effective and feasible, they would give support to more efficient pricing regimes.

How Should the State Set Tariffs?

What should the state's approach be to pricing higher education, transportation, and water supply? Beginning with water, the DWR and the state's many urban and agricultural districts might revise their pricing policies to promote water conservation. This means using increasing block rate tariffs in urban areas and linking them with CIMIS to adjust tariffs to weather conditions. Agricultural pricing can promote more flexibility in cropping patterns and do a great deal to develop best-practice irrigation. As the U.S. Bureau of Reclamation has discovered, there is no reason why agricultural water users should pay less than the full cost of providing their water. This is an easy way to bring cropping patterns and groundwater use in rational connection with local climatic conditions. California should continue to promote conservation through pricing and regulation.

Transportation is another matter. The state's reliance on user fees and taxes to fund highways has broken down. We now are using sales taxes and General Fund resources to finance infrastructure. This approach breaks the link between users and payers and makes it more difficult to manage demand and reduce congestion. The challenge facing the transportation sector is to increase gasoline taxes and vehicle registration fees and to implement a range of programs to promote transit and carpooling. Higher parking fees, telecommuting, and nonauto alternative forms of transportation would make great sense. The biggest challenge is to implement a congestion pricing system on the state's congested bridges and highways. A demonstration project to address equity effects should be launched.

Higher education is even more problematic, as it is the quintessential merit good. However, there are ways of adjusting prices to increase revenues while maintaining and enhancing quality. Tuition should be means-tested, with scholarships and financial aid given to those who need it. Fees should encourage students to move through the system—pricing should be used to speed up the time to degree in the UC and CSU systems. Fees for courses in community colleges should differ between vocational and university preparatory courses and those aimed at senior and leisure markets. The fees of professional schools and colleges should be increased to more closely approximate actual costs, particularly in areas were students receive high starting salaries. Exceptions and fee waivers could be given to students willing to enter public or community service careers upon graduation.

Fee structures should be altered to place more of the financial burden on users and beneficiaries. This will generate the necessary resources to support statewide growth, modernization, and the provision of truly meritorious goods such as K–12 education and health care. However, this must be combined with lifeline rate and ability-to-pay offset programs. Infrastructure tariff-setting policies need to balance two distinct and competing goals: (1) cost recovery and (2) ensuring that low- and moderate-income users have access to services.

8. Financing California's Infrastructure

According to the Department of Finance, California's total capital requirements between 1999 and 2009 come to $82.2 billion (Table 8.1).[1] This figure does not include the deferred maintenance and upgrading needed to remove backlogs or to bring water facilities into compliance. When these costs are added, total needs are likely to exceed $150 billion.

To meet these capital requirements, California has three basic financial options: pay-as-you-go, long-term financing, and leasing and private provision. In the first two options, the government or the community purchases the assets and facilities that provide the infrastructure service. In the third option, the government rents the facility providing the service or procures the service from a nongovernmental provider. The advantages and disadvantages of each option are discussed in Dowall (2000).

Table 8.1

Ten-Year Capital Requirements, 1999–2009

Category	Requirement ($ billions)	Percent
Business and transportation	27.6	37.6
Higher education	15.4	21.0
K–12 education	8.9	12.1
Corrections	9.5	12.9
Resources	9.0	12.2
Other	3.1	4.2
Total	82.2	100.0

SOURCE: Legislative Analyst's Office (1998b).

[1]The state plans to spend $56 billion between 2002 and 2007 on capital outlay (California Department of Finance, 2002).

Policymakers must decide which combination of these methods is most appropriate. In general, a balance of pay-as-you-go and long-term financing, with some limited emphasis on private provision, provides the most efficient means for procuring and financing infrastructure. In cases where federal government transfers are available, these funds are typically used to finance developments on a pay-as-you-go basis. For services generating user and beneficiary fees, long-term financing or private provision is helpful for producing predictable cash flows. Services that generate no income streams may be financed from general funds on a pay-as-you-go or on a general obligation bond, debt-financed basis. Private provision or public-private partnerships are typically used to leverage government resources to develop capital projects. As project financing becomes more complex, infrastructure banks and financial advisors play an important role in facilitating financial arrangements.

In California, as elsewhere, local governments have been shifting infrastructure capital costs from general fund sources to user and beneficiary groups. According to a 1993 survey of 79 cities and nine counties in California, 60 percent of the respondents indicated that they had shifted costs on to users between 1987 and 1992. Of those stating that they had shifted costs, 62 percent indicated that they have implemented user fees and charges to finance services. Seventy-five percent of cost shifters said that they required developers to finance infrastructure projects (International City/County Managers Association, 1993).

Improving Infrastructure Finance

Both the California Budget Project and the Legislative Analyst's Office have uncovered a range of limitations in California's infrastructure finance system (see California Budget Project, 1999, and Legislative Analyst's Office 1998a, 1998b). Perhaps the most serious limitation is the ad hoc manner in which capital outlay planning and budgeting takes place in Sacramento (Legislative Analyst's Office, 1998b). Although the adoption of AB 1473 helps link strategic planning and capital budgeting, most agencies do not keep up-to-date records of infrastructure condition and maintenance needs, and they have not developed rigorous strategic planning processes to prepare capital budgets. Without well-articulated programmatic plans and justifications for infrastructure investment, the Department of Finance has no systematic method for prioritizing capital investment needs across agencies and sectors.

Unpredictable funding levels from the state compounds the ad hoc planning problem. With the exception of state highway construction, no infrastructure sector is provided with a stable source of pay-as-you-go or debt financing. Each year, the state budgeting process adjusts capital funding in light of revenues. During much of the 1990s, General Fund expenditures for debt payments totaled $11.5 billion and General Fund appropriations for capital outlay totaled $735 million. Over this period, these appropriations accounted for less than 0.3 percent of total General Fund revenues (Legislative Analyst's Office, 1998b). As a result, capital funding for many sectors was based on the voter approval of bond authorizations. Other agencies have no access to bond financing propositions and therefore must rely on the state's General Fund. Many programs that are fortunate enough to have dedicated sources of funding—state highways and higher education, for example—have seen the real value of their charges deteriorate over time. As we discussed in Chapter 7, taxes and user fees for highways have not kept pace with inflation since the 1950s. In the case of higher education, real inflation-adjusted fees were erratic but flat from 1963 to the later 1980s, increased precipitously between 1989 and 1994, and since then have fallen in real terms by 20 percent.

Another serious problem with the current system is a lack of clarity regarding state and local responsibilities. Although the state is solely responsible for providing adequate facilities for state-operated programs, Sacramento has gradually become a major funder of local government capital facilities, especially since the passage of Proposition 13. The state's real per capita funding of local government has increased from less than $500 in the 1960s to over $1,200 in the 1990s. Approximately two-thirds of the state's $35 billion in bond financing since 1986 has gone to support nonstate facilities. A good deal of this financing has funded local school facilities.

The current state-local division is based largely on financial exigencies rather than sound principles. As the purchasing power of state and federal gasoline taxes has eroded, for example, many local governments have levied local sales taxes. Although this shift makes pragmatic sense, it is neither equitable nor efficient. The sales tax is regressive—low-income households pay proportionately more sales tax than affluent ones. Also, all payers of sales taxes, regardless of their highway usage, pay to finance highway systems. Finally, this system does not provide incentives for users to adjust their usage to the real costs of maintaining the roads.

Another problem with California's infrastructure financing is that the state does not seek to optimize the ratio of pay-as-you-go and debt financing. In some cases, capital outlays are completely driven by pay-as-you-go. In other cases, financing is based on the passage of bond authorizations. Overreliance on pay-as-you-go places the full cost of facilities on the current users, an approach that raises questions of intergenerational equity. Debt-based financing, in contrast, spreads costs over the full lifecycle of the facility and imposes costs on all users over time.

Given these problems, five broad, interrelated, and strategic recommendations could do much to improve the state's system of infrastructure finance.

Recommended Actions

Base Infrastructure Programs on Sound, Long-Range Financing Plans. Long-range planning includes lifecycle costing, a subject explored more fully in Chapter 10. For now, it suffices to note that the agency or department responsible for service should be required to forecast the funds required to cover the full cost of the project, including maintenance, over the course of its lifecycle. The plan should define how the monies will be raised—through user charges, tax revenues, or bond proceeds. If the project or program requires financing, the plan should forecast the annual revenues needed to repay the bonds as well as to cover operations and maintenance costs. As noted above, the DWR prepares such a plan for the management of the State Water Project (California Department of Water Resources, 1999c).

Improve the Predictability of Infrastructure Funding. The state's ad hoc approach to infrastructure planning creates an erratic pattern of infrastructure funding. Each year, agencies must guess how much money they will receive from the state budget for capital outlay. The funding of higher education, for example, ranged from $25 million in 1983–84 to $1 billion in 1993–1994 to $77 million in 1994–1995 (Figure 8.1). Funding can be made more predictable if agencies could charge fees for services or, in the case of merit goods, receive a fixed capital appropriation per unit of service provided. Although gasoline tax revenues do not cover the costs of road construction, repair, and maintenance, the transportation sector benefits from a predictable flow of funding for highways. If higher education capital expenditures were funded on a fee-based or fixed-capital appropriations method, UC, CSU, and CCC could more effectively plan for capital expansion and renewal.

To provide an example of how these plans might look, we refer to the LAO's recent proposal for K–12 capital funding. This plan would establish a California Annual School Allotment (CASA) for funding capital expenditures for school facilities. The CASA would be based on estimated actual capital costs per student. LAO estimates a fee of $550

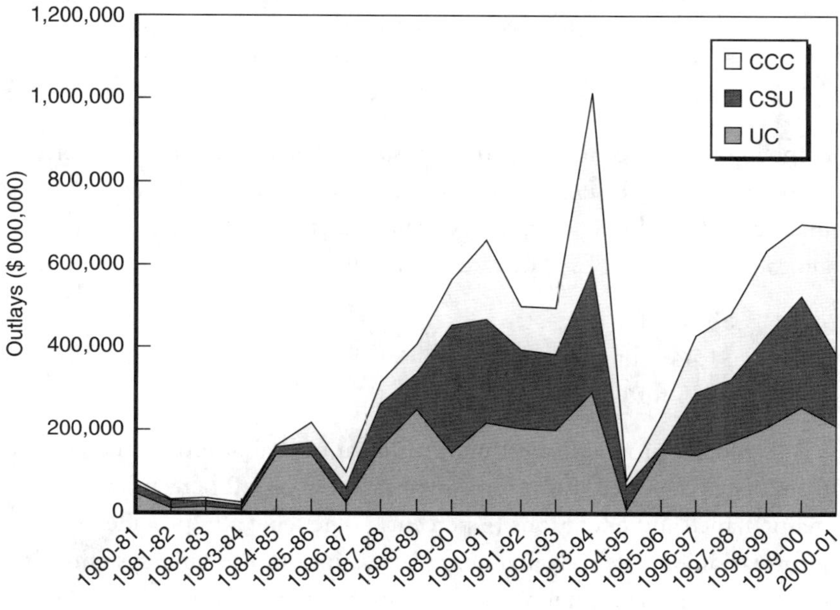

Figure 8.1—State Funding of Higher Education Capital Outlay, 1980–2001

per student based on past funding levels and a presumed economic life of 50 years for facilities (with a one-time modernization at 25 years). LAO suggests splitting the CASA into a local match and a state contribution. Local school districts would have flexibility over the use of the CASA, but each district would have a predictable stream of income to plan its capital programs. Such a model could also be applied to higher education. Each system could receive an annual allotment based on FTE enrollment—an approach that resembles the funding structure now in place for higher educational operating expenses.

It would be important to ensure that the allocation is based on the full lifecycle costs of facilities. For example, instead of gearing the allocation to design and construction only, the allocation would reflect the annualized full lifecycle costs. (See Chapter 10 for a discussion of lifecycle costing.) In Chapter 6, we presented estimates of capital facilities costs for UC, CSU, and CCC. The capital costs of adding one additional FTE capacity was

- $73,576 per FTE for the UC system,
- $28,861 per FTE for the CSU system, and
- $14,700 per FTE for the CCC system.

Applying a 5 percent rate to these costs—2 percent for amortization (based on a 50-year life) of the initial capital costs and 3 percent for maintenance and renewal costs, we can estimate an annual capital allocation fee per FTE. The rates are as follows:

- $3,678 for UC,
- $1,443 for CSU, and
- $735 for CCC.

Table 8.2 provides an estimate of the annual allocation results for the three systems broken down for capital replacement (2 percent) and maintenance and operations (3 percent). The table also provides information on recent capital outlay allocations to the three systems. It illustrates that the capital replacement estimates are fairly close to the total actual capital outlay received by the three systems. However, the estimates suggest that the allocation across the three systems may be biased toward UC and CSU. The maintenance and renewal component

Table 8.2

Estimates of Capital Allocation Spending for Higher Education Institutions

System	FTE Capital Allocation	Total FTE	Capital Replacement (2%) ($ 000)	Maintenance and Renewal (3%) ($ 000)	Total Allocation ($ 000)	1999–00 Actual State Capital Outlay ($ 000)
UC	3,678	161,400	237,503	356,126	593,629	257,059
CSU	1,443	273,928	158,117	237,161	395,278	266,033
CCC	735	960,081	282,264	423,396	705,660	304,432
Total	1,214	1,395,409	677,884	1,016,683	1,694,567	827,524

SOURCE: Authors' estimates.

is much greater than the present level of funding received by the three systems for budgeted maintenance.

Rebalance State-Local Infrastructure Financing. Like most states, California uses state funds to finance K–12 school facilities. Although the state's current policy is to fund 50 percent of new school construction projects and 80 percent of modernization projects, most districts can apply for hardship standing and receive 100 percent funding. Under the CASA plan, the state would strictly limit its funding to 50 percent, thereby reducing its K–12 capital outlay obligations by half (California Business Roundtable, 1998).

In higher education, community college districts have access to local property taxes and draw most of their students locally. These facts suggest that local participation should be significant. Before the passage of Proposition 13, local community college districts accounted for roughly 50 percent of the total capital outlay funds. Since 1989–1990, however, virtually 100 percent of capital funding for CCC has come from the state. To make the financing of CCC facilities more predicable and equitable across districts, funding for CCC might be structured along the same lines as the LAO's CASA proposal—a 50 percent match.

Neither UC nor CSU has access to local property taxes, and their student bodies, particularly in the case of UC, are composed of students from across the state. It is therefore more appropriate to draw on state funds for facilities. However, both systems have proven that they can raise nonstate support in the form of fees, donations, and research contracts. Over the past ten years, UC has raised nearly $5 billion in nonstate support for its capital projects—an average of 73 percent of total capital outlays (California Postsecondary Education Commission, 1999). Although CSU has been less successful in raising funds, it has generated $461 million over the same period, or 21 percent of its total capital outlay. For these two systems, some form of state participation makes sense. Funding for teaching and instruction might be fully funded, but support for research facilities might be limited. Both systems should be granted far more flexibility to raise nonstate resources—in partnership with the private sector or with federal programs.

Rely More on User and Beneficiary Fees. Many analysts have recommended that fuel tax rates be adjusted for inflation and that revenue per VMT be held constant (Brown et al., 1999). The state would double its tax collections if it raised state gasoline taxes to reflect their 1950 levels.[2] In terms of taxes per gallon of gasoline, the current tax is approximately $0.18 per gallon. Doubling the tax would increase the amount to $0.36 a gallon. Assuming a vehicle mileage rate of 22 miles per gallon, the typical driver traveling 15,000 miles per year would pay $245 per year in taxes. Since the current fuel economy of vehicles is now much greater, and consumers now purchase fewer gallons to travel 15,000 miles, the effect of the increase on drivers would be less than if it were imposed in 1950. The higher tax would slightly increase the overall cost of gasoline. Since the demand for gasoline is price inelastic, total tax receipts would increase.

As mentioned above, there is also scope for more user and beneficiary charges in higher education, especially in combination with expanded financial aid programs. If fees were increased to cover 20 percent of the capital outlay and maintenance requirements of the three systems between 1999 and 2009, the effects would be as follows:

- UC student facilities fee of $735,
- CSU student facilities fee of $289, and
- CCC student facilities fee of $147.

---

[2]This figure adjusts for inflation and increased fuel economy.

Table 8.3 illustrates the effects of these fee increases in terms of current fees and total revenues raised. If these fee increases were implemented, they would generate $339 million in funding for capital projects. This would have accounted for 41 percent of total state funding of capital outlay in FY 1999–2000. The increases in fees would range from 15.8 to 44.1 percent. Note that we have not factored in the effects of the price elasticity of demand for higher education services. The effects of the price elasticity are likely to vary by sector. For UC and CSU, the falloff in demand is likely to be very low, since demand is strong. In the case of CCC, the increase in fees might generate a reduction in applications. Clearly, increasing fees for higher education must be approached with extreme care. Offsetting programs of financial aid would be needed to preserve access. Given these factors, the estimates in Table 8.3 should be viewed as upper-bound estimates.

Table 8.3

Possible Effects of Student Facilities Fees, 1999–2000

System	Annual Student Fee ($)	Percentage Increase in Current Fees	Total FTE	Total Fees Raised by Increase ($ 000)	1999–00 Actual State Capital Outlay ($ 000)	Student Fees as a Percentage of State Capital Outlay
UC	735	18.9	161,400	118,629	257,059	46.1
CSU	289	15.8	273,928	79,165	266,033	29.8
CCC	147	44.1	960,081	141,132	304,432	46.4
Total			1,395,409	338,926	827,524	41.0

SOURCE: Authors' estimates.

Enhance the Equitableness of Infrastructure Finance. More user and beneficiary fees risk unacceptable equity effects. However, it is possible to use graduated payment schemes to minimize the burden on the poor. We have outlined several examples of lifeline tariffs for water service. Financial aid for students in higher education can mitigate the adverse equity effects of higher fees. In K–12 education, the effects of LAO's CASA program on poor districts can be mitigated by offering exceptions to districts that have limited financial resources. For example, the LAO suggests including an ability-to-pay adjustment program for qualifying districts (Legislative Analyst's Office, 2001, pp. 13–15). In the transportation sector, the equity effects of user fees and congestion pricing could be offset by offering tax rebates or cash grants to low-income automobile users. It could also employ a voucher system that would provide qualifying households with scrip to use for transit, tolls, or fuel.

In virtually every case, these offsets can easily be built into the pricing or tax systems. They are not likely to be prohibitively expensive. For example, the LAO estimates that its ability-to-pay adjustment program would cost the state $250 million to $350 million annually—approximately 20 percent of the total cost of the CASA program. In higher education, if the financial aid practices of the UC system were applied to CSU and CCC, ability-to-pay offsets would account for about 33 percent of the total program cost. In neither case are these additional costs "deal-killers." In Chapter 7, we illustrated how UC, PG&E, and EBMUD currently offer ability-to-pay offsets to low-income students and customers. Their experience suggests that it is feasible to address the adverse equity effects of increased user fees.

These broad areas of policy reform are the critical areas that should command the attention of the state's policymakers. It is our belief that policymakers should rigorously assess the financial and political feasibility of using ability-to-pay offsets.

9. Enhancing Project and Service Delivery

The delivery of water supply, transportation, and educational facility projects in California is far from optimal. As Chapter 4 suggests, projects typically cost significantly more and take far longer to complete than planned. These problems are not unique to California. In fact, a recent international survey of major transportation infrastructure projects concludes that cost overruns are endemic (Flyvbjerg et al., 2002). This chapter explores how to improve the planning, programming, and construction of new infrastructure investments. In particular, it examines a range of techniques used to create more value, accelerate project delivery, and make projects and services more responsive to consumer needs. To the fullest extent possible, we have tried to identify best-practice cases from California.

Better Project Execution

Infrastructure projects typically require years of planning and design and lengthy review procedures to ensure that their construction will not significantly damage the environment. Project planning and delivery therefore play a critical role in shaping outcomes. Two recent success stories show the importance of enhanced planning.

Santa Clara County Traffic Authority

In response to unrelenting traffic congestion and increased travel times, the citizens of Santa Clara County took a bold and unprecedented step in 1984 to take control of their highway-building destiny (Razo et al., 1996). The Santa Clara County Traffic Authority (SCCTA) was created by Measure A, a ballot initiative to address traffic congestion in the county. Measure A outlined a specific set of transportation projects to widen 26 miles of Highway 101, extend Highway 85 for 18 miles, and upgrade Route 237 to freeway status. The program marked the first time in the state that a local jurisdiction opted to devote its own funds to finance state highway improvements. The measure passed with 54 percent of the vote, ratifying a one-half cent sales tax over a ten-year period that would fund $1.1 billion in highway improvements.

The measure called for the formation of the SCCTA, an independent agency, to administer and manage the program. Figure 9.1 illustrates the organizational structure of the Santa Clara County Traffic Authority Program Management Model. Both the authority and the advisory board are composed of local elected officials. The five-member authority sets policy guidelines and priorities for implementing Measure A. The 16-member advisory board fosters communications between the authority and local communities and advises the authority and its executive staff on policy options. The ballot measure limited funds available for the executive staff, which augmented its capacity by retaining consultants. Bechtel Civil Company was retained to provide program management support to the authority. Working with subconsultants, Bechtel's brief covered cost control, design coordination, construction coordination, and administrative support. Approximately 40 Bechtel employees were assigned to the project.

The authority began its work in December 1984. Initially, it considered having Caltrans manage the project, and it invited the state

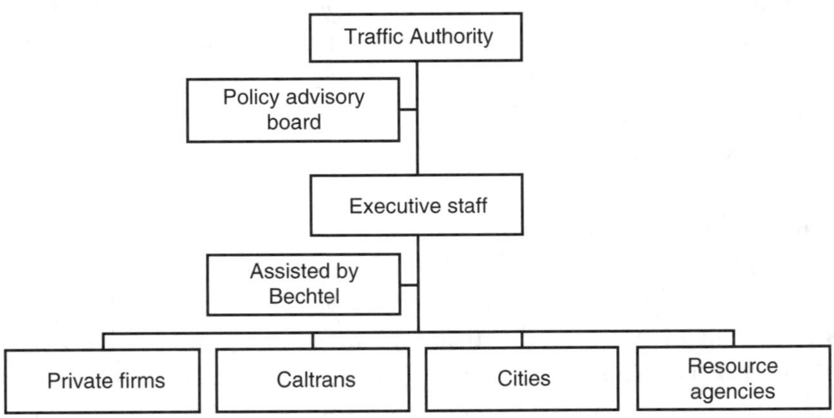

Figure 9.1—Santa Clara County Traffic Authority Management Model

agency to make a proposal. In February 1985, Caltrans proposed a completion time of 23 years. The authority pressed Caltrans for a more expeditious proposal, and the final proposal was 14 years. When the authority realized that Caltrans could not meet its objective of completing the project within ten years, it turned its attention to forming a partnership with public and private sector participants. Over the next several months, the authority forged a complex set of agreements with Caltrans, local jurisdictions, Bechtel, and various resource agencies. Caltrans agreed to provide support for right-of-way acquisition. It also agreed to cooperate with the authority on securing the necessary environmental reviews and approvals. Caltrans was assigned the lead role in the preparation of the environmental impact report for the project, setting the scope of work and technical standards for environmental review. Caltrans and the authority used private consultants to prepare assessments. Finally, Caltrans agreed to provide design oversight and review of engineering plans and specifications.

Extra care was taken to ensure that community concerns were quickly and fully addressed by the authority, which developed close relations with local jurisdictions likely to be affected by the project. A performance agreement was developed and used to ratify and achieve consensus. The authority also formed an outreach program to identify and resolve community issues. The authority also maintained close and regular contact with other federal and state agencies involved with the project. Frequent coordination meetings were held to quickly identify issues and resolve them.

Design development and value engineering played a critical role in keeping the project on time and on budget. The authority's commitment to value engineering—changing designs to reduce cost while satisfying concerns for safety—yielded a $116 million savings in total project cost. The authority was able to maintain its ten-year schedule by using a fast-track process of development. Unlike Caltrans, which is required to proceed one step at a time, the authority was able to commence work on right-of-way engineering, preliminary design, and environmental reviews simultaneously. The authority also used Critical Path Method scheduling to develop plans, specifications, and estimates.[1]

Overall, the experience with Measure A was extremely positive. Through innovative project management and implementation, Santa Clara County was able to implement the project in less than one-half the time stipulated by Caltrans and with a savings of $116 million.

California State University System

In 1995, the Chancellor's Office at CSU commissioned a study of its Capital Outlay Program. Carried out by Coopers and Lybrand, the study covered the entire range of the project cycle, including

- Needs assessment,
- Capital budgeting,
- Design,
- Bid and award,
- Construction, and
- Commissioning.

Based on extensive interviews, case studies of ten recently completed projects, and process mapping, the study found that the capital outlay process consisted of a cumbersome system of multiple reviews and handoffs. On average, it took CSU nine years to move through the process cycle. State capital outlay requirements and multiple reviews provided few opportunities for expediting projects. The typical project required 28 internal reviews, four outsourced reviews, and six state reviews. The Department of Finance's funding process (preliminary design, working drawings, and construction funding) slowed down the process and hindered the development of multiple projects. The study found that the review process constituted 42 percent of the design time and 19 percent of the total project cycle while not significantly improving design quality or functionality. Coopers and Lybrand also

---

[1]The SCCTA did not fully exploit the possibility of a design-build process, which combines the design and construction of the project into one step (Moore et al., 2000). This approach, which uses a single contract to clearly establish responsibility for design as well as construction, might have generated even more savings.

found that 32 percent of all CSU projects proposed were not approved by DOF.

Handoffs (switching of responsibility from one management team to another) also slowed the process. Coopers and Lybrand found, on average, 17 handoffs in the needs assessment phase, 21 in the capital-budgeting phase, 40 in the design phase, 20 in the bid and award phase, an indefinite number during construction, and 20 during the commissioning phase. An extensive amount of time was devoted to design-bid-construction—typically 4.5 years, about 50 percent of the total time to identify, plan, design, and construct the project.

Through interviews, widespread dissatisfaction was found with the capital outlay process across the CSU system. Customers and users in particular were dissatisfied with the quality and functionality of the projects. Respondents noted that the capital outlay process was inflexible and incomprehensible; the overall process did not produce satisfactory results; communication lines were complex; and information was not widely shared. Coopers and Lybrand found that CSU considered the state and campus facilities planners in their process but that insufficient attention was paid to the ultimate users and their concerns. This problem was aggravated by the fact that the capital outlay process was too centralized at the Chancellor's Office, far removed from the end user.

After making this assessment, Coopers and Lybrand and the Chancellor's Office proposed two models for reforming CSU's capital outlay process. CSU responded by streamlining its process and reducing approval requirements (Table 9.1). It also obtained lump-sum funding from Sacramento. The restructured program gives campuses authority to directly manage the entire capital outlay process from budgeting through design and construction and increases funding flexibility to manage capital outlay appropriations on a holistic rather than line item basis. A number of accountability measures have been developed including certifications of eligibility, required financial record-keeping, certification of project compliance during project phases, performance reviews, and financial accountability measurements. Campuses that do not want management authority, or those that do not achieve certification, will

Table 9.1

CSU's Restructured Capital Outlay Process

Process Phase	Prior Process	Restructured Process
	Budget	
Annual Capital Outlay Program and Five-Year Capital Improvement Program	Prepared by Physical Planning and Development (PPD), using program information supplied by each campus	No change
Project feasibility studies	Funding is requested from the state as part of the annual capital outlay budget request	*Campuses will be responsible for funding these studies* from existing resources to support capital outlay requests
Fund allocation	Upon receipt of funds, PPD allocates Group II equipment funds to the campuses and retains management responsibility for all preliminary planning, working drawings and construction fund allocations for each approved project	*Upon receipt of funds, campuses with management authority will be allocated lump-sum funding,* i.e., preliminary planning, working drawings, and construction funds, as well as Group II equipment funds
	Design	
Appointment of project architect and engineer	PPD maintains a prequalified listing of design professionals and provides lists to campuses for preselection interview; campuses submit listing of recommendations; PPD processes recommendations through a screening committeee and forwards a recommendation to the Board of Trustees for appointment; board appoints	PPD will continue to maintain a prequalified listing of design professionals and provide lists to campuses; *campuses conduct interviews, make selection of preferred design professional, and carry out appointment process*
Architect's and engineer's contract preparation	PPD enters into professional services contracts with all design professionals commissioned to design capital outlay projects	*Using PPD standard forms, campuses enter into professional service contracts* with all design professionals they commission

Table 9.1 (continued)

Process Phase	Prior Process	Restructured Process
Service agreements	PPD enters into all service agreements, such as soils testing, concrete testing, consulting specialists, project inspection, and any others that may be required to develop and implement a capital outlay project	*Using PPD standard forms, campuses enter into all service agreements*
Schematic plans	Campuses submit schematic plans to PPD for review and submission to the Board of Trustees for approval	No change
Preliminary plans	Campuses submit completed preliminary plans to PPD for review and submission to DOF and the State Public Works Board for approval and authorization to proceed to working drawings	Campuses submit completed preliminary plans to PPD for review; *campuses will be permitted to continue with the design process without further approval; in addition campuses must certify that the project is within the scope, budget, and schedule, as defined in the Budget Act Supplemental Language, or define how they intend to meet those criteria*
Working drawings	Campuses submit completed working drawings to PPD for review and submission to DOF for approval to proceed-to-bid stage; PPD is responsible for directing the design professional to secure approvals through appropriate agencies	Campuses submit 100 percent complete working drawings, including all required plan approvals to PPD; *campuses will be permitted to continue with the design process without further approval; in addition, campuses must certify that the project is within the scope, budget, and schedule, as defined in the Budget Act Supplemental Language, or define how they intend to meet those criteria*

Table 9.1 (continued)

Process Phase	Prior Process	Restructured Process
	Construction	
Prebid	PPD carries out the prebid process, including contractor prequalification, advertising, prebid conferences, and related activities	*Campuses will carry out the prebid process*, including advertising, prebid conference, and related activities; *PPD will continue to prequalify contractors*
Bid	PPD accepts bids and prepares all contracts and related documentation for processing, including the approval-to-award request to DOF	*Campuses will accept bids and, using PPD standard forms, prepare all contracts and related documentation* for processing; *no further approval is required*
Award	PPD prepares all appropriate contract documents, reviews contractor submissions, and certifies compliance with Minority, Women, Disabled Veteran Business Enterprises (MWDVBE) requirements and submits to CSU Office of General Counsel for approval as to form	*Campuses will prepare all* appropriate contract documents, review contractor submissions, and certify compliance with MWDVBE requirements and submit to CSU Office of General Counsel for approval, if required
Construction	PPD carries out all construction management activities required to complete the project, including stop-notice activity and contractor payment requests; PPD processes all augmentation requests and any scope changes that may be deemed necessary; PPD manages construction claim disputes as part of this responsibility	*Campuses will carry out all construction management activities required to complete the project, including stop-notice activity and contractor payment requests; PPD will report any scope changes that may be deemed necessary; there will be no state or Chancellor's Office augmentations; campuses will manage construction claim disputes with PPD assistance, as requested*
Building commissioning	PPD authorizes beneficial occupancy, records notice of completion, and closes out the project through completion of the project punch-list items	*Campuses will be responsible for all aspects of this step*

SOURCE: Restructuring the California State University Capital Outlay Process: Final Report of the Building Design and Construction Task Force (1996).

follow the prior process, with Physical Planning and Development (PPD) managing the program. The certification review board comprises two campus representatives, two Chancellor's Office representatives, and one outsider.

The PPD maintains its policy role in administering the systemwide Capital Outlay Program, represents the capital budget presentations, and acts as liaison with all state agencies that interact with CSU in capital outlay matters. In addition, PPD serves as facilitator for campuses that receive certification and as a center for specialized professional consultation and specialized training. All but three (Los Angeles, Monterey Bay, and Maritime Academy) of the 22 campuses are certified.

Several other unique features of CSU's project execution could potentially benefit other infrastructure sectors. During the project design phase, CSU takes advantage of site-specific studies and an independent team of top-notch engineers to review facility designs. Some time ago, CSU commissioned site-specific seismic studies of all its campus properties. These studies afford CSU designs a greater margin of safety in the event of an earthquake than other sectors, such as the CCC. The CCC lacks site-specific information, and therefore must rely on one set of statewide standards from the Field Act—a set of standards that does not take into account a building's proximity to faults or orientation in relation to faults. CCC (and K–12) designs offer less safety and can be expected to incur greater damage in earthquakes. Because of these oversights, the Field Act should be revised.

CSU hired consultants to generate cost-estimating standards for all their facilities. These standards set out, item-by-item, the cost of materials per unit that may be used in constructing CSU facilities. The benefits from these standards are far-reaching. Completion time for bid review and project design is shortened. Contractors may vary bids only according to labor costs. Fewer change orders can be expected from design and procurement problems. CSU's procurement managers can now establish relationships with suppliers and have more leverage to negotiate price because they know in advance the typical materials used in construction.

Another important feature of CSU's new program applies after project construction. It is widely understood in the construction industry that contractors may submit bids far below their actual cost to win the job, only to follow up with a series of expensive change orders once construction has begun. The managing entity would incur significant costs to undergo another bid process or change contractors and is reluctant to do so. To circumvent this practice, CSU monitors construction and change orders, documenting the source of change orders and widely disseminating postconstruction evaluations of contractor performance. Contractors with poor performance records may be disqualified from future bidding. Our research suggests that other state entities have not tracked performance, and as a result, cost overruns are common.

CSU's new project delivery process is a significant step forward. It works to shorten the project delivery cycle, reduces handoffs, and increases accountability. By doing so, it may reduce project cycle timelines by as much as 2.5 years. Although decentralization is still new, CSU's administration has suggested that the system has saved between $13 million and $15 million in one year as a result of the streamlined process. This new process could go further, however; in particular, it could consider using a design-build process to expedite project delivery (Moore et al., 2000).

Joint-Use Facilities

Many agencies providing public infrastructure develop their needs assessments and facilities requirements without considering whether they could partner with other sister public agencies or private entities. This pattern is understandable given the pressures of meeting mandated program responsibilities and conserving resources. However, in some instances cooperation and joint use of facilities make good sense, both programmatically and financially. In this section, we outline a few examples of joint-use projects and suggest how the state might develop the concept further.

In 1992, when San Jose State University hired Campus Librarian James Schmidt, its library facilities were housed in two separate buildings. The campus wanted to combine them in one modern facility to improve access and provide room for expansion. In 1994, however, California voters rejected a statewide bond issue, indefinitely postponing all new construction on the 22 campus California State University system. Schmidt and Campus President Handel Evans made a dramatic proposal to then–City of San Jose Mayor Susan Hammer—the development of a joint CSU and city library. Both the campus library and the city library were under severe financial strain. During the late 1980s and early 1990s, the campus's library funding declined 25 percent, and its rate of acquisitions slipped by 50 percent. The City of San Jose Library was spending a $22 per person for library operations, much less than other comparable cities spend across the state. The proposal called for a joint-use facility on the edge of the downtown campus, complete with state-of-the-art information technology that would demonstrate the kind of creativity and innovation one expects from the Silicon Valley. The planned facility is large (twice the size of the new San Francisco Main Library), and it marks what is probably the most significant collaboration between a major city and a university.

There are several potential benefits of jointly operating the facility, including reduced staffing, the elimination of redundant volumes, and shared operational costs. Reduced capital costs and accelerated project approval also drew both the city and the university together. Facility costs of $177.5 million are split between the university ($91 million), the city ($70 million), and private donations ($16.5 million). By using the university's existing land, both the city and the university avoided a lengthy site selection process. By teaming with the university, the city could accelerate its redevelopment process while sharing a portion of the planning and development costs with the university. The university, meanwhile, can tap redevelopment district bond funds and leverage its scarce resources to move the badly needed expansion forward.

Despite these benefits, the project had its share of critics. Many faculty were concerned about the concept of a joint municipal and university library. Skeptics pointed out that the types of users from the community and campus would be dramatically different. The university and its academic senate worked closely together to address these concerns, and in February 1998, the Faculty Senate adopted principles for proceeding. In May 1998, the city and the university signed a memorandum of understanding for the project. In November of that year, state voters approved a bond issue for higher education that funded most of the university's portion of the project.

Other joint-use projects are now under development across the state, including a new library project linking Sonoma State University and the Rohnert Park-Cotati Unified School District. In 1996, California Polytechnic and State University at San Luis Obispo jointly developed a performing arts center with the City of San Luis Obispo. In the future, CSU may link with the CCC to develop joint facilities.

There are also real opportunities for cooperative sharing in the case of K–12 facilities. An innovative project in Orlando illustrates the combined benefits of facility sharing and creative partnering with the private sector. NorthLake Park Community School/Center combines three important community functions into one project—a K–5 elementary school, a YMCA with child-care and fitness facilities, and a community wellness center run by the City of Orlando. Designed around one common entrance lobby, each function is separate. Concerns about the safety and security of students were addressed by the deployment of a full-time receptionist in the lobby to monitor visitor access. The project is a preengineered steel structure with a second floor of traditional composite beam and metal deck construction. From groundbreaking to substantial completion, the 133,700 square foot project took 47 weeks and $9.7 million to construct. The local real estate developer provided the site and offered a five-year lease-purchase option to the Orlando County Public Schools.

This project offers several important lessons. First, it illustrates the benefits of combining compatible users into one structure. By combining activities, the city, the school district, and the YMCA were able to secure space for their operations at lower costs than if they had gone out on their own. Second, the innovative design using a preengineered metal structure for the first floor kept costs very low. Third, the developer was willing to provide excellent financing to the school district so that the school facility was open and ready to go before the neighborhood was developed. This arrangement was very attractive to the school district because it enabled them to better accommodate growth. It was also attractive to the developer, who could more readily market housing to young families. The deal allowed the school to acquire the facility at a fixed price ($9.7 million) but not incur debt for five years, and the lease payments during the five years allowed the developer to finance the structure for the lease period.[2]

NorthLake is a promising example of creative cooperation and public-private partnering that may have applicability to California's school districts. (See Taylor and Snell, 2000, for other examples of innovative partnerships for school construction.) Some of this cooperation may occur in California; we note that former Mayor Richard Riordan of Los Angeles led a task force that proposed solving the city's classroom shortage by inviting private developers to build schools in the city.

Public-Private Partnerships

Examples of public-private cooperation in California higher education include UC Davis's joint effort with the Ecumenical Association for Housing of San Rafael to build 181 apartments. Also, UC Irvine (UCI) has teamed with Catellus Development Corporation to develop a 1,100-unit housing project on the Irvine campus (UC Irvine, 2000). UC Irvine's Research Park also leases sites to research-oriented companies that are interested in developing linkages with university researchers. The park, consisting of 85 acres, has been leased to the Irvine Corporation, the company that donated the land to create UCI over 25 years ago. Under the terms of the agreement, Irvine develops and leases research space to firms that promise to participate in university research projects and to make best efforts to offer internships to UCI students. UCI has authority to veto leases. The trend to establish research partnerships between universities and private industry is growing across California and includes Caltech's Biochemistry Center and Claremont Graduate University's new School of Information Science. Governor Davis's initiative to create four new science institutes at UC San Diego, UC Los Angeles, UC San Francisco, and UC Berkeley by leveraging state funding with private investment is a bold and important step toward forming new partnerships on UC campuses.

---

[2]Phone interview with Steve Kuhn, Centex Rooney Company, 2000.

Another prominent example of university-private partnerships is the Sansom Common Project at the University of Pennsylvania (University of Pennsylvania Facilities Services, 2000). The project, located in the heart of the campus, includes a 50,000 square foot University Bookstore operated by Barnes and Noble, additional retail space, and a 250-room hotel with supporting facilities. The university and LaSalle Partners are jointly managing the project. The intent is to introduce the mixed-use project as a catalyst to revitalize and invigorate the core campus. In addition, the university will receive rental income and ground rent from the tenants.

Partnerships are well developed and widely used in the transportation sector. Many transit operators have discovered that it is extremely cost-effective to partner with private transportation service providers. As a recent issue of *Transit California* pointed out,

> The California public transportation industry is a large and complex system of agencies and organizations working together to provide vital transportation services to California's citizens. Contrary to some commonly-held myths about transit, these services are not provided only by monolithic public agencies employing scads of government apparatchiks. In fact, the diverse transit industry in this state reflects a commitment by government agencies to utilize the goods and services of the private sector to carry out the mission of moving California's people efficiently, effectively and safety (Hurwitz, 1996, p. 6).

San Diego offers a good example of active and ongoing partnering between public and private sector transportation service providers. In 1972, the City of Chula Vista contracted its transportation services to a private company. After the passage of Proposition 13 in 1978, many other San Diego County communities followed suit. In the early 1980s, the region's many transit providers have been grouped under the Metropolitan Transit Systems. In 1995, 63 percent of fixed bus routes in the Metropolitan Transit Development Board (MTDB) region were operated by contractors. The remaining 37 percent were operated by San Diego Transit. All general dial-a-ride, specialized paratransit, and Coaster Express Feeder van services were provided by private vendors. Services are coordinated by the MTDB, including route planning, fare and transfer policies, marketing, capital programming, funding, and compliance with the Americans with Disabilities Act.

What has emerged over the years is a competitive system of both public and private transit operation in the region. Service contracts are awarded competitively. In some cases, bus routes are awarded to the public San Diego Transit and in other cases service contracts go to private operators. Most operating contracts run for three to five years and are then reopened to competitive bidding. This competitive process forces both public and private operators to closely watch costs.

The MTDB has a policy of annually reviewing routes for possible competitive award. The reviews are conducted by a committee composed of MTDB, San Diego Transit, a private sector operator, a member of the local bus drivers' union, and a citizen representative. Route selection is not based on rigid quotas or formula. Instead, the committee looks at poor performing routes and routes that need to be restructured. In the course of selecting routes for bid, the committee also considers the potential effects on bus drivers' unions.

According to Elliot Hurwitz, San Diego's approach to fostering competitive partnerships has been very cost-effective and has not generated major labor disruption. Cost savings realized from contracting out services has fostered the expansion of transit services in the region while maintaining a fare box cost recovery rate of nearly 50 percent (Hurwitz, 1996).

Outsourcing, Competition, and Accountability

Outsourcing, or the procurement of inputs from vendors outside the organization, can be an effective method for increasing cost-effectiveness. Quite often it is possible to acquire services or products from vendors that are considerably less expensive than those produced internally. In most cases, it is not readily apparent that outside costs are lower because most agencies do not routinely assess procurement costs of internally provided goods and services. Outsourcing can be linked with competitive procurement, whereby incumbent internal providers are forced to compete with outside suppliers on price and quality. Many governments around the world have developed competitive procurement methods. The most common approach taken is to shift from "making" services to "buying" them—outsourcing. However, another viable option is to create competitive markets for procurement and allow existing government departments the right to compete to provide services.

A recent survey of state highway departments revealed extensive use of outsourcing. Table 9.2 provides a tabulation of outsourcing activities by area. Although the survey did not provide responses for individual states, Caltrans outsources very little of its activities and has been entangled in a series of court cases to block and ballot initiatives to foster outsourcing (Witheford, 1997).

Table 9.3 presents trend data for state and local government contracting out by type of activity. As it illustrates, contracting out has been expanding across the country over the past 12 years.

Considerable evidence suggests that contracting out saves costs through the reduction of overhead, fixed costs, and lower direct production costs. It can also help to increase public sector cost efficiency (U.S. General Accounting Office, 1997). According to the Organization for Economic Cooperation and Development's (OECD) Public Management Advisory Group, successful contracting out is one of the principal market-type mechanisms applied in member countries. Evidence suggests that contracting out can lead to efficiency gains while maintaining or increasing service quality (Organization for Economic Cooperation and Development, 1997a). The Reason Foundation has extensively studied outsourcing and has identified a range of important

Table 9.2

Overview of Outsourcing by State Highway Departments, 1997

Activity Area	% of Respondents Outsourcing All or Part of Activity	Total Outsourced Activities	Activity Most Frequently Outsourced
Administration	46.7	11	Training
Planning	63.3	12	Research
Design	90.0	9	Plans and specifications
Right-of-way	56.7	5	Appraisals
Construction management	60.0	7	Construction management
Operations	53.3	9	Pavement marking
Maintenance	70.0	17	Road surfaces
Other	66.7	12	Rest areas

SOURCE: Witheford (1997).

Table 9.3

Trends in State and Local Government Service Outsourcing

Function	Percentage of Activities Outsourced		
	1987	1990	1995
Major construction projects	100	100	100
Janitorial services	52	62	70
Solid waste collection	30	38	50
Building maintenance	32	37	42
Security services	27	33	40
Parking garages	20	26	35
Park maintenance	18	25	32
Tree trimming	17	23	31
Street maintenance and repair	19	21	37
Ambulance services	11	13	20
Bill collection	10	12	20
Street sweeping	9	11	18

SOURCE: Mercer Management Consulting (1995).

requirements for ensuring successful outsourcing (Eggers, 1997, 1998; Moore et al., 2000). These include

- Top management involvement and commitment to reengineering,
- Focus on staff concerns and issues,
- Monitoring performance and fostering cooperative relationships, and
- Ensuring valid comparisons between in-house and outside proposals.

Not all outsourcing is successful, especially when oversight is poor. Government guarantees can leave the public sector shouldering more than acceptable risks for contractor performance. Recurrent contracting, and contracting for highly specific assets, can erode competition, as the winners of initial contracts benefit from first-mover advantages and information asymmetry, where those advantages can be used to raise barriers to entry (Sclar, 2000; Williamson, 1985). Noncompetitive and loosely controlled contracting of projects can lead to inefficiencies, cost overruns, and corruption (Bloomfield et al., 1998).

Whereas outsourcing and competitive procurement are used to acquire specific services, management contracting is the wholesale (although temporary) transfer of management responsibility from incumbent public managers to outside private or nonprofit entities. Management contracting is increasingly occurring in the areas of municipal wastewater collection and treatment and water supply and distribution. In 1998, the City of Milwaukee entered into a ten-year operations and maintenance (O&M) contract with United Water. The management contract, with a value of $350 million, is the largest wastewater O&M agreement reached to date in the United States. It guarantees 30 percent annual savings to ratepayers, estimated to total $145 million (Reason Public Policy Institute, 1999). The City of Atlanta also recently took steps to contract out the operation of its water supply and wastewater treatment system. Looking at 100 percent rate increases to bring its system up to state and federal water quality standards, the city negotiated a 20-year agreement with Lyonnaise des Eaux and United Water to operate and maintain its system and to bring it into compliance with applicable water quality standards. The city retains ownership of the system and will continue to control rates and to finance capital expenditures (Reason Public Policy Institute, 1999). In both cases, the cities structured competitive tendering procedures to attract firms to bid for contracts. The use of competitive bidding enabled both to procure lower-cost alternatives for managing and operating their utility systems. It is interesting to note that both winning bidders agreed to hire all public water and wastewater employees and keep them on payroll (Reason Public Policy Institute, 1999).

Leasing and concessions offer another option for creating competition to improve the efficiency of infrastructure operations. Concessions and leases are used when the company or the infrastructure service requires significant capital investment. The government leases the existing facility to the private operator, requiring that the facility be upgraded to a specified level of service and then operated for a fixed time period. At the end of the lease or concession period, the facility, including improvements, is returned to the government. In some cases, concessions do not reflect the full economic value of the assets being leased and therefore provide indirect subsidies to private entities (U.S.

General Accounting Office, 1996). Great care must be taken in monitoring concessionaire performance if the full benefits of concessions are to be realized (Burns and Estache, 1998).

As the cases in this chapter illustrate, state departments may be able to look within California for efficient forms of project delivery, such as the Santa Clara County Traffic Authority and the California State University system. Alternatively, the state may realize cost savings by engaging in more joint-use projects with either public or private partners, as in the case of the San Jose Library, or the NorthLake Elementary School. The most complex form of management utilizes competition to reduce cost. Here, also, the San Diego Metropolitan Transit Development Board provides leadership from within California.

As projects are delivered, accurate record-keeping remains essential. As explained in the following chapter, without documentation explaining construction materials and completed design, routine maintenance can easily escalate into wholesale rehabilitation.

10. Deferred Maintenance

Until recently, most state and local governments made little attempt to monitor public sector assets. Unlike the private sector, where asset valuation and condition are carefully monitored and measures for depreciation are included in accounting statements, governmental accounting did not require such bookkeeping. Because most public sector planners and policymakers had little knowledge of facilities' condition, it was easy for them to defer maintenance costs. Deferred maintenance has been defined as "the extent of maintenance, repair, rehabilitation, etc., that is needed to bring capital assets from a sub-par condition to needed service levels" (Urban Institute, 1994). It can be quantified as the estimated cost of maintenance and repair needed to bring a facility up to a minimum acceptable condition (National Research Council, 1998).

Without accurate assessments of infrastructure condition and utilization, it is difficult if not impossible to make efficient resource allocation decisions. In some cases, governments provide more infrastructure than is needed. Lack of information about facilities also makes it difficult to effectively plan maintenance and renewal. Public facilities are typically not well maintained, receiving service only when there is a breakdown or system failure. Making repairs and doing maintenance only when the system is broken is expensive and disruptive. Periodic maintenance and renewal is much more cost-effective.

Attention began to focus on deferred infrastructure maintenance with the publication of *America in Ruins* (Choate and Walters, 1981) and several highly publicized infrastructure failures. Gradually, a variety of government agencies began to give maintenance issues more scrutiny. In 1996, the Federal Accounting Standards Advisory Board enacted Standard Number 6, Accounting for Property, Plant and Equipment, the first-ever governmentwide initiative requiring that federal agencies report dollar amounts of deferred maintenance (1996). In 1999, the

Government Accounting Standards Board (GASB) approved Statement 34—"Basic Financial Statements and Management's Discussion and Analysis—for State and Local Governments." GASB 34 requires that state and local governments report on the value of their infrastructure assets, including roads, bridges, water and sewer facilities, and dams. The new standard affects more than 84,000 state and local governments (Dornan, 2000). As concern grew at the national level, many states, including California, began to assess their maintenance backlogs.

California's Deferred Maintenance Backlog

California's stock of infrastructure assets is enormous and although no precise estimate of its value exists it is clearly close to a trillion dollars—higher educational facilities, highways, water supply systems, parks, office buildings, equipment, and so on. The state's ownership of such facilities carries with it the responsibility to ensure that they are properly maintained to provide services.

Inevitably, these facilities or the various components that make up these facilities deteriorate with time and use. Their life and usefulness can be optimized if they are properly maintained and repaired. On the other hand, by delaying or deferring maintenance, managers can diminish the quality of service that a building or facility provides. Ultimately in the long run deferred maintenance leads to a shortened life and reduced asset value (American Public Works Association, 1992).

Maintenance refers to the act of keeping facilities (buildings, physical plant, and equipment) in acceptable condition. It consists of preventive maintenance, normal repairs, replacement of parts and structural components, and other activities so that the asset continues to provide acceptable levels of service over its expected life. Maintenance does not include actions or repairs that aim to increase an asset's level of service or capacity. Deferred maintenance is defined as maintenance that was not performed when it should have happened—this includes failure to perform scheduled maintenance on a facility and repair of malfunctioning parts or components.

Deferred maintenance has been defined as "the extent of maintenance, repair, rehabilitation, etc., that is needed to bring capital assets from a sub-par condition to needed service levels" (Urban Institute,

1994). Deferred maintenance can be quantified as the estimated cost of maintenance and repair needed to bring a facility up to a minimum acceptable condition (National Research Council, 1998). As the Urban Institute points out, the existence of deferred maintenance is significant in that it implies that the quality and reliability of service provided by infrastructure on which maintenance has been deferred is lower than it should be. Infrastructure with deferred maintenance backlogs is therefore not adequately serving the public (Urban Institute, 1994). Figure 10.1 illustrates the relationships between deferred maintenance and service performance.

How much maintenance do facilities need? The answer depends on many factors—building size and complexity, types of finishes, mechanical and electrical system technology, established safety and environmental standards, climate, turnover and type of user, age, labor, energy, and materials prices. Facilities specialists will tell you that the most effective approach to maintenance is based on a combination of strategies—preventive maintenance, programmed major maintenance,

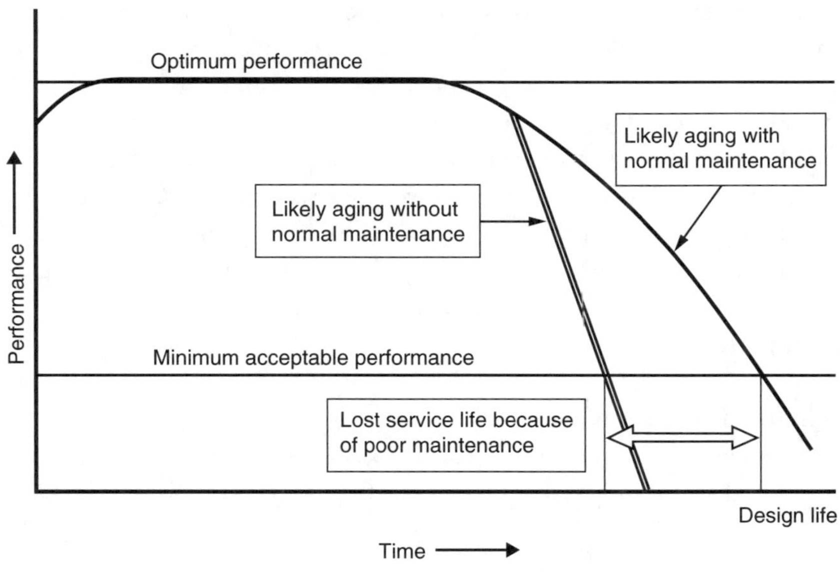

Figure 10.1—Effect of Adequate and Timely Maintenance and Repairs on the Service Life of an Asset

predictive testing and inspection, routine repairs, service calls, and run to failure (Federal Facilities Council, 2001).

If facilities are not properly maintained, they will perform suboptimally. Poor roads reduce productivity—vehicle speeds will fall and operating costs will increase. Transportation costs will increase, reducing society's welfare. In the case of higher education, UC may begin to experience a "brain-drain" of its faculty if lab and research facilities are not maintained. Even students may eventually vote with their feet and seek training in private institutions or decide to go out of state. Certainly, poor maintenance in the state's water supply and distribution systems will generate substantial costs. Lack of water reliability, because of system failures, could generate substantial losses in agriculture, tourism, and business activities.

Although most policymakers are focused on "ribbon-cutting" new infrastructure investment, the evidence clearly suggests that maintenance and renewal are critical components of infrastructure management. In fact, one big lesson that the World Bank learned in the 1990s was that it needed to put more emphasis on infrastructure management and maintenance (World Bank, 1994). Its review of infrastructure investments in the 1980s revealed massive failures in costly transportation and water supply investments. For example, in Ghana it used to take about two hours to drive from Accra to Kumasi; now, because the road is so poor, it takes well over six hours. California may not be Ghana, but it will certainly feel the effect of poorly maintained infrastructure. So how serious is the problem? The next section examines infrastructure backlogs and renewal issues in higher education, transportation, and water supply.

Higher Education

Recent assessments of deferred maintenance in higher education have produced astonishing results. As the LAO reported (1996b):

> Over the past 10 to 15 years, California's three public higher education systems have been in a state of constant maintenance deferral. As a result, the UC estimates that its deferred maintenance backlog exceeds $480 million, of which about $251 million are priority-one projects. (Priority-one deferred maintenance projects are those requiring immediate action to return a facility

to normal operation, stop accelerated deterioration, or correct a cited safety hazard.) The CSU estimates that its deferred maintenance backlog exceeds $325 million, of which about $108 million are priority-one projects. The CCC Chancellor's Office estimates that the statewide community college deferred maintenance backlog is about $90 million.

More recent estimates suggest that the higher education deferred maintenance figures are much higher. UC Berkeley alone estimates that its deferred maintenance requirements now top $500 million.

Professional groups concerned with the management and operation of facilities, such as the Building Operators and Managers Association, the Federal Facilities Council, and the National Association of Corporate Real Estate Executives generally agree that physical plant (office buildings, hospitals, laboratories, and residential rental units) should spend between 3 and 6 percent of the replacement cost per year on maintenance and renewal expenditures. Figure 10.2 illustrates the actual 1999 levels of facilities spending for UC Berkeley, the UC systemwide average, two private California universities, basic survival, and corporate standards.

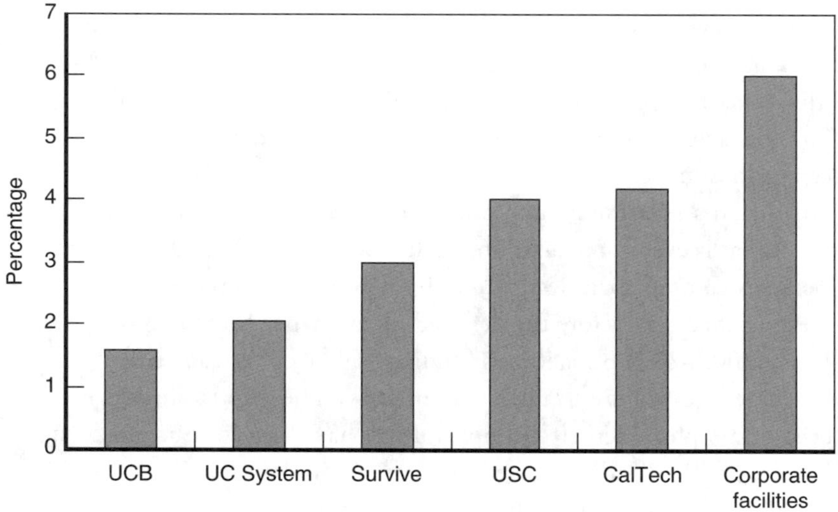

Figure 10.2—Facilities Maintenance Expenditures Versus Replacement Cost, 1999

Most facilities specialists argue that spending 3 percent of replacement value on maintenance is the bare minimum. The private and corporate real estate sectors maintain that 6 percent is more appropriate. The UC system, however, averages about 2 percent in terms of facilities expenditures versus replacement cost. UC Berkeley is lower, averaging 1.6 percent. In contrast, CalTech and USC, both private universities, spend approximately 4 percent, about twice the average for the UC system. The campus has a present replacement value of approximately $3 billion. At a minimum it should be spending $90 million a year (3 percent). If it were to approach the comparable spending levels of private universities—4 percent, it should be spending about $120 million per year on maintenance. In 1994–1995, the Berkeley campus spent $51.5 million on operation and maintenance of plant. Deducting operational costs, the campus spent $33 million on maintenance. Of this amount, $7.6 million was for deferred maintenance—catch-up. Therefore, the campus spent about $25 million on maintenance in 1994–1995, which amounts to about 20 percent of what is necessary to match private comparable universities and about 28 percent of what is necessary to fund maintenance and renewal at a survival rate of 3 percent. The campus needs to spend between $90 million and $120 million a year on maintenance—not $25 million. Since its actual funding of maintenance as well as deferred maintenance catch-up is inadequate, the total deferred maintenance backlog is growing at an alarming rate—well in excess of $50 million a year.

What is even more alarming is that between 1998 and 2001, the UC Berkeley campus spent less than $20 million a year on deferred maintenance—therefore the deferred maintenance backlog is increasing. In the 2002–2003 budget, this funding will be completely cut.

One significant effect of this shortfall can be seen in almost any classroom on the Berkeley campus. Most have broken seats, inadequate lighting, broken audiovisual equipment, or similar problems. Consider Evans 10, a large lecture hall. As a result of years of deferred maintenance, the seat cushions failed. Instead of replacing them, maintenance staff removed the cushions and painted the fiberglass seats. As a result, it is nearly impossible to hear lectures because the acoustics of the room have been so degraded. In other cases, the campus has spent literally millions of dollars improving the seismic safety of a building while failing to fix leaky roofs.

Another significant effect of the maintenance shortfall has to do with capital outlay decisionmaking. Buildings that should have been torn down—Wurster and Barrows Hall, for example—are being seismically upgraded because campus administrators are not considering deferred maintenance backlogs in their capital outlay decisions. A seismically upgraded building with $15 million in deferred maintenance is still a building with $15 million in deferred maintenance. The architectural and historic value of a structure may warrant upgrading instead of replacement, but deferred maintenance must be incorporated into decisionmaking in either case.

Given the advanced age of buildings and facilities on most UC, CSU, and CCC campuses, we can expect the deferred maintenance backlog to mushroom over the next 20 years. As campus buildings and infrastructure age, a greater percentage of replacement costs must be programmed to maintenance. If not, the backlog will grow. The current deferred maintenance backlog in the higher education sector probably stands at about $2 billion.

Transportation

Estimates of deferred maintenance of the Caltrans highway network are orders of magnitude higher. The Streets and Highways Code Section 167(a) defines operations, maintenance, rehabilitation, and safety as the top priorities for state highway expenditures. Caltrans prepares a ten-year SHOPP plan covering the following types of projects:

- Resurfacing and pavement rehabilitation,
- Bridge rehabilitation and replacement,
- Roadside rehabilitation, including drainage, planting and rest areas,
- Protective betterments to forestall chronic problems, most often from erosion or drainage,
- Safety improvements, including those for the roadway, intersections, and roadside,

- Traffic operations improvements, to help traffic move more smoothly, and
- Lands and buildings improvements, including maintenance facility modernization.

Rebuild California recently reported that the state ranked 48th in the nation in terms of road condition. The study found that 50 percent of the roads are in poor or mediocre condition. Potholes, ruts, and rough pavements are estimated to cause the average driver to pay out roughly $354 per year in added vehicle maintenance and operating costs. This totals $7.4 billion per year for the state (Rebuild California, 2001).

Despite the planning and maintenance efforts of Caltrans and local governments across the state, maintenance expenditures have not kept pace with increases in VMT. Table 10.1 provides inflation-adjusted expenditures for maintenance from 1978 to 1996. Figure 10.3 illustrates trends in real maintenance expenditures per VMT. The state is spending less on maintenance per VMT now than it has since 1983. These low levels of maintenance spending are problematic because most of the state's roads and highways are reaching the end of their useful lives.

Table 10.1

Trends in Highway Maintenance

Year	Annual VMT (millions)	Lane Miles	Real Maintenance Expenditure ($ millions)	Real Maintenance Expenditure/ Lane Mile ($)	Real Maintenance Expenditure/ 100 VMT ($)
1978	85,806	47,511	59.9	1,261	0.0698
1980	87,610	47,623	46.6	979	0.0532
1981	91,343	47,690	46	965	0.0504
1983	96,758	47,855	80.4	1,680	0.0831
1985	106,833	48,096	80.3	1,670	0.0752
1987	121,722	48,257	135.3	2,804	0.1112
1989	134,371	48,530	94.1	1,939	0.0700
1992	141,687	49,138	132.5	2,696	0.0935
1995	146,155	49,893	99.4	1,992	0.0680
1996	149,569	50,040	103.2	2,062	0.0690

SOURCE: Caltrans, various years.

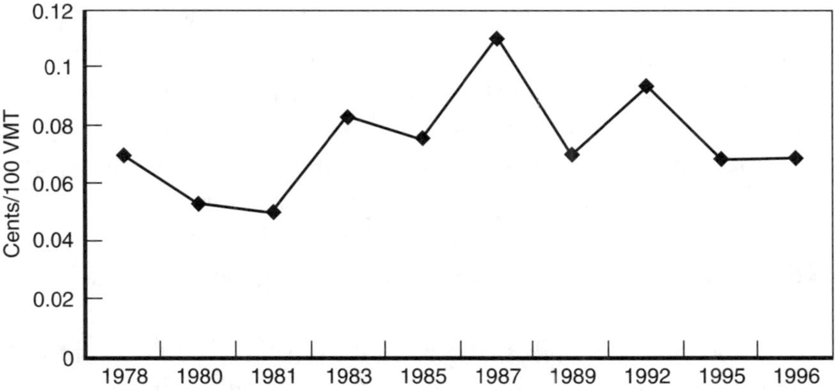

Figure 10.3—Real Road Maintenance Expenditures per 100 VMT

The 1999 California Transportation Commission *Inventory of Ten-Year Funding Needs for California's Transportation Systems* provides a long list of state highway repairs and rehabilitation projects. The total projected needs are $12.5 billion. Of this amount, $7 billion is funded under the current SHOPP. The remaining $5.5 billion is unfunded at the present time.

The California Transportation Commission estimates that, in the long term, the total deferred maintenance backlog for local streets and roads is $10.5 billion (California Transportation Commission, 1999b). The backlog for local bridge repair and replacement is $600 million.

Considering both state and local roads, the Metropolitan Transportation Commission in the San Francisco Bay Area estimates that the region's deferred maintenance backlog doubled between 1981 and 1999. The total backlog in 1999 was estimated at $1.6 billion. By 2010, the backlog is expected to exceed $2 billion—approximately $300 per person. Local governments are charged with the responsibility of maintaining 91 percent of the region's roads, and although they spend about $13,000 per lane mile per year on maintenance, it is estimated that they should be spending over 50 percent more—$20,000 per lane mile per year (Metropolitan Transportation Commission, 2000). Local and state funds for street maintenance and repair have increased over the last decade, but they have not kept pace with traffic volumes or repair and maintenance costs. Compounding this problem is the fact that transportation agencies around the region do not have a sound and consistent strategy for road maintenance. Many jurisdictions do not keep adequate information on road conditions. Some focus on fixing the worst roads first—an ineffective and costly approach. Others simply do not accord road condition as a top priority and therefore defer maintenance. One skeptical assessment suggests that politicians allow potholes to grow to motivate voters into approving inordinately large transportation packages.

Because SHOPP funds are taken off the top of STIP funds, Caltrans and the California Transportation Commission give the impression that maintenance is indeed a priority for the state. However, Caltrans is probably spending significantly higher amounts to maintain each project than it should. At completion of construction, for example, contractors should be required to submit detailed drawings showing the condition of the highway as it was actually built—"as-built drawings," in industry parlance. Unfortunately, Caltrans separation between construction and maintenance is so complete that Caltrans construction managers have rarely if ever required as-built records of projects with enough information to guide maintenance contracting. Contractors bid on maintenance from the SHOPP, and Caltrans accepts these bids without adequate information as to the materials and thickness of the existing roadway. As a result, it is almost impossible to truly assess the lifespan of Caltrans projects, to adequately prioritize maintenance, and to control the cost of maintenance. Contractors end up literally tearing up the pavement to see what is inside, and rebuilding beyond what could have been necessary.

A key concept in street and road maintenance is early intervention. During the first 15 years of its life, a road deteriorates by 40 percent (Dornan, 2000). After this point, deterioration rapidly accelerates. Another 40 percent deterioration occurs over the next 2.4 years. If pavements can be managed so that preventive maintenance can be applied before this rapid decline, overall maintenance costs can be minimized. Early intervention costs about 20 percent less than maintenance efforts made during the last 25 percent of a road's life.

Better maintenance generates higher-quality road and street performance. Table 10.2 and Figure 10.4 illustrate the relationship between annual investment in pavement maintenance and repair and

Table 10.2

Pavement Expenditure and Pavement Condition Index

Jurisdiction	Average Expenditure per Mile, 1981–1995 ($)	1996–1997 Pavement Condition Index
Foster City	24,932	77
Mountain View	22,338	78
Fremont	20,376	74
Benicia	16,945	71
Santa Clara	16,581	79
Pleasanton	14,921	70
Alameda County	14,869	73
Livermore	14,416	75
Sunnyvale	14,372	75
Hercules	14,150	71
Danville	13,076	72
Mill Valley	12,990	65
Belmont	12,929	66
Campbell	10,726	60
Santa Clara County	10,266	65
Sausalito	10,079	62
Richmond	9,758	67
Menlo Park	9,597	53
Orinda	9,331	55
Contra Costa County	8,778	64
Napa	8,315	66
Los Gatos	8,209	60
Sonoma County	6,950	46
Calistoga	6,157	44
Berkeley	6,059	61
El Cerrito	5,802	55
Marin County	5,678	45
Los Altos Hills	5,361	58
East Palo Alto	5,316	58
Petaluma	5,181	40
Solano County	4,931	51

SOURCE: Metropolitan Transportation Commission (2000).

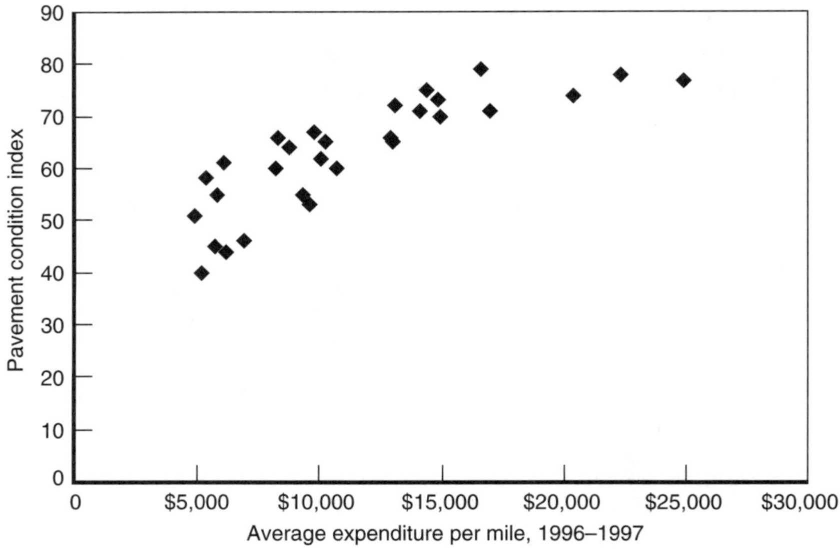

Figure 10.4—Metropolitan Transportation Commission Pavement Condition Index Versus Maintenance Expenditures per Mile, 1996–1997

pavement condition. As these two displays illustrate, you get what you pay for—better roads for more spending.

A promising approach for tackling maintenance problems is to have private road contractors guarantee pavement conditions. In New Mexico, the state highway department recently contracted with Koch Industries to expand a 121-mile section of Corridor 44. Under the contract, Koch agreed to design, construct, and warranty the new facility. Koch agreed to guarantee the road from subbase to surface and to maintain the road for 20 years at no additional cost to the state. By linking design, construction, performance warranty, and maintenance, the contract provides powerful incentives for Koch to provide a facility that will offer a high quality at the lowest lifecycle cost (Moore et al., 2000).

Overall in the transportation sector, deferred maintenance is estimated to stand at $12.5 billion for the state-managed roads and bridges and $10.5 billion for local streets and bridges. This total amount—$23 billion—is what California needs to spend just to keep its facilities in adequate shape. Unfortunately, much of the actual funding of maintenance comes from sales taxes, and these are about to sunset unless extended. If these taxes are not extended or if the gasoline tax is not significantly increased, highway maintenance spending will plummet.

Water Supply

The state's water supply sector is better maintained than either the higher education or transportation sector. Both the State Water Project (under DWR) and the Central Valley Project (under the U.S. Bureau of Reclamation) have statutory authority to levy fees and charges to support maintenance, operations, and capital costs (California Department of Water Resources, 2001). As we explained in Chapter 7, water tariffs are based on actual costs. As a result, funding to support system maintenance is adequate. However, increasing water quality standards mandated under the U.S. Safe Drinking Water Act are placing severe financial pressures on local water districts. These increased standards require advanced treatment facilities for water supply and wastewater treatment. Moreover, as urbanization puts pressure on the state's surface and groundwater supplies, more sophisticated and costly water treatment facilities will be required. All of this means that water distribution and supply systems need expensive infrastructure upgrades. As Rebuild California (2001) points out:

> Our present water collection and distribution system is consistently safe and reliable, but not risk-free. Between 1994 and 1995 alone, drinking water systems around the state reported 570 health violations or . . . Environmental Protection Agency violations for inadequate filtration or disinfection. In 1999, the state Department of Water Resources' 10-year capital improvement forecast called for more than $1.6 billion in spending to ensure delivery of clean water.

The state's water supply and treatment systems need to be overhauled to support water-recycling programs. This means more investment. This comes at a time when the California Resources Control Board estimates a need for $8.4 billion for local wastewater treatment improvements. It also comes at a time when many of our cities have water mains, sewers, and storm drains that are more than 100 years old or that have not expanded enough to meet new demands. For example, the Hetch Hetchy water system that serves 2.3 million people in the Bay Area needs $4.6 billion in repairs, prompting water officials to announce that customers' water rates would have to double to provide funds for the repairs. The alternative is for voters in San Francisco and the 29 suburban agencies that buy Hetch Hetchy water to pass millions of dollars in new bonds to replace the system's aging water pipes. In 1997, San Francisco voters authorized $300 million in system repair bonds, but the city has not issued them pending final improvement designs.

Taken together, deferred maintenance in higher education, transportation, and water supply are monumental: on the order of $65 billion.

What Should the State Do About Deferred Maintenance?

In its study of deferred maintenance in higher education, the LAO called for several initiatives:

- Increased funding for ongoing maintenance,
- More accountability at the agency level,
- Prohibiting the addition of new projects to existing deferred maintenance backlogs, and
- Starting a process to eliminate the backlog.

These proposals make sense, but additional recommendations are needed. First, agencies need to do a better job of recording facilities' condition and maintenance requirements. Databases and more systematic assessments of conditions are needed (Syme and Oschrin, 1996). Second, agencies should be required to place more emphasis on lifecycle costs as opposed to first costs.

Lifecycle Maintenance

Lifecycle maintenance involves setting up financing to cover maintenance costs with initial project financing. For agencies able to charge user fees, those fees should be brought to levels adequate to accommodate maintenance expenses for the foreseeable lifespan of the facility. For agencies unable to charge user fees, long-term financing must include sinking funds devoted to maintenance expenses. During the design phase, contractors and state engineers should be required to take into account the maintenance costs of their designs and strive to reduce those costs. Simple examples of designs for reduced maintenance costs include the installation of solar panels and the design of open interior overhead systems for wiring, such as overhead brackets for phone, cable, and computer networking that allow facility maintenance workers to reroute systems without the need to damage or reconstruct ceiling tiles or drywall. For existing structures, detailed knowledge of age and condition can inform estimates of the remaining useful lifespan of the structure. Structures and roads can differ dramatically in the amount of maintenance investment required. Some facilities built in the early 1900s have considerably longer lifespans than those constructed after 1960, as the price of construction materials escalated considerably from this point on, and departments sought out cheaper materials as a way to cut costs.

Lifecycle maintenance also takes into account the fact that the lifespan of a building and its constituent parts requires investments that can and should change, on a set pattern, from year to year. For example, heating, ventilation, and air conditioning systems may require replacement every ten years, carpets every five years, and the roof every 15 years. For each building, these expenses must be charted out and budgeted in an overall maintenance program that accounts for the full lifecycle of the building. This process may sound difficult to institute, but in reality it is not. Contractors responsible for designing facilities should simply be required to develop a companion maintenance schedule with these details. Knowledge of probable maintenance costs is the first step in modifying design to minimize the effect of maintenance. With this information come cost estimates for replacing various systems, with inflation factored in. Records of actual replacements are kept alongside those planned in an automated accounting system. For all the state's existing facilities, some type of inspection of facility conditions will be required in any case to meet generally accepted accounting principles and GASB 34 reporting requirements. Maintenance plans should be prepared in conjunction with these inspections.

The fact that California's budgeting system allows operations and maintenance funds to compete with one another places maintenance on the losing side of a never-ending battle. During economic slumps, departments will always drop maintenance to keep their employees. In the best of all worlds, maintenance funds are not only protected from the effect of growing staff and salaries but also planned for separately from operations. California should seize the opportunity established by AB 1473 to institute a companion five-year statewide maintenance plan for infrastructure.

11. Policy Recommendations

As the foregoing chapters indicate, the state faces an array of daunting infrastructure challenges. Given the downturn in the economy in the fall of 2001, it will be particularly difficult to overcome them rapidly. But if we look forward over the next two to five years, there is a range of possibilities that could put California back on track. This chapter presents recommendations and ideas about how state policymakers might proceed.

As a starting point, the state needs to introduce strategic planning and link it to the capital planning done by agencies. This process is under way with the implementation of AB 1473. However, the state also needs to think about how to foster multisectoral investment planning. We have suggested that the state develop a vision for the future growth of California and use it to plan and prioritize infrastructure investments in water supply, transportation, education, and other areas.

This could be carried out in a number of ways. One way is to develop a series of regional or metropolitan plans that consider how to link transportation and land-use planning with other infrastructure services. The plans could be then integrated to form the basis of a statewide strategic plan for California. A more centralized approach would be to develop a statewide development plan. Two past examples come to mind—*The California Tomorrow Plan* (Heller, 1972) and the Brown administration's *An Urban Strategy for California* (Office of Planning and Research, 1978).

Our general recommendations, then, are as follows.

Define California's Vision for the Future and Use It to Plan Infrastructure Investments. The state government needs to define and implement its vision of performance-based, efficient government service delivery. It needs to link agency-related goals and missions with the capital decisionmaking process for infrastructure investment. This means being absolutely sure that the new investment is needed and that the performance gap cannot be met in some other way. It means carefully assessing whether there are ways to shift the provision of the service to other entities. It means determining whether there are ways to finance required infrastructure more creatively or to develop collaborative partnerships to provide services. Finally, it means determining how to most efficiently provide services by enhancing project delivery.

Introduce Demand Management to Infrastructure Planning. Given the projected infrastructure needs facing California, the state must manage demand as well as increase supply strategically. Among other things, demand management means fostering water conservation in the urban and agricultural sectors; implementing road pricing to mitigate traffic congestion; and encouraging carpooling, off-peak travel, mass transit, telecommuting, and other forms of travel besides single-occupancy auto trips. In the case of higher education, operating year-round makes good sense, as does providing students with incentives to move through colleges and universities faster.

Review and Adjust User Fees and Charges While Developing Ability-to-Pay Offsets. Where the state uses fees and charges to finance infrastructure, it needs to raise rates to recover from years of stagnation. The DWR and the myriad of urban and agricultural districts need to revise their pricing policies to promote water conservation. This means using increasing block rate tariffs in urban areas and linking them with CIMIS to adjust blocks to weather conditions. Agricultural pricing needs to promote more flexibility in cropping patterns and to develop best-practice irrigation.

The challenge facing the transportation sector is to increase gasoline taxes and vehicle registration fees and to implement a range of programs to promote transit and carpooling. Higher parking fees, telecommuting, and nonauto alternative forms of transportation would make great sense. The biggest challenge is to implement a congestion pricing system on the state's congested bridges and highways. A demonstration project to address equity effects should be launched.

Although higher education is the quintessential merit good, there are ways to adjust prices to generate more revenues while maintaining quality and access. Tuition could be based on means testing, with scholarships and financial aid given to those needing it. Fees could encourage students to move through the system—pricing could be used to foster faster time to degree in the UC and CSU systems. Fees for courses in community colleges could differentiate between vocational and university preparatory courses and those aimed at senior and leisure markets. The fees of professional schools and colleges could be increased to more closely approximate actual costs, particularly in areas where students receive high starting salaries. Exceptions and fee waivers could be given to students willing to enter public or community service careers upon graduation. If fee structures placed a greater burden on users and beneficiaries, more resources would be available to support the growth and modernization of the system.

Exceptional care needs to be taken to ensure that fee adjustments do not limit the access of low- and moderate-income households to services. This will require that the state offer a range of offsets, including lifeline rates, financial aid, and tax rebates.

Make Capital Funding More Predictable. Sacramento needs to move beyond its current method of allocating funds for capital investment. In particular, capital outlays need to be geared to strategic capital planning. For example, the LAO's proposal for a K–12 grant system looks expensive, but if it is balanced with an increase in user fees and local taxes, it can work.

Increase Accountability to Foster Enhanced Project Delivery. Partly because many state agencies face little or no competition for their services, they are less accountable to clients than might otherwise be the case. To increase accountability, state agencies should develop agency strategic plans that establish goals and standards of performance for meeting client needs. These goals and standards could be regularly used to assess agency performance.

Accountability alone will not deliver improved service, however. The state needs to provide clear and strong incentives to reward high-level performance. Personnel reviews, salary merit increases, and bonuses could play a useful role. Competition should also be introduced, so that public service providers are forced to compete with private firms for the right to provide client services (Goldsmith, 1999).

Introduce Lifecycle Costing and Management. A preoccupation with first costs has distorted capital outlay decisionmaking. A better approach is to focus on the total costs of building, operating, and maintaining a capital asset over its lifetime. This lifecycle approach looks beyond procurement costs and considers ongoing maintenance costs. These costs would be included as part of the budget for the facility. Funding for maintenance should be encumbered when an asset is put in place.

The state also needs to hold agencies accountable for the maintenance of their capital facilities. At a minimum, this requires much better reporting of facilities' condition. Agencies should be required to report deferred maintenance backlogs and to develop five-year plans for eliminating deferred maintenance. We note that GASB 34 provides important incentives for better accounting of infrastructure condition.

Where Should the State Start?

These recommendations are very broad in scope. How might they be implemented in the short, medium, and long term? Under AB 1473, the governor is required to submit a Five-Year Capital Plan to the legislature. This plan should serve as the basis for charting out the course of actions that need to be taken. The plan should be divided into three phases: immediate steps to relieve costly congestion and infrastructure effects, near-term efforts to begin to address infrastructure service shortfalls over a two- to five-year period, and a long-term overhaul to remove structural and institutional impediments to infrastructure provision.

Immediate Actions—Demand Management and Pricing

Demand management interventions will have the quickest effects. They can create capacity in weeks or months and they do not rely on capital outlays. In areas of the state that face extreme and costly traffic congestion, we propose implementing congestion pricing pilot projects. In the Bay Area, for example, peak-hour tolls should be imposed for a one-year trial. In conjunction with this tolling, the state should offer commuters discounted (or perhaps even free) vouchers for public transit use.

The state's gasoline taxes could be scheduled for a 20 percent increase per year over the next five years. The state could also consider requiring that local governments levy parking excise taxes on all municipal and private parking lots and structures.

The state could aggressively encourage the rollout of urban water conservation programs to all municipal districts. This could be brought about by requiring that urban water districts adopt the DWR MOU on urban water conservation. The CIMIS program that automates landscape watering in Irvine should be expanded across the state. Similar action is needed for agricultural water districts as well. The state should accelerate the conversion of water tariffs to a full cost recovery basis.

For K–12 education, year-round schooling could be encouraged through incentives or mandated for schools experiencing the effects of high growth. For higher education, the state should mandate a thorough review of capital planning at the CCC and UC systems. Such a review should be modeled on the recent assessment carried out for CSU. Student fees should be increased for all systems and additional financial aid should be offered on a means-tested basis. At CSU and UC, students should be encouraged to graduate in four years.

Medium-Term Actions—Institutional and Financial Restructuring

Over the next five years, the state should work to restructure its infrastructure institutions. The AB 1473 process should be used to foster more strategic planning and a closer link to strategic and capital planning. Funding allocation systems for transportation and education need to be made more equitable and efficient. The state needs to develop accountability systems to measure agency performance. Incentives (both positive and negative) need to be developed to spur more efficacious performance. GASB 34 provides a starting point for the state to develop rigorous reporting of state and local infrastructure conditions. The state should also design and disseminate state-of-the-art legislation on public-private partnership formation.

Over the next two to five years, the state should restructure its systems of infrastructure finance. This should include dedicated full funding of maintenance, programming of capital outlay grants to sectors based on demand, and a balancing of pay-as-you-go and debt financing to introduce more predictability to infrastructure capital investment.

Long-Term Actions—Articulate a Vision and Make Infrastructure Policy More Integrated and Multisectoral

Over the next two decades, the state should develop a vision for the future economic and physical development of California. The vision should link land-use and environmental planning with economic development and infrastructure investment. The vision and the plan should also serve as a basis for planning and programming multisectoral infrastructure investments. What is important is to start the process of integrated planning. As President Dwight Eisenhower said, "Plans are nothing, planning is everything." We need the process if we are to ensure prosperity for tomorrow's Californians.

Bibliography

American Public Works Association, *Plan, Predict, Prevent: How to Reinvest in Public Buildings,* Special Report #62, Chicago, Illinois, 1992.

Angelides, Phil, *Smart Investments: A Special Update on California's Debt Affordability Report,* State Treasurer's Office, Sacramento, California, 1999.

Association of California Water Agencies, *The State's Looming Water Crisis: A Status Report,* Sacramento, California, 1999.

Association of Commuter Transportation, *TDM Case Studies and Commuter Testimonials*, Transportation Demand Management Institute, Washington, D.C., 1997.

Auerback, Alan J., Laurence J. Kotilikoff, and Willi Leibfritz, *Generational Accounting Around the World*, University of Chicago Press, Chicago, Illinois, 1999.

Baumann, D. D., J. J. Boland, and W. Michael Hanemann (eds.), *Urban Water Demand Management and Planning*, McGraw-Hill, New York, 1998.

Blakely, Edward J., and Mary Gail Snyder, *Fortress America: Gated Communities in the United States*, Brookings Institute, Washington, D.C., 1999.

Bloomfield, Pamela, David Westerling, and Robert Carey, "Innovations and Risk in a Public-Private Partnership: Financing and Construction of a Capital Project in Massachusetts," *Public Productivity & Management Review*, Vol. 21, No. 4, 1998, pp. 460–471.

Brown, Jeffrey, Michele DiFrancia, Mary C. Hill, Philip Law, Jeffery Olson, Brian D. Taylor, Martin Wachs, and Asha Weinstein, *The*

Future of California Highway Finance, The California Policy Research Center, Berkeley, California, 1999.

Bryson, John, and Robert Einsweiler, *Strategic Planning: Threats and Opportunities for Planners,* American Planning Association Press, Chicago, Illinois, 1988.

Burns, Phil, and Antonio Estache, *Information, Accounting and the Regulation of Concessioned Infrastructure Monopolies*, World Bank Discussion Paper 2034, Washington, D.C., 1998.

CALFED Bay-Delta Program, *Framework Agreement Between the Governor's Water Policy Council of the State of California and the Federal Ecosystem Directorate*, Sacramento, California, 1994.

CALFED Bay-Delta Program, *California's Water Future: A Framework for Action,* Sacramento, California, June 2000a.

CALFED Bay-Delta Program, *Final Programmatic Environmental Impact Statement/Environmental Impact Report*, Sacramento, California, July 2000b.

CALFED Bay-Delta Program, *Programmatic Record of Decision*, Sacramento, California, August 2000c.

CALFED Bay-Delta Program, "CALFED Bay-Delta Program Overview," 2001, available at http://calfed.ca.gov/general_info.html, 2001.

California Budget Project, *Critical Choices for California: The 1999–2000 State Budget*, Sacramento, 1999.

California Business Roundtable, *Building a Legacy for the Next Generation*, Sacramento, 1998.

California Community Colleges, Board of Governors, *New Criteria for Prioritizing Capital Outlay Projects*, Sacramento, 1999.

California Community Colleges, Board of Governors, *Capital Outlay Planning,* Sacramento, 2000.

California Community Colleges, "Facilities Planning Manual," 2002, available at http://www.cccco.edu/divisions/fiscal/references/fac_pln_mnl.htm.

California Department of Education, "Year-Round Education Statistics 1998–1999," 1998a, available at http://www.cde.ca.gov/facilities/yearround/yrestats.htm.

California Department of Education, "School Facilities Fingertip Facts," 1998b, available at http://www.cde.ca.gov/dmsbranch/sfpdiv/docs/facts.htm.

California Department of Finance, *State Administrative Manual,* Sacramento, 1953.

California Department of Finance, *Capital Outlay and Infrastructure Report 1996,* Sacramento, 1996.

California Department of Finance, Demographics Research Unit, "State and County Projected K–12 Enrollment and High School Graduates," 1999, available at http://www.dof.ca.gov/HTML/DEMOGRAP/drupubs.htm.

California Department of Finance, "Economic and Demographic Statistics," 2000, available at http://www.dof.ca.gov.

California Department of Finance, *California Statistical Abstract, 2001,* Sacramento, 2001a.

California Department of Finance, "Governor's Budget Summary, 2001–2002," 2001b, available at http://www.dof.ca.gov/HTML/Budgt01-02/K-12-T.htm.

California Department of Finance, *California's Five Year Infrastructure Plan, 2002,* Sacramento, 2002.

California Department of General Services, Office of Public School Construction, "New Construction Commensurate Requirement," 1999, available at http://www.opsc.dgs.ca.gov/stateallocationboard/sab-policies.asp.

California Department of General Services, Office of Public School Construction, "School Facility Program: Approval History of the

School Facility Program Regulations," 2001, available at http://www.opsc.ca.gov/Regulations/history_reg_approvals.asp.

California Department of General Services, Office of Public School Construction, "State School Facilities Program Overview," 2002, available at http://www.opsc.dgs.ca.gov/Programs/Default.htm.

California Department of Housing and Community Development *Raising the Roof,* Sacramento, 2000.

California Department of Transportation, "Ten-Year State Highway System Rehabilitation Plan: 1998–99 through 2007–08, and Recommendation for Funding Within the 1998 State Transportation Improvement Program Fund Estimate," 1998a, available at http://www.dot.ca.gov/hq/transprog/reports/tnyrplan.pdf.

California Department of Transportation, Office of the Director, *Interregional Transportation Strategic Plan: A Plan to Guide Development of the Interregional Transportation System,* Sacramento, 1998b.

California Department of Transportation, *How Caltrans Builds Projects*, Sacramento, 1998c.

California Department of Transportation, "Mass Transit Program, California Transit Passenger Services," 1999a, available at http://www.dot.ca.gov/hq/MassTrans/ctps9798.html.

California Department of Transportation, *State Transportation Improvement Plan,* Sacramento, 1999b.

California Department of Transportation, "District 11 Cost Estimating Improvements" (draft, not for publication), Sacramento, 2001a.

California Department of Transportation, "Fact Sheet: Important Events in Caltrans History," 2001b, available at http://www.dot.ca.gov/hq/paffairs/about/chist.htm.

California Department of Transportation, Division of Transportation System Information, "Table 2-3-3" and "Table 2-2-1," 2002, available at http://www.dot.ca.gov/hq/tsip/docs.htm.

California Department of Water Resources, Division of Resources Planning, *The California Water Plan,* Bulletin 3, Sacramento, 1957.

California Department of Water Resources, *California's Groundwater,* Bulletin 118, Sacramento, 1975.

California Department of Water Resources, *California Water: Looking to the Future*, Sacramento, 1987.

California Department of Water Resources, "California Water Management: Ground Water," *Water Facts: California Water Management*, Sacramento, 1993.

California Department of Water Resources, *General Comparison of Water District Acts*, Sacramento, 1994.

California Department of Water Resources, "California Water Management: Adjudicated Ground Water Basins in California," *Water Facts: California Water Management*, Sacramento, 1996a.

California Department of Water Resources, "California Water Management: Groundwater Management Districts or Agencies in California," *Water Facts: California Water Management*, January 1996b.

California Department of Water Resources, *Strategic Business Plan*, Sacramento, 1997.

California Department of Water Resources, *Management of the California State Water Project,* Report 132-1998, Sacramento, 1998a.

California Department of Water Resources, Division of Planning and Local Assistance, *Technical Elements of CIMIS: The California Irrigation Management Information System*, Sacramento, 1998b.

California Department of Water Resources, *California Water Plan Update,* Bulletin 160-98, Sacramento, 1999a.

California Department of Water Resources, *Groundwater Management in California: A Report to the Legislature Pursuant to Senate Bill 1245 (1997),* Sacramento, 1999b.

California Department of Water Resources, *Management of the California State Water Project,* Bulletin 132-98, Sacramento, 1999c.

California Department of Water Resources, "California Department of Water Resources," Brochure No. OSP 00 43490, Sacramento, 2000.

California Department of Water Resources, *Management of the State Water Project,* Bulletin 132-99, Sacramento, 2001.

California Government Code Section 11800.

California Government Code Section 13104.

California Legislature, Assembly Office of Research, *Rusty Hinges on the Golden Gate,* Sacramento, 1983.

California Little Hoover Commission, *To Build a Better School,* Sacramento, 2000a.

California Little Hoover Commission, *Special Districts: Relics of the Past or Resources for the Future?* Sacramento, 2000b.

California Postsecondary Education Commission, *The Infrastructure Needs of California Public Higher Education,* Sacramento, 1987.

California Postsecondary Education Commission, *Higher Education at the Crossroads,* Sacramento, 1990.

California Postsecondary Education Commission, *Prospects for Long-Range Capital Planning in California Public Higher Education,* Sacramento, 1992a.

California Postsecondary Education Commission, *A Framework for Statewide Facilities Planning,* Sacramento, 1992b.

California Postsecondary Education Commission, *A Capacity for Growth: Enrollments, Resources, and Facilities for California Higher Education, 1993–94 to 2005–06,* Sacramento, 1995a.

California Postsecondary Education Commission, *The Challenge of the Century,* Sacramento, 1995b.

California Postsecondary Education Commission, *Toward a Unified State System: A Report and Recommendations on the Governance of the California Community Colleges,* Sacramento, 1998.

California Postsecondary Education Commission, *Fiscal Profiles, 1999*, Sacramento, 1999.

California Postsecondary Education Commission, *Providing for Progress: California Higher Education Enrollment Demand and Resources into the 21st Century*, Sacramento, 2000.

California Postsecondary Education Commission, *The Condition of Higher Education in California, 2002,* Sacramento, 2002.

California Secretary of State, "California Official Voter Information Guide, General Election Date Tuesday, November 5, 2002," 2002, available at http://voterguide.ss.ca.gov, 2002.

California State University, Office of the University Auditor, *Restructuring the California State University Capital Outlay Process: Final Report of the Building Design and Construction Task Force*, Long Beach, 1996.

California State University, *Cornerstones Report*, Long Beach, 1998a.

California State University, "1998–1999 Budget Index," 1998b, available at http://www.calstate.edu/tier3/Budget/1998_99BudIndex/SpptBud/PhysPlnt.html.

California State University, "State University Administrative Manual," 2002, available at http://www.calstate.edu/CPDC/SUAM.html.

California State Water Resources Control Board, *1995 Bay Delta Water Quality Control Plan*, Sacramento, 1995.

California State Water Resources Control Board, *Final Environmental Impact Report for Implementation of the Bay Delta Water Quality Control Plan*, Sacramento, 1999.

California State Water Resources Control Board, *State Water Resources Control Board: Ground Water in California*, Sacramento, n.d.

California Transportation Commission, *1999 Annual Report to California Legislature: Volume 1, Key Issues for 2000*, Sacramento, 1999a.

California Transportation Commission, *Inventory* of *Ten-Year Funding Needs for California's Transportation Systems,* Sacramento, 1999b.

Choate, Pat, and Susan Walters, *America in Ruins: Beyond the Public Works Pork Barrel,* The Council of State Planning Agencies, Washington, D.C., 1981.

Christian, John, and Amar Pandeya, "Cost Predictions of Facilities," *Journal of Management in Engineering*, Vol. 13, No. 1, January–February 1997, pp. 52–61.

Commission for the Review of the Master Plan for Higher Education, *The Master Plan Renewed: Unity, Equity, Quality, and Efficiency in California Postsecondary Education*, Sacramento, California, 1987.

Commonwealth Competition Council, *Annual Report*, Commonwealth of Virginia, Richmond, 1998a.

Commonwealth Competition Council, *The Privatization/Competition Manual*, Commonwealth of Virginia, Richmond, 1998b.

Coopers and Lybrand, *California State University System NACUBO Benchmarking Project II,* California State University, Long Beach, California, 1995.

Dornan, Daniel L., *GASB 34's Impacts on Infrastructure Management, Financing and Reporting,* Infrastructure Management Group, Inc., Bethesda, Maryland, 2000.

Dowall, David E., *California's Infrastructure Policy for the 21st Century: Issues and Opportunities,* Public Policy Institute of California, 2000, available at http://www.ppic.org/publications/PPIC130/PPIC130.pdf/index.html.

Downs, Anthony, *Stuck in Traffic: Coping with Peak-Hour Traffic Congestion,* Brookings Institution, Washington, D.C., 1992.

East Bay Municipal Utility District (EBMUD), "Customer Assistance Program (CAP)," 2002, available at http://www.ebmud.com/services/

account_information/making_payments/customer_assistance_program/default.htm.

Eggers, William D., *Performance-Based Contracting: Designing State-of-the-Art Contract Administration and Monitoring Systems,* Policy Study 17, Reason Public Policy Institute, Los Angeles, California, 1997.

Eggers, William D., *Competitive Neutrality: Ensuring a Level Playing Field in Managed Competitions,* How-to Guide 18, Reason Public Policy Institute, Los Angeles, California, 1998.

Federal Accounting Standards Advisory Board, "Accounting for Property Plant, and Equipment, Statement of Recommended Accounting Standards," No. 6, 1996, available at http://www.financenet.gov/financenet/fed/fasab/concepts.htm.

Federal Facilities Council, *Deferred Maintenance Reporting for Federal Facilities,* Technical Report 141, Washington, D.C., 2001.

Federal Highway Administration, *Highway Statistics 1925–1995*, Washington, D.C., 1996.

Fidell, Megan, Peter H. Glieck, and Arlene K. Wong, "Converting to Efficient Drip Irrigation: Underwood Ranches and High Rise Farms," in Lisa Owens-Viani, Arlene K. Wong, and Peter H. Gleick (eds.), *Sustainable Use of Water: California Success Stories*, Pacific Institute, Oakland, California, 1999.

Fishbein, Gregory, and Suman Babbar, *Private Financing of Toll Roads*, The World Bank, Washington, D.C., 1996.

Flyvbjerg, Bent, Mette Skamris Holm, and Søren Buhl, "Underestimating Costs in Public Works Projects: Error or Lie?" *Journal of the American Planning Association,* Vol. 68, No. 3, Summer 2002, pp. 279–295.

Gleick, Peter H., P. Loh, S. V. Gomez, and J. Morrison, *California Water 2020: A Sustainable Vision,* Pacific Institute, Oakland, California, 1995.

Goldsmith, Stephen, *The 21st Century City,* Rowan & Littlefield, New York, 1999.

Gómez-Ibáñez, Jose A., and Kenneth Small, "Road Pricing for Congestion Management: A Survey of International Practice," *Synthesis of Highway Practice 210*, Transportation Research Board, National Academy Press, Washington, D.C., 1994.

Gottlieb, Robert, and Margaret Fitzsimmons, *Thirst for Growth: Water Agencies as Hidden Government in California*, University of Arizona Press, Tuscon, 1991.

Government Accounting Standards Board, "Statement 34—Basic Financial Satements and Management's Discussion and Analysis for State and Local Governments," Norwalk, Connecticut, 1999.

"The Government Performance and Results Act," 1993, available at Gopher://ftp.fedworld.gov/pub/results/results.htm.

Haasz, Dana, "Reducing Water Use in Residential, Industrial and Municipal Landscapes," in Lisa Owens-Viani, Arlene K. Wong, and Peter H. Gleick (eds.), *Sustainable Use of Water: California Success Stories,* Pacific Institute, Oakland, California, 1999.

Heller, Alfred, *The California Tomorrow Plan,* California Tomorrow, Los Altos, California, 1972.

Hurwitz, Elliot, "San Diego's Strong Public-Private Partnership," *Transit California,* February 1996, pp. 6–10.

International City/County Managers Association, *Special Data Issues: Local Government Infrastructure Finance*, Washington, D.C., 1993.

Irvine Ranch Water District website, 1998, available at http://www.irwd.com.

Jepsen, Christopher, and Steven Rivkin, *Class Size Reduction, Teacher Quality, and Academic Achievement in California Public Elementary Schools,* Public Policy Institute of California, San Francisco, California, 2002.

Johnson, Robert, "The Colorado River: History and Contemporary Issues of a Complex System" (white paper, not for publication), n.d.

Kawada, Kim, *San Diego's Interstate 15 Value Pricing Project*, San Diego Association of Governments, San Diego, California, 1998.

Legislative Analyst's Office, "Higher Education Cross-Cutting Issues: Analysis of the 1995–1996 Budget Bill," 1995, available at http://www.lao.gov.

Legislative Analyst's Office, "Deferred Maintenance. Analysis of the Budget Bill," 1996a, pp. F13–F22, available at http://www.lao.ca.gov.

Legislative Analyst's Office, "Rethinking the State's Approach to Deferred Maintenance. LAO Analysis of the 1995–6 Budget Bill: Higher Education Crosscutting Issues," 1996b, available at http://www.lao.ca.gov.

Legislative Analyst's Office, "A Primer on State Bonds," 1998a, available at http://www.lao.ca.gov.

Legislative Analyst's Office, "Overhauling the State's Infrastructure: Planning and Financing Process," 1998b, available at http://www.lao.ca.gov.

Legislative Analyst's Office, "Year Round Operations in Higher Education," 1999, available at http://www.lao.ca.gov.

Legislative Analyst's Office, *Analysis of the 2000–01 Budget Bill: Report from the Legislative Analyst's Office to the Joint Legislative Budget Committee*, Sacramento, California, 2000a.

Legislative Analyst's Office, *California Travels: Financing Our Transportation,* Sacramento, California, 2000b.

Legislative Analyst's Office, *California's Changing Income Distribution,* Sacramento, California, 2000c.

Legislative Analyst's Office, "A New Blueprint for California School Facility Finance," 2001, available at http://www.lao.ca.gov.

Liaison Committee of the State Board of Education and The Regents of the University of California, *A Master Plan for Higher Education in California, 1960–1975*, California State Department of Education, Sacramento, 1960.

Litman, Todd, Charles Komanoff, and Douglas Howell, *Road Relief: Tax and Pricing Shifts for a Fairer, Cleaner, and Less Congested*

Transportation System in Washington State, Energy Outreach Center, Olympia, Washington, 1998.

Littleworth, Arthur, and Eric Garner, *California Water*, Solano Press, Point Arena, California, 1995.

McWilliams, Carey, *California: The Great Exception,* Current Books, New York, 1949; University of California Press reprint, 1999.

Mercer Management Consulting, *1995 Privatization Study,* Washington, D.C., 1995.

Metropolitan Transportation Commission, *The Pothole Report,* Oakland, California, 2000.

Metropolitan Water District of Southern California, "California's Colorado River Allocation," 2001, available at http://www.mwd.dst.ca.us/mwdh2o/pages/yourwater/supply/colorado/colorado04.

Moore, Adrian T., Geoffrey F. Segal, and John McCormally, *Infrastructure Outsourcing: Leveraging Concrete, Steel, and Asphalt with Public-Private Partnerships,* Policy Study 272, Reason Public Policy Institute, Los Angeles, California, 2000.

National Center for Educational Statistics, *Baccalaureate and Beyond Longitudinal Study: 1993/97*, U.S. Department of Education, Office of Educational Research and Improvement, Washington, D.C., 1999.

National Research Council, *Committing to the Cost of Ownership: Maintenance and Repair of Public Buildings*, Building Research Board, National Academy Press, Washington, D.C., 1990.

National Research Council, *Stewardship of Federal Facilities: A Proactive Strategy for Managing the Nation's Public Assets*, Washington, D.C., 1998.

Nelson, Arthur C., *System Development Charges for Water, Wastewater and Stormwater Facilities,* Lewis Publishing, Boca Raton, Florida, 1995.

Neuman, Michael, and Jan Whittington, *Building California's Future: Current Conditions in Infrastructure Planning, Budgeting, and*

Financing, Public Policy Institute of California, San Francisco, California, 2000.

New Jersey State Planning Commission, *The New Jersey State Development and Redevelopment Plan: Infrastructure Needs Assessment, Executive Summary,* Trenton, 2001a.

New Jersey State Planning Commission, "The New Jersey State Plan," 2001b, available at http://www.state.nj.us/osp/plan2/execsum/sdrp2esfull.htm.

Obra, Joan, Stacy Schwandt, and Peter Woodall, "Corporate Donors' Influence Spilling into UC Classrooms," *San Francisco Chronicle*, June 26, 2001.

Office of Financial Management, *The Capital Planning Process—Summary,* Olympia, Washington, 2002.

Office of the Governor of the State of Minnesota, "Strategic Capital Budget Plan," 2001, available at http://www.finance.state.mn.us/.

Office of the Governor of the State of Minnesota, "The Big Plan—Healthy, Vital Communities," 2002, available at http://www.mainserver.state.mn.us/governor/healthy_vital_communities.html.

Office of Management and Budget, *Capital Programming Guide: Supplement to OMB Circular A-11, Part 3: Planning, Budgeting and Acquisition of Capital Assets,* Washington, D.C., 1997.

Office of Planning and Research, *An Urban Strategy for California,* Sacramento, 1978.

Organization for Economic Cooperation and Development, *Contracting Out Government Services: Best Practice Guidelines and Case Studies*, Public Management Occasional Papers No. 20, Paris, 1997a.

Organization for Economic Cooperation and Development, *Privatization of Utilities and Infrastructure*, Paris, 1997b.

Orr, Jim, "Madera Water-Bank Idea at Death's Door," *The Fresno Bee*, March 26, 1999.

Owens-Viani, Lisa, "Marin Municipal Water District's Innovative Integrated Resource Management Program," in Lisa Owens-Viani, Arlene K. Wong, and Peter H. Gleick (eds.), *Sustainable Use of Water: California Success Stories,* Pacific Institute, Oakland, California, 1999.

Pacific Gas and Electric, CARE (California Alternative Rates for Energy) Program website, 2002, available at http://www.pge.com/001_res_svc/financial_assistance/care.shtml.

Park, George S., and Robert J. Lempert, *The Class of 2014: Preserving Access to California Higher Education*, RAND, Santa Monica, California, 1998.

Parker, D., D. Zilberman, D. Cohen, and D. Osgood, *The Economic Costs and Benefits Associated with the California Irrigation Management Information System (CIMIS): Final Report,* Department of Agricultural and Resource Economics, University of California, Berkeley, 1996.

Peterson, George E., *American's Urban Capital Stock: An Urban Institute Series,* The Urban Institute, Washington, D.C., 1979.

Peterson, George E., Ted Miller, Nancy Humphrey, and Christopher Walker, *Infrastructure Needs Studies: A Critique*, The Urban Institute, Washington, D.C., 1986.

Rapoport, Roger, *California Dreaming: The Political Odyssey of Pat & Jerry Brown,* Nolo Press, Berkeley, California, 1982.

Razo, Armando, David Murray, and Rachel Sumi, *How the Santa Clara Traffic Authority Succeeded in Implementing Measure A Highway Improvement Program—Ahead of Schedule and Under Budget,* Metropolitan Transportation Commission, Oakland, California, 1996.

Reason Public Policy Institute, *Privatization 1999: The 13th Annual Report on Privatization*, Los Angeles, California, 1999.

Rebuild California website, 2001, available at http://www.rebuildca.org.

Renwick, Mary, Richard Green, and Chester McCorkle, *Measuring the Price Responsiveness of Residential Water Demand in California's Areas: A Report*, Sacramento, 1998.

Sacramento Bee, "The Gold Rush Lives: State Court Upholds Me-First Water Ethic," August 24, 2000.

San Jose State University–City of San Jose, "A Library Like No Other, for a Community Like No Other," 2000, available at http://www.library.sjsu.edu/jointlibrary.

Schreffler, Eric N., Theresa Costa, and Carl B. Moyer, "Evaluating Travel and Air Quality Cost-Effectiveness of Transportation Demand Management Projects," *Transportation Research Record*, No. 1520, 1996.

Schwartz, Peter, *The Art of the Long View*, Doubleday, New York, 1996.

Sclar, Elliott D., *You Don't Always Get What You Pay For: The Economics of Privatization,* Cornell University Press, Ithaca, New York, 2000.

Seik, F. T., "An Effective Demand Management Instrument in Urban Transport: The Area Licensing Scheme in Singapore," *Cities*, Vol. 14, No. 3, 1997, pp. 155–164.

Select Committee on the Master Plan for Higher Education to the Coordinating Council for Higher Education, *The California Master Plan for Higher Education in the Seventies and Beyond*, Sacramento, 1972.

Senate of the State of California, Master Plan Survey Team, "A Master Plan for Higher Education in California, 1960–1975," 1960, available at http://www.sen.ca.gov/ftp/SEN/COMMITTEE/JOINT/MASTER_PLAN/_home/historical.htp.

Sonstelie, Jon, Eric Brunner, and Kenneth Ardon, *For Better or For Worse? School Finance Reform in California*, Public Policy Institute of California, San Francisco, California, 2000.

Space Assignments and Capital Improvements Committee, *Tabulations of UC Classroom and Teaching Lab Utilization,* University of California, Berkeley, 1997.

Sterngold, James, "California Governor Sees an End to Freeway Building," *New York Times*, August 21, 2001.

Sullivan, Edward C., *Evaluating the Impacts of the SR91 Variable-Toll Express Lane Facility,* California Polytechnic State University, Department of Civil and Environmental Engineering, San Luis Obispo, 1998.

Syme, Preston T., and Jay Oschrin, *How to Inspect Your Facilities and Still Have Money Left to Repair Them,* Association of Higher Education Facilities Officers (APPA), Alexandria, Virginia, 1996.

Taylor, Matthew D., and Lisa Snell, *Innovative School Facility Partnerships: Downtown, Airport, and Retail Space,* Policy Study 276, Reason Public Policy Institute, Los Angeles, California, 2000.

Texas Transportation Institute, *Metropolitan Mobility Reports,* College Station, 2001.

Transit Cooperative Research Program, *TCRP Report 40: Strategies to Attract Auto Users to Public Transportation,* 1998.

UC Irvine, "University of California, Irvine, Faculty and Staff Housing," 2000, available at http://www.icha.uci.edu.

University of California, Office of the President, *Systemwide Tabulations of Classroom Facilities,* Oakland, 1997.

University of California, Office of the President, "UC Facilities Manual," 2002, available at http://www.ucop.edu/facil/fmc/facilman/volume2/intro.html.

University of California Regents, *The University of California Student Fee Policy,* Oakland, 1994.

University of Pennsylvania Facilities Services, "Sansom Common: A New Heart for the Campus," 2000, available at http://www.upenn.edu/fm/projs/cancom.html.

Urban Institute, *Issues in Deferred Maintenance: The Federal Infrastructure Strategy Program,* Alexandria, Virginia, 1994.

U.S. Bureau of Reclamation, History Program, "The Central Valley Project American River Division, The Folsom and Sly Park Units, The Auburn-Folsom South Unit," 1994, available at http://www.dataweb.usbr.gov/html/cvpamriv.html.

U.S. Bureau of Reclamation, Lower Colorado Region, *Description and Assessment of Operations, Maintenance, and Sensitive Species of the Lower Colorado River: Biological Assessment*, 1996.

U.S. Bureau of Reclamation, *Strategic Plan 2000–2005*, Washington, D.C., 1999.

U.S. Bureau of Reclamation, Mid-Pacific Region, *Mid-Pacific Region Overview*, Sacramento, California, 2000.

U.S. Bureau of Reclamation, *FY 2002 Annual Performance Plan: FY 2000 Annual Performance Report,* Washington, D.C., 2001a.

U.S. Bureau of Reclamation, Mid-Pacific Region, and U.S. Fish and Wildlife Service, California-Nevada Operations Office, *Record of Decision: Central Valley Project Improvement Act, Final Programmatic Environmental Impact Statement*, 2001b.

U.S. Bureau of Reclamation, "Regional Map," 2002, available at http://www.usbr.gov/main/what/regionalmap/index.html.

U.S. Bureau of Reclamation, Central Valley Project, California, and California Department of Water Resources, State Water Project, "Agreement Between the United States of America and the State of California for Coordinated Operation of the Central Valley Project and the State Water Project," 1986, available at http://www.dwr.water.ca.gov/dir-general_informationR2/DWR-MilestonesR2.

U.S. General Accounting Office, *Concession Contracting: Government-Wide Rates of Return*, Washington, D.C., 1996.

U.S. General Accounting Office, *Privatization: Lessons Learned by State and Local Governments*, Washington, D.C., 1997.

U.S. General Accounting Office, *Executive Guide: Leading Practices in Capital Decision-Making,* Washington, D.C., 1998.

Vickery, William, *Statement to the Joint Committee on Washington Metropolitan Problems*, U.S. Congress, Washington, D.C., 1959.

Walker, Chris, *Partnerships for Parks: Lessons from the Lila Wallace–Reader's Digest Parks Program*, The Urban Institute, Washington, D.C., 1999.

Washington State Budget and Accounting Act (RCW 43.88).

Washington State Community, *Trade and Economic Development, Infrastructure,* discussion paper 7, Olympia, 2002.

Washington State Department of Transportation, "TDM Success Story: Washington's Commute Trip Reduction Law & Statewide CTR Program Deliver Results," 2000, available at http://www.wsdot.wa.gov/mobility/TDM/TDMsuccess.html.

Water Education Foundation, *Layperson's Guide to the Central Valley Project,* Sacramento, California, 1998.

WestEd and U.S. Department of Education, "California Charter School Information," 2001, available at http://www.uscharterschools.org/pub/sp/1.

Williamson, Oliver E., *The Economic Institutions of Capitalism*, Free Press, New York, 1985.

Witheford, David K., *Outsourcing of State Highway Facilities and Services, National Cooperative Highway Research Program Synthesis of Highway Practices 246,* Transportation Research Board, National Research Council, National Academy Press, Washington, D.C., 1997.

Wong, Arlene K., "Promoting Conservation with Irvine Ranch Water District's Ascending Block Rate Structure," in Lisa Owens-Viani, Arlene K. Wong, and Peter H. Gleick (eds.), *Sustainable Use of Water: California Success Stories,* Pacific Institute, Oakland, California, 1999.

World Bank, *World Development Report,* The World Bank, Washington, D.C., 1994.

About the Authors

DAVID E. DOWALL

David Dowall is a professor of city and regional planning at the University of California, Berkeley, and a visiting fellow at the Public Policy Institute of California. He is a leading expert on urban economics and infrastructure policy and frequently consults for the World Bank, Asian Development Bank, United Nations Development Programme, and the U.S. Agency for International Development. He has served as a policy advisor to local and central governments and businesses in over 40 countries. His books include *The Suburban Squeeze*, *The Land Market Assessment*, and *The Warsaw Economy in Transition*. He holds a B.S. in economics from the University of Maryland and both a master's degree in urban and regional planning and a Ph.D. in economics from the University of Colorado.

JAN WHITTINGTON

Jan Whittington is a Ph.D. student in city and regional planning at the University of California, Berkeley. Before beginning her doctoral studies, she was a senior planner at Bechtel, where she managed large-scale infrastructure developments in Asia and the Americas. She holds an M.C.R.P. from California State Polytechnic University, San Luis Obispo, and B.A. degrees in biology and environmental studies from the University of California, Santa Cruz.

Related PPIC Publications

Metropolitan Growth Planning in California, 1900–2000
Elisa Barbour

California's Infrastructure Policy for the 21st Century: Issues and Opportunities
David E. Dowall

Federal Transportation Policy and the Role of Metropolitan Planning Organizations in California
Paul G. Lewis and Mary Sprague

Local Economic Development in Southern California's Suburbs: 1990–1997
Max Neiman, Gregory Andranovich, and Kenneth Fernandez

Building California's Future: Current Conditions in Infrastructure Planning, Budgeting, and Financing
Michael Neuman and Jan Whittington

PPIC publications may be ordered by phone or from our website
(800) 232-5343 [mainland U.S.]
(415) 291-4400 [Canada, Hawaii, overseas]
www.ppic.org